The Dawn at My Back

The Constructs Series examines the ways in which the things we make change both our world and how we understand it. Authors in the series explore the constructive nature of the human artifact and the imagination and reflection that bring it into being.

Series Editors: H. Randolph Swearer • Robert Mugerauer •Vivian Sobchack

Publication of this book was aided by a generous subsidy from the Houston Endowment and by individual gifts from Danah Fayman, Madeline Goldberg, and Kathleen MacLeod.

The Dawn at My Back

Memoir of a Black Texas Upbringing

Carroll Parrott Blue

 University of Texas Press, Austin

University of Texas Press, Austin

Requests for permission to reproduce material from this work should be sent to Permissions, University of Texas Press, P.O. Box 7819, Austin, TX 78713-7819.

∞ The paper used in this book meets the minimum requirements of ANSI/NISO Z39.48-1992 (R1997) (Permanence of Paper).

Library of Congress Cataloging-in-Publication Data

Blue, Carroll Parrott.
   The dawn at my back : memoir of a Black Texas upbringing
/ Carroll Parrott Blue.
      p.   cm. — (Construct series)
   ISBN 0-292-70913-7 (alk. paper)
   1. Blue, Carroll Parrott.   2. Photographers—United States—Biography.
   3. African American photographers—Biography.
   4. Motion picture producers and directors—United States—Biography.   I. Title.   II. Series
   TR140.B385   A3   2003
   791.43'023'092—dc21
                                                    2002002335

INJG:119

Dedicated to Mollie Carroll Parrott

Contents

CORPORATION LIMITS OF INDEPENDENCE HEIGHTS

Part I **Prologue**

Southern trees bear a strange fruit,
Blood on the leaves and blood at the root,
Black bodies swinging in the Southern breeze,
Strange fruit hanging from the poplar trees.

—Abel Meeropol
(a.k.a. Lewis Allan)

Hell

I smell the peanut shells turn brown. My mother turns, opens the oven door, and shakes them. Some turn over, specks of black on the undersides appearing.

"A large white ball rushes fiercely down a steep hill. It is soft, spongy, porous. But it's not gravity propelling it. It's being driven from inside by an appetite to devour. In the front, in its path, is its prey. A small, frightened black ball. Hard and shiny, like coal." She's telling me another version of her recurring dream.

"This time it wasn't like before. But then, every ending is always different." This dream first appeared when she was around my age. Since then it's managed to possess her sleep, mysteriously popping up in her dreams at its own will, especially when she least expects it.

This particular dream arrived the night before, leaving her in such pain today that she's forced to recount its horror. She often uses me to tell her dreams to, only because she has no friends she trusts with her vulnerability. She doesn't trust me either, but I am a child and weaker than she. So, without my permission, she forces me to listen to her nightmares.

"Last night," she continues, "the white ball caught the black one, swallowing it . . . whole." She pauses for effect as her hands shape a circle. "Like an amoeba," she dramatizes, "capturing something helpless, surrounding it, and then slowly sucking the life out of it—for food." Her metaphor of eating comes naturally. She's now shelling the roasted peanuts, popping them whole into her mouth and chewing them up with a tremendous gusto. "Yep, it gulped that tiny ball whole, leaving no trace."

I shudder.

Outside the kitchen window it's winter. The sky is a single opaque cloud painting its entire expanse a full-on gray. Slivers of arctic winds stream through tiny cracks in the tightly shut windows. Clusters of bare tree branches reach hungrily through the cold to the notion of a sun above.

My mother's determined to use her talk and me to get to some other side—a side unknown to me. But I don't ask about that; I've learned to be silent when she's like this. Stealing a look at her, I realize she's no longer present at our table. I follow her gaze out the window on up to the motionless sky. Here I pause to squint. There is absolutely nothing out there before us. Unsettled, I grow afraid.

I am only seven years old on this biting cold day. I am terrified because my mother is teaching me how to be like her. I am learning how to be afraid, to know that any minute I could be swallowed whole. Her white ball is my world. That black ball is certainly me. And I am powerless. My hard-won essence could well be absorbed by this mighty white mass that she lays at the trembling feet of my soul.

Then it will be my turn. My energy will feed its power, help it grow bigger, stronger, better. Its digestive juices burning like acid into my disintegrating body and soul, dissolving traces of me, of my history, and of my contribution to its ever-growing capacity.

And there's more. While my mother pours out her grief, a grief too adult for me to handle, she also leaves a space between her words where I can read her unspoken message. I must face this battle alone. Of course she won't be there for me. How could she be? No one had ever been there for her. How could she possibly find any space in her heart to help me? Every ounce of her energy is locked up in her private war to remain functionally sane.

Greedily, she pushes the fear that runs rampant through every crevice of her body, invading even her most sacred boundaries, on to me. Why, it even follows her into her sleep, where the fear lurks in hidden places, watching for her to dare, even secretly, to dream. And once inside the sweetness of her dream time, it takes special pleasure in slapping her back into an embittered, sleepless reality.

Her gaze steadies; her silence stills the air. I watch her observing the inside of the sky, and I wonder where has she gone. Years later, when I'm full-grown, I'll resent her abandoning me, leaving me with the legacy of her paranoia.

But right now, in my seventh winter on this planet, I encounter Hell. It is not a vast territory of silently licking red-orange flames. It is an unforgiving dead and barren land, with a freezing north wind pushing the trees' stark-naked branches up against the frigid sky. Here I encounter my mother's eyes. I watch them die at their center.

And from where I sit, the ice harbored in the air freezes the blood in my veins.

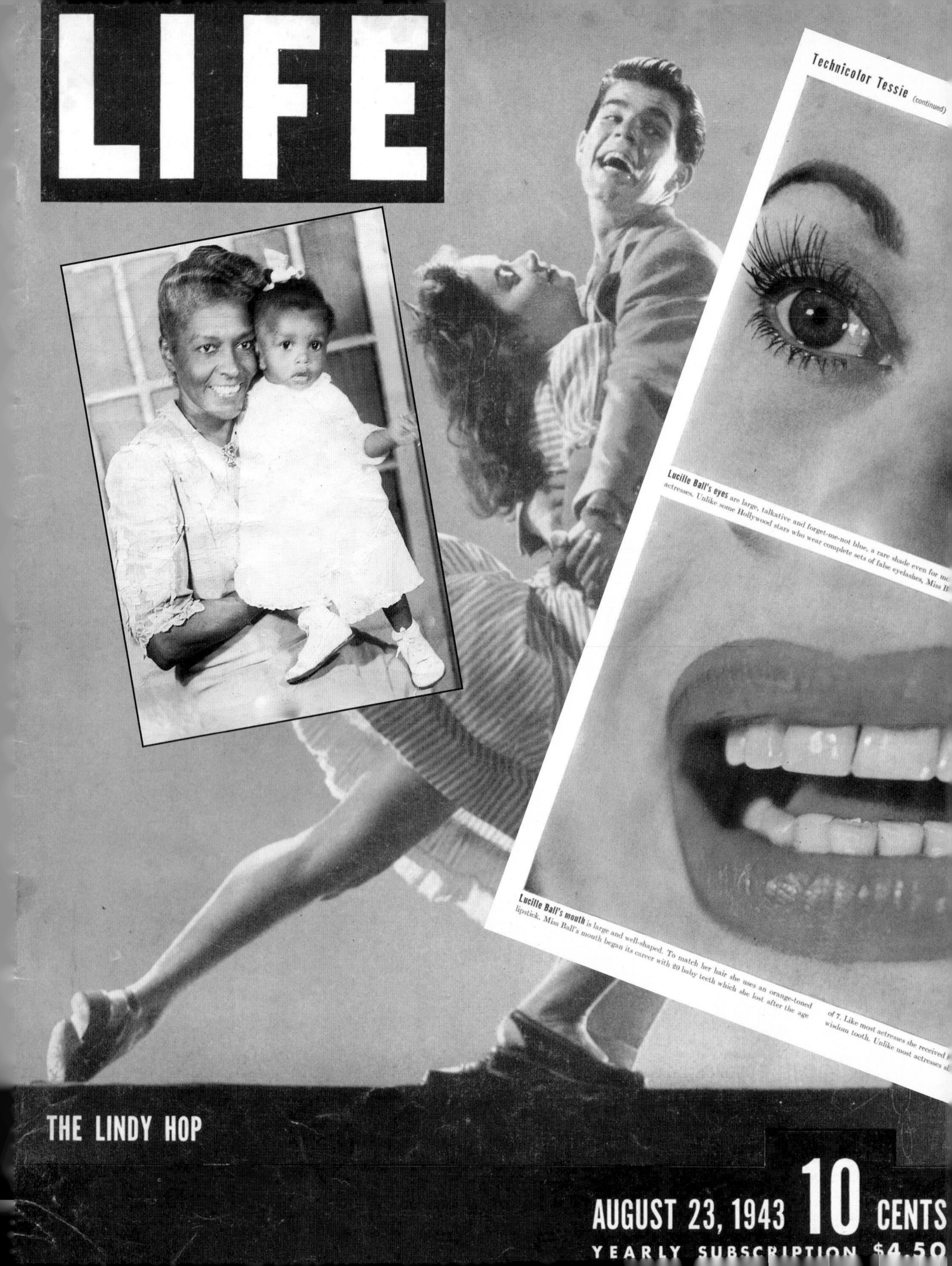

LIFE

Technicolor Tessie (continued)

Lucille Ball's eyes are large, talkative and forget-me-not blue, a rare shade even for me actresses. Unlike some Hollywood stars who wear complete sets of false eyelashes, Miss B

Lucille Ball's mouth is large and well-shaped. To match her hair she uses an orange-toned lipstick. Miss Ball's mouth began its career with 20 baby teeth which she lost after the age of 7. Like most actresses she received ∥ wisdom tooth. Unlike most actresses sh

THE LINDY HOP

AUGUST 23, 1943 **10** CENTS

YEARLY SUBSCRIPTION $4.50

My life will be seen as a thread winding in and out of the story.

—Erik Barnouw,
Media Marathon: A Twentieth-Century Memoir

Part II **Life**

only the outer half of her eyelid. This gives a plumed upward tilt to her al.
s. Note the difference between her apricot-colored hair and dark eyebrows.

32 adult teeth, losing only one
ps in order to beautify them.

NEGRO DIVISION
It prepares to go overseas

.G DESERT HEAT, IMMEDIATELY AFTER A 28-MILE HIKE, NEGRO SOLDIERS OF THE 93RD DIVISION MARCH ON THE PARADE GROUND AT FORT HUACHUCA, ARIZ.

When German prisoners recently were sent to a U. S. prison camp, they said that the best fighters they encountered in North Africa were Australian troops and American Negro troops. Actually, the number of Negroes engaged in combat in Africa was small, but more and more of them are now being sent overseas to help in the fighting. For instance, the 93rd Infantry Division shown here, which was the first all-Negro combat division to be organized, has reached a state of training where it is ready to move out of the country at a moment's notice, Negroes remain essentially untried as fighters. During World War I

more than 90% of the Negroes in the U. S. Army served in labor battalions. Even today the majority of Negroes in the Army are still in such battalions. But an increasing percentage of them are being put into combat units. They are admitted to all branches of the Army, including the Air Forces, and two all-Negro divisions have been activated. Approximately 3,000 Negroes are officers, almost three times as many as in World War I.

The 93rd Division consists of 16,000 enlisted men, all colored, and a thousand officers, half of whom are colored, Cooperation between the whites and the Negroes throughout the division is generally considered to be excellent.

CONTINUED ON NEXT PAGE

37

COL. THOMAS F. TAYLOR AND HIS STAFF OF NEGRO AND WHITE OFFICERS REVIEW A RETREAT PARADE. HIGHEST RANKING NEGRO COMBAT OFFICER IN DIVISION IS A MAJOR

Letter writing is part of your education.

DR. FRED D. PARROTT
Dentist

419½ MILAM STREET   SUITE 5
HOUSTON, TEXAS

OFFICE PHONE C. 4-5228
RESIDENCE PHONE L. 7056

My dear son;

Your letters are so interesting that we look forward to receiving them with such pleasant anticipation. We were amused at your use of the colloquial term (youl.) We thought you were such a middle westerner that you had in this time forgotten all of our southern words and even our southern accent, (laugh, laugh) I do want to emphasize care in spelling. if you are not sure about a word look it up in the dictionary, if there is no dictionary in the house, buy one. Now this is self improvement. I think you are big enough, and mentally alert enough to do this because you want to do so. (Read) Re-read your letters to detect mistakes and correct the mistakes found therein even when you write us far by so doing you will soon be able to see mistakes at a glance and such mistakes will become negligible (This comes out of my experience for I am a poor speller. When I was your age I spell have to hatter and let's test —

Letter writing is part of your education

DR. FRED D. PARROTT
Dentist

419 1/2 Milam Street Suite 5   Office Phone C. 4-5228
Houston, Texas   Residence Phone L. 7056

My dear son:

Your letters are so interesting that we look forward to receiving them with such pleasant anticipation. We were amused at your use of the colloquial term. (youl.) We thought you were such a middle westerner that you had in this time forgotten all of our southern words and even our southern accent. (laugh, laugh) I do want to emphasize care in spelling if you are not sure about a word look it up in the dictionary, if there is no dictionary in the house, buy one. Now this is self improvement. I think you are big enough, and mentally alert enough to do this because you want to do so. (Read) re-read your letters to detect mistakes and correct the mistakes found therein even when you write us for by so doing you will soon be able to see mistakes at a glance and such mistakes will become negligible (This comes out of my experience for I am a poor speller. When I was your age I spell have to—hafter—and let's—lest—)

We were thrilled to know that you went to Grant Park, the museum and had the motor boat ride.

Fred, we want you to work and earn money—you know me, I believe in work as a tonic for the mind, but now and with you there seeing things (at your age) is most important for about eighty percent of what we learn is through the eye and the ear—so keep your eyes open and your ears attuned to what is about you.

Yes, Fred, there is segregation in Chicago—there is segregation or discrimination either by word, sign or action all over the United States. That is why we want you exposed to all worthwhile things so when you are a man you can fight this condition in order that your children will not have to face what you face—that is why we want you to go to a mixed school early in life so you can learn how the white boys and girls think and feel then you will know better how to work with them when they and you are men and women. Fred, that condition (segregation) that you have met is why Mother is always so serious, that is why I go to so many clubs, that is what I spend my leisure time doing—trying to fight in a small way that very condition so you will not have to face what I had to face.

It is grand that you have such an intelligent guide and guard as Mrs. Spears. She understands what we are trying to do. She knows our every hope, desire and ambition for you and do not think one time that she is not constantly aware. My letters, I expect are a little grown-up for you but ask some other grown-up what I mean if you do not get the import of all my statements—I am remembering that you do have a sort of matured mind yourself. (bragging on my own child)

My, my, my you are some BIG SHOT taking two girls out—Gee, gee No wonder you lost five dollars—it's a wonder you didn't lose your head two girls—in a ballroom like the Parkway Ball Room walking on carpet that sinks down an inch at a time would make Daddy lose his head to say nothing about his money. (Laugh, laugh) Were the girls pretty with good hair? Remember we won't have any ugly girls in our circle—you know you told me that I would have to bring you a pretty sister. So, also will you have to bring up pretty girl acquaintances for Daddy and me. That they must be good, intelligent girls goes without saying. (Grin)

I don't mention your going to school up there anymore because Daddy is coming up as soon as <u>Carroll Ann</u> comes, then you can discuss it pro and con. You notice everything and think through everything and you will know exactly what to say to him because your observations, conclusions and decisions will govern Daddy's actions to a large extent (a boy who has only a mind of a 16 year old—Smart, eh?)

We are glad you gave Aunt Minnie five dollars. Give her money every week. Daddy said "Maybe he will take care of you until you are 18, <u>then</u> Uncle Sam says you are old enough to fight so you must be a man <u>then</u> you must hit it for yourself (Smile, I just made that up. Daddy didn't say that—just some fun.)

Well so much for this "jive" (Listen at mother using slangs—but I have to try to speak my big shot son's language). I hope and think I'll not write any more until Carroll Ann or Ann Carroll (whichever way you & Daddy want) comes. We are glad you were thoughtful to have Mrs. Spears for dinner. Sorry you did not invite Mrs. Sayles.

Mother

DR. FRED D. PARROTT
Dentist

419½ MILAM STREET   SUITE 5
HOUSTON, TEXAS

OFFICE PHONE C. 4-5228
RESIDENCE PHONE L. 7056

We were thrilled to know that you went to Grant Park, the museums and had the motor boat ride.

Fred, we want you to work and earn money — you know me, I believe in work as a tonic for the mind, but now and with you there seeing thing (at your age) is most important for about eighty per cent of what we learn is through the eyes and ears — so keep your eyes open and your ears attuned to what is about you.

Yes, Fred, there is segregation in Chicago — there is segregation or discrimination either by ward, sign or action all over the United States. That why we want you exposed to all worthwhile things so when you are a man you can fight this condition in order that your children will not have to face

DR. FRED D. PARROTT
Dentist

419½ MILAM STREET   SUITE 5
HOUSTON, TEXAS

OFFICE PHONE C. 4-5228
RESIDENCE PHONE L. 7056

what you face — that is why we want you to go to a mixed school early in life so you can learn how the white boys and girls think and feel then you will know better how to work with them when they and you are men and women. Fred, that condition (segregation) that you have met is why Mother is always so serious, that is why I go to so many clubs, that is what I spent my leisure time doing — trying to fight in a small way that very condition so you will not have to face what I had to face.

It is grand that you have such an intelligent guide and guard as Mrs. Spears. She understands what we are trying to do. She knows our

DR. FRED D. PARROTT
Dentist

419½ MILAM STREET   SUITE 5
HOUSTON, TEXAS

OFFICE PHONE C. 4-5228
RESIDENCE PHONE L. 7056

every hope, desire and ambition for you and do not think one time that she is not constantly aware. My letters, I expect are a little grown up for you but ask some other grown ups what I meant if you do not get the import of all of my statements — I am remembering that you do have a sort of matured mind yourself. (bragging on my own child.)

My, my, my you are some SHOT taking two girls out — gee, gee (big) (Shot) No wonder you lost five dollar — it's a wonder you did lose your head two girls — in a ball room like the Parkway Ball Room walking on carpet that sinks down an inch at a time would make Daddy loose his

DR. FRED D. PARROTT
Dentist

419½ MILAM STREET   SUITE 5
HOUSTON, TEXAS

OFFICE PHONE C. 4-5228
RESIDENCE PHONE L. 7056

his head to say nothing about his money (laugh, laugh) Were the girls pretty with good hair? Remember we won't have ugly girls in our circle — you know you told me that I would have to bring you a pretty sister. so, also will you have to bring up pretty girl acquaintances for Daddy and me. That they must be good, intelligent girls go without saying. (Grin)

I don't mention your going to school up there any more because Daddy is coming up and as soon as Carroll Ann comes, then you can discuss it pro and con. You notice everything and think through everything and you will know exactly what to say to him because your observations

DR. FRED D. PARROTT

Dentist

419½ MILAM STREET   SUITE 5
HOUSTON, TEXAS

OFFICE PHONE C. 4-5228
RESIDENCE PHONE L. 7056

Conclusions and decisions will govern Daddy's actions to a large extent (a boy who has only a mind of a 16 year old — Smart. Smart. eh?

We are glad you gave Aunt Minnie five dollars. Give her money every week. Daddy said "Maybe he will take care of you until you are 18, then Uncle Sam says you are old enough to fight so you must be a man then you must hit it for yourself (Smile) (I just made that up. Daddy didn't say that — just some fun.)

Well so much for this "jive" (Listen at mother using slang — but I have to try to speak my big shot son's language). I hope and think I'll not write any more until Carroll Ann or Ann Carroll (which your way you + Daddy want it) comes. We are glad you were thoughtful to have Mrs. Spears for dinner. Sorry you did not invite Mrs. Sayles. Was sweet of Aunt Minnie to let you invite her. What does she need over

R. FRED D. PARROTT
Dentist
419½ MILAM STREET
HOUSTON, TEXAS

Fred D. Parrott
6152 So. Elizabeth
Chicago, Ill

Chapter I **Life**

I am Carroll Parrott Blue. I was born on August 23, 1943.

My mother, Mollie Carroll Parrott, and my father, Frederick Douglas Parrott, Senior, were the first in each of their families to obtain advanced college degrees. They were professionals. My mother was an elementary school teacher, my father a dentist. Both their fathers were dirt-poor farmers; my mother's parents were born slaves. Knowingly, my parents dismissed the consequences of their humble origins. Their raw energy to achieve was their main capital. They turned that into hard work and determination. Then they made both courageous and foolish bids to become part of this country's middle class.

Months before my arrival, my parents moved my brother, Frederick Douglas Parrott, Junior, to Chicago, Illinois. He was sixteen years old. My mother was especially keen on him graduating from an integrated high school. For her, his Chicago relocation held a promise that Fred's northern high school diploma could provide a door of opportunity for him to move up in a racist world. In fact, my brother did become an upstanding community member, a very successful doctor and entrepreneur.

Some ten days before my birth, my mother and brother corresponded. At the time, she was quickly becoming a middle-aged woman; her hair had begun to gray. In those days, old women simply did not have babies. She was ashamed to be pregnant. She was trapped with a philandering husband in a fading marriage. She faced what was to her the very unsavory prospect of raising yet another child.

I was one responsibility that she clearly did not want. She felt it was particularly unfair to be bound to the responsibility of motherhood in her fifties and sixties, the twilight years of her largely unfulfilled life.

Her life's goal was to be free. She yearned for and now wanted to work toward a better world for herself, her family, and the Negro race. In her letter to her now older child, she poignantly expresses her values, hopes, and aspirations.

"My dear son," my mother opens her letter. And so she begins instructions to my brother as to how he is to live his life. For her, academic degrees were the key to achieving a better standard of living. And age was not a factor to her continuing dreams of success. Shortly after my birth, she returned to college to obtain a master's degree in special education. At the time, she was fifty years old, with me, a six-year-old, in tow. To the very end of her life I observed her becoming all that she extolled her son to be in her August 1943 letter to him. She taught the same values to me. How my mother lived her life became my greatest model.

"Now this is self improvement," she tells him. Diligently, she maintained a lifelong record of the same quality of self-improvement and community activism that she describes as a pathway for her son in this letter to him. Over time, my parents did achieve a modicum of success. They enjoyed a certain quality of status as professionals and community leaders in Third Ward, one of Houston's Black neighborhoods. Yet their rugged, tough-love brand of optimism faced what to this day seems to me to be eternal obstacles. I do believe the challenge was too great for them. The story of their struggle seems to have disappeared with their deaths. For this reason, I am compelled to write our story.

Born poor, my parents were burdened by a lifetime of debt; there was never enough money. And they had no access to the sometimes life-affirming perks that race provided if one was born poor and white. My mother carried an additional burden of being old, female, and stuck with the responsibility of raising a small child alone while enduring the trials that come with an increasingly distant husband.

Her biggest challenge was to make the best of her life in a deeply embedded racist environment. The world surrounding her life had been so assuredly arranged to destroy her spirit. In time, the multiple rejections daily visited upon her conspired to take their toll on her zest for life. Her justified anger at these inequities had nowhere to go but inward.

"Yes, Fred, there is segregation in Chicago—there is segregation or discrimination either by word, sign or action all over the United States." My mother's letter to her son reveals her anguish over the eventual effects of racism on her child. Her fear of its power forced her to expel her sixteen-year-old boy from her Houston home and send him to the North. In Chicago she felt that he could learn firsthand about white people.

If you were Black and lived in the South, you especially could not escape the punishment that came with being Black. At the turn of the twentieth century, there had been a great migration of Blacks to the North to escape this tyranny. When my parents were teenagers in Houston, the Black press pointed out to them the logic of this mass migration:

> Some are decrying this exodus and scoring the Negroes for doing what they believe to be best for them. Every man ought to make an effort to improve his condition. But there is a reason why these people are leaving the south in such numbers and going to the North. (*Houston Observer,* October 21, 1916)

My parents did move unsuccessfully to the North in the 1930s, only to be forced for financial reasons to return back home. Here they stayed. Yet, they encouraged both their children to leave the South.

"Were the girls pretty, with good hair?" My mother tells my brother that the woman he chooses to mother his children must look white and have "good" or straight hair. She denies her children even a casual enjoyment of the beauty and company of black-skinned people with woolly hair. She requires that my brother keep uppermost in his mind that his future children must conform in appearance to white standards in order to fare well in this society.

She, in turn, will continue "to fight in a small way that very condition." She names this "condition" as segregation. This "condition" drove my mother to a form of self-repulsion. Her denial of her own Blackness and her simultaneous need to be a "race woman" propelled her into a just-below-the-surface, persistent anger that I label as a kind of lunacy.

The invisible quality of the nature of racism makes it difficult for me to get at the impact of its entangled, complicated, and deeply entrenched roots—roots that grew outside the reach of my parents. I suspect racism's consolidated power is frozen inside the values, goals, and aspirations of our very institutions. It can be traced, in part, to the values and cultures that come from the combined, yet largely uncoordinated, work of Congress, courts, corporations, churches, schools, prisons, and mass media. My story concentrates on the cumulative effects of mass media's racist stereotypes on my life.

As I tell my story, certain values extracted from events, books, magazines, entertainers, songs, television, and film begin to surface. And so my personal history is joined with a larger, more public story. This larger narrative is one of my society's history. It is a mass cultural, collective vision of values based on appearance (the right race, sex, and class) and the ability to consume. Appearance counts; money counts; things count.

LIFE

THE LINDY HOP

AUGUST 23, 1943 **10** CENTS

YEARLY SUBSCRIPTION $4.50

REG. U. S. PAT. OFF.

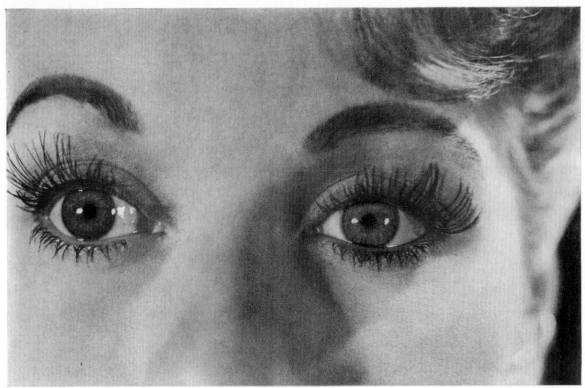

24

Lucille Ball's eyes are large, talkative and forget-me-not blue, a rare shade even for movie actresses. Unlike some Hollywood stars who wear complete sets of false eyelashes, Miss Ball uses them on only the outer half of her eyelid. This gives a plumed upward tilt to her already large eyes. Note the difference between her apricot-colored hair and dark eyebrows.

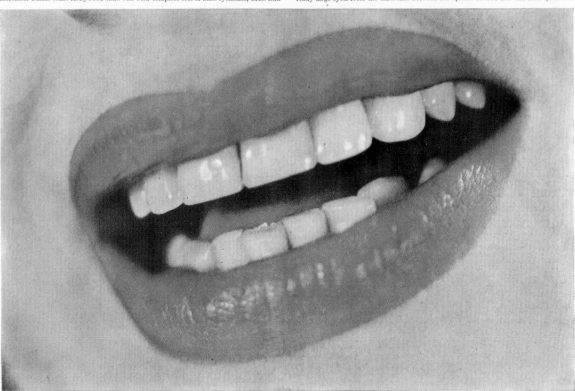

Lucille Ball's mouth is large and well-shaped. To match her hair she uses an orange-toned lipstick. Miss Ball's mouth began its career with 20 baby teeth which she lost after the age of 7. Like most actresses she received her full complement of 32 adult teeth, losing only one wisdom tooth. Unlike most actresses she uses no artificial caps in order to beautify them.

IN SWELTERING DESERT HEAT, IMMEDIATELY AFTER A 25-MILE HIKE, NEGRO SOLDIERS OF THE 93RD DIVISION MARCH ON THE PARADE GROUND AT FORT HUACHUCA, ARIZ.

NEGRO
DIVISION

It prepares to go overseas

When German prisoners recently were sent to a U. S. prison camp, they said that the best fighters they encountered in North Africa were Australian troops and American Negro troops. Actually, the number of Negroes engaged in combat in Africa was small, but more and more of them are now being sent overseas to help in the fighting. For instance, the 93rd Infantry Division shown here, which was the first all-Negro combat division to be organized, has reached a state of training where it is ready to move out of the country at a moment's notice.

In spite of what the Germans say, however, Negroes remain essentially untried as fighters. During World War I more than 90% of the Negroes in the U. S. Army served in labor battalions. Even today the majority of Negroes in the Army are still in such battalions. But an increasing percentage of them are being put into combat units. They are admitted to all branches of the Army, including the Air Forces, and two all-Negro divisions have been activated. Approximately 3,000 Negroes are officers, almost three times as many as in World War I.

The 93rd Division consists of 16,000 enlisted men, all colored, and a thousand officers, half of whom are colored. Cooperation between the whites and the Negroes throughout the division is generally considered to be excellent.

COL. THOMAS F. TAYLOR AND HIS STAFF OF NEGRO AND WHITE OFFICERS REVIEW A RETREAT PARADE. HIGHEST RANKING NEGRO COMBAT OFFICER IN DIVISION IS A MAJOR

CONTINUED ON NEXT PAGE

"If you're so smart, how come you aren't rich?" • "Champagne tastes, beer money." • "Bullshit talks, money walks." • "I've been unhappy poor and unhappy rich. I'd rather be unhappy rich." • "When a woman is twenty, it's her body. When she's thirty, it's her personality. When she's forty, it's her wisdom. When she's fifty, it's cold, hard cash."

Appearance and money determine how much power I can really possess. And so I use these values in movies, magazines, newspapers, music, and television as mirrors to learn about me, my story, and my culture. What I am learning about is the power of a culture's persuasive mass-media techniques and, conversely, the power and ability of people to challenge that authority.

In 2000, America on Online (AOL) bought Time-Warner, one of America's largest media corporations. At the time, the sale turned this American conglomerate into a global entertainment and information dynasty. Other companies followed suit with larger mergers which have, over time, yielded lackluster results. But even before AOL-Time-Warner existed, its original product, *Life* magazine, came to my house weekly through the mail. *Life* magazine and I were even historically linked.

Life's August 23, 1943, issue appeared on my actual birthday. This particular *Life* magazine illustrates the stereotyping of Black and white in the world that I entered. The Lindy Hop, a Black-initiated dance, is portrayed on the cover by a delicately posed white couple shot in high-key lighting while inside the magazine a primitive, wildly posed Black couple with animal-like facial expressions is submerged in low-key lighting. "Lindy" is short for Charles A. Lindbergh, an international hero who was also a known Nazi sympathizer. In another article, Lucille Ball's pink skin, red hair, and blue eyes are shown as the standard for testing and measuring the exposure range in Technicolor film. Elsewhere, *Life* magazine issues an official denial countering the claim of the German Nazi soldiers that "the best fighters they encountered in North Africa were Australian troops and American Negro troops."

How can I trace the movement of such an elusive negative energy or chart the invisibility of the injustice or even begin to outline the impact of such an inaccessible power? The story I write here is a journey through my memory and the remaining odd scraps of letters, photographs, and cultural artifacts, coupled with information gleaned from interviews with those still alive to explore my past. Eventually, my family was fractured by these powers outside our grasp.

These earlier, grandiose 1943 assumptions have finally been proven false, and the proof comes from the contributions of ordinary people. The Lindy Hop evolved into Rap and Hip-Hop, the financial salvation and creative infusion of an anemic global music industry. Film's exposure range in motion picture cinematography has broadened. Black skin's dusky golden highlights and shadows are illuminated in the cinematic visions of today's Black independent filmmakers such as Spike Lee, Euzhan Palcy, Charles Burnett, Julie Dash, and Haile Germina, among others.

And the incredible contributions of African Americans to this country's military history are beginning to appear in films like Norman Jewison's *Glory*, Sidney Poitier's *Buck and the Preacher*, Charles Haid's *Buffalo Soldiers*, and Paul Espinosa's *The Hunt for Pancho Villa*. As to *Life* magazine's August 23, 1943, claim that "Negroes remain essentially untried as fighters," time has proven the report false. I know this because on July 16, 2000, I was there in Sommocolonia, a tiny Italian village, watching this village pay tribute to the African American soldiers who courageously fought to save it from the Germans in December 1944.

In Sommocolonia's case, for close to sixty years a group of African American soldiers who survived that battle and the Italian villagers they rescued persisted in telling anyone who would listen their account of the events that transpired. Ultimately, their version has reached the world. In the early summer of 2000, the writer Solace Sheets e-mailed a press release to major world press organs about Sommocolonia's upcoming celebration. Through a collection of press clippings, we can trace this story's journey from her e-mail to a front-page article in the Sunday, July 16, 2000, edition of the *New York Times*.

In my fifty-eight-year lifetime, everything assumed as true in *Life*'s 1943 magazine has been proven false in 2000, simply because people designated as powerless have successfully challenged the assumptions. Success in situations like this remind me that all of us must tell our stories.

Ill-equipped and unlettered in the ways of power, my mother still triumphed. She taught me how to fight back. Yet how she succeeded and failed was based on what she had learned from those before and around her. This memoir summarizes both the painful and joyful lessons that I've learned in return from her struggles and triumphs.

I want to finally make sense of the tragedy that racism made of our lives. For me, *Life* magazine maps the contours of a madness that devastated our family as we passed through the twentieth century. My hope is that the story told here will serve as one more blueprint for those who follow us. With all this in mind, I begin our story.

My mother, Mollie Carroll Parrott, was born January 21, 1900.

27

28

Some of Philadelphia's Negro Soldiers. Photo of colored troops who were wounded or gassed in the fighting in France. They are all from Philadelphia.

To: Carroll Blue
From: Carroll Blue
Subject: "La Rocca alla Pace"
Cc:
Bcc:
X-Attachments:

1

Date: Wed, 02 Aug 2000 21:51:10
From: Solace Sheets
Reply-To:
To: Carroll Blue
Subject: "La Rocca alla Pace"

Dear Carroll,

I am leaving here tomorrow and realized I wanted to send you some info. Below is the press release that I sent out before the Sommocolonia event. There were several articles you may be interested in checking out: Newsweek of July 24, The New York Times front page article Sunday, July 16, 2000 and the San Francisco Chronicle of July 13. This last mentioned article by Frank Viviano is excellent and should be helpful to you.

I hope you had a pleasant stay in Lucca. I'm sorry I missed meeting you there. Good luck with your book -- it sounds interesting -- I will look for it.

Best,
Solace

PRESS RELEASE:

WWII Heroism of African American soldiers overlooked for half century by nation it served -- Now Black vets honored in Tuscan village

contact Solace Wales:

Sommocolonia, Italy

The dawn after Christmas 1944, the future of Europe hung in the balance as a handful of black American soldiers stood alone against the Wehrmacht in one of the final German offensives of World War II. Very few lived to tell their story -- and it was soon lost in the mist of haphazard U.S. history and stark racial indifference.

But the people of Sommocolonia never forgot the black GIs who fed them that terrible winter and died defending their village. Next month, on July 16, they will honor the black soldiers in a way that their own country failed to for more than half a century. Seven African American veterans -- among the last survivors of the segregated U.S. Army division that held this strategic Tuscan mountain ridge on the southern front -- will gather here to help initiate a monument to peace on the site of the Battle of Sommocolona. They are coming to remember their own participation in the action and to honor their

---

compatriots who died here.

Vastly outnumbered by attacking troops from an elite Austrian alpine unit, and cut off from supplies and any possibility of relief, the seventy "Buffalo Soldiers" -- the popular nickname for men of the all black 92nd Infantry Division -- at Sommocolonia held out until nearly two thirds of them were dead and many of the others wounded. Finding his outpost surrounded by enemy soldiers, the forward observer, Lt. John Fox, called in a massive artillery assault on his own position.

Until 1997, when President Clinton posthumously awarded the Congressional Medal of Honor to Fox -- fifty-two years after he died in Sommocolonia -- the heroism of these men was completely overlooked by the nation it served. Not a single black American received the Medal of Honor in the immediate aftermath of WWII.

The Buffalo soldiers' own commanding general, who was white, was openly opposed to their deployment on the Italian front. A small coterie of black veterans struggled for decades to win recognition for Fox. In the end, it took a special act of Congress in 1996 to secure the Medal of Honor for him and six other black Americans who served in the Allied effort.

Among those coming to Sommocolonia this July is Arlene Fox, Lt. John Fox's widow. She will be accompanied by her daughter, who was two years old when her father died, and by two grandchildren.   About twenty-five black Americans will be present at the initiation of "La Rocca alla Pace" (Rock to Peace), a medieval fortress site at the top of the village which will become a monument/park.

At the site to honor the Buffalo Soldiers and Fox family, will be the American Consul General to Florence, Hilarian Martinez and key Italian officials of the region, along with Sommocolonian villagers who lived through the disastrous battle. Among the participating veterans are Otis Zachary, who was ordered to fire the cannons at his close friend, John Fox, and Rothacker Smith, a medic who, himself wounded early in the battle, still managed to bandage others in his company. Smith was then taken prisoner and shipped to Germany in a boxcar.

FOR FURTHER INFORMATION ON THE MONUMENT:
contact Solace Wales

"LA ROCCA ALLA PACE" IN SOMMOCOLONIA, ITALY

Greatly outnumbered and outgunned, Lt. John Fox and the other African American soldiers could not prevent the Axis from breaking through the "Gothic Line" at Sommocolonia. But they did succeed in dramatically slowing the last great Nazi counteroffensive in southern Europe. Fox's Headquarters in the valley below was only obliged to withdraw a mile and a half, a much less significant retreat than if the Germans had met with little resistence. Some German military analysts had hoped to advance all the way to the critical port of Livorno, which could have put the entire Allied invasion in chaos. Instead,

LA NAZIONE

QN *Quotidiano Nazionale*

RITAGLIA
IL BOLLINO

LUCCA

✚ OGGI QUOTIDIANO NET ➔

WWW.LANAZIONE.IT

ANNO 142 • N. 195

DOMENICA 16 LUGLIO 2000 • Lire 2.000 a Toscana, Umbria e prov. La Spezia in abbonamento obbligatorio con GENTE Lire 1.500 nelle altre zone di diffusione

Trapezista vive da vegetale in una roulotte

Montecatini: abbandonato da moglie e figli. I genitori chiedono aiuto

SERVIZIO A PAGINA 5

La «Buffalo» torna a Barga Festa dei veterani

La mitica divisione americana oggi in Garfagnana, liberata nel '44

PAGINA A PAGINA 10

DOMANI
in regalo
I TASCABILI
CON LINUS, SNOOPY, CHARLIE BROWN...
LA NAZIONE

Divisione Buffalo, ultimo urrah
Il ritorno dei «liberatori»

Sopra il presidente Clinton conferisce a Vernon Baker, uno dei sopravvissuti della Buffalo, la medaglia d'onore. A fianco, la vedova del tenente Fox con il sindaco di Barga e nel riquadro Fox 50 anni fa

di Paolo Pacini

...stri!

...ché oggi nel pa-...ocolonia, sulle ...ano i veterani ...la mitica divi-...i rese protago-...nosa battaglia ...Quello fu un ...Sommocolo-...sere stato l'ul-...ve si è com-...ra mondiale. ...civili, soldati ...italiani e te-...queste parti ...eppure oltre

...ella «Buffa-...npati a quel ...nuovo qua ...ti in trenta

per partecipare alla cerimonia che vuole ricordare quella battaglia e tutti i suoi morti, a cominciare dal tenente John Fox che cadde eroicamente nel paese. Molti dei veterani hanno vissuto direttamente quel tragico episodio e oggi, sebbene ormai ottantenni, sono voluti tornare per rivivere quei momenti. Momenti così lontani, ma ancora impressi nella memoria. E per qualcuno anche nella carne. Con loro anche la vedova del tenente Fox, la signora Arlene. Il marito è stato uno dei primi soldati di colore ad essere insignito della «Medaglia d'onore», la più alta onorificenza americana dal presidente Clinton, nel 1997. Fino ad allora, il contributo eroico dei «black» alla guerra di liberazione, era stato ingiustamente relegato in secondo piano.

La cerimonia si terrà stamani alle 11,30 a Sommocolonia dopo la celebrazione di una messa (ore 10,30), in occasione della Festa della Madonna del Carmine. Assie-

me ai veterani saranno presenti i partigiani che combatterono in paese, i civili che vissero quei momenti e numerose autorità civili e militari italiane e americane. Seguirà un ritrovo conviviale e alla sera a Sommocolonia le celebrazioni si chiuderanno con la tradizionale processione per la Madonna del Carmine. Il tutto per lanciare un messaggio importante: il progetto della «Rocca alla Pace», il monumento che dovrà nascere in paese, sui resti dell'antica rocca. Un'opera che ricorderà non solo i morti di quella terribile battaglia del '44, ma tutti i morti della guerra. Di una parte e dell'altra, quale segno di pacificazione e di riconciliazione tra i popoli.

Ieri, intanto, la vedova Fox e i veterani della «Buffalo» con i loro familiari, sono stati ricevuti ufficialmente nella sala consiliare di Barga dal sindaco Umberto Sereni. Con loro anche molti giornalisti americani. Pronti a cogliere la lacrima furtiva del soldato Ryan.

Carroll Blue,10/21/00 1:00 PM -0800,"La Rocca alla Pace"

compatriots who died here.

Vastly outnumbered by attacking troops from an elite Austrian alpine unit, and cut off from supplies and any possibility of relief, the seventy "Buffalo Soldiers" -- the popular nickname for men of the all black 92nd Infantry Division -- at Sommocolonia held out until nearly two thirds of them were dead and many of the others wounded. Finding his outpost surrounded by enemy soldiers, the forward observer, Lt. John Fox, called in a massive artillery assault on his own position.

Until 1997, when President Clinton posthumously awarded the Congressional Medal of Honor to Fox -- fifty-two years after he died in Sommocolonia -- the heroism of these men was completely overlooked by the nation it served. Not a single black American received the Medal of Honor in the immediate aftermath of WWII.

The Buffalo soldiers' own commanding general, who was white, was openly opposed to their deployment on the Italian front. A small coterie of black veterans struggled for decades to win recognition for Fox. In the end, it took a special act of Congress in 1996 to secure the Medal of Honor for him and six other black Americans who served in the Allied effort.

Among those coming to Sommocolonia this July is Arlene Fox, Lt. John Fox's widow. She will be accompanied by her daughter, who was two years old when her father died, and by two grandchildren. About twenty-five black Americans will be present at the initiation of "La Rocca alla Pace" (Rock to Peace), a medieval fortress site at the top of the village which will become a monument/park.

At the site to honor the Buffalo Soldiers and Fox family, will be the American Consul General to Florence, Hilarian Martinez and key Italian officials of the region, along with Sommocolonian villagers who lived through the disastrous battle. Among the participating veterans are Otis Zachary, who was ordered to fire the cannons at his close friend, John Fox, and Rothacker Smith, a medic who, himself wounded early in the battle, still managed to bandage others in his company. Smith was then taken prisoner and shipped to Germany in a boxcar.

FOR FURTHER INFORMATION ON THE MONUMENT: contact Solace Wales

"LA ROCCA ALLA PACE" IN SOMMOCOLONIA, ITALY

Greatly outnumbered and outgunned, Lt. John Fox and the other African American soldiers could not prevent the Axis from breaking through the "Gothic Line" at Sommocolonia. But they did succeed in dramatically slowing the last great Nazi counteroffensive in southern Europe. Fox's Headquarters in the valley below was only obliged to withdraw a mile and a half, a much less significant retreat than if the Germans had met with little resistence. Some German military analysts had hoped to advance all the way to the critical port of Livorno, which could have put the entire Allied invasion in chaos. Instead,

Carroll Ann

At 3 yrs.

31

I believe corporatization has been the key political issue since the conquistadors. Corporations were created to enable the exploitation of the New World by profit-seeking commercial entities....Bear in mind that the American colonies rose up not against the tyranny of a crazed King George, but against the rule of his chartered corporations....In essence, America was created to end corporate abuse. That we have become what we feared is ironic, and would be merely of historical interest were it not for the fact that corporate activity today threatens life itself.

—Paul Hawken, "Down to Business: Paul Hawken on Reshaping the Economy"

We could define *All About My Mother* as a screwball drama. Delirious drama, baroque, filled with extreme characters, beat up by chance...

—Pedro Almodóvar on *All About My Mother*

Chapter II **All about My Mother**

Spain figures somewhere in there, near the beginning of my own story. My story's beginning is centuries old. It's also a story encased in the institution of slavery, the African holocaust. Spain is part of me. It is the country that financed Christopher Columbus's trip to the New World. In a roundabout way, I wouldn't be here if it weren't for Spain. That country's greedy quest for wealth and expansion led to both its conquest and its eventual loss of the Americas. This is the part of my story that is centuries long. Spain's initial aggression led to my ancestor's captivity. Spain's desire is how my mother ended up rubbing salve into her father's back. A former slave, my grandfather suffered in old age from battered skin full of crust-filled cracks from old whip marks.

Early on, I found out about Spain for myself. I read about it when I was eleven years old. It happened almost by accident. Curiosity motivated my efforts. I wondered about my mother's strange reaction to Spain. I wanted to know why this place so far away from us could cause such an odd reaction on her part.

My mother had been reading about Spain's history. Some days I imagine that my mother might have been a formidable intellectual if she had been trained properly. She was so hungry for the life of the mind. Such lofty notions on how to live in full debate with ideas were given a very short shrift for any young Black woman like my mother who was born in the segregated South at the beginning of the twentieth century. The South was where my mother became this Negro woman jailed inside a segregation full of separate and unequal institutions. It was a prison

where "great ideas," my mother would often say, "were scarcer than a hen's teeth."

So she hunted down culture with an inventiveness that bordered on cunning. She enlisted the services of the United States Postal system by subscribing to every major print organ she could afford. Her choices were eclectic. Primary for her was her membership in the Book-of-the-Month Club. Then there were the magazines—*National Geographic, Harper's, Atlantic Monthly, Daily Word, Look, Life,* and *Time.* Books, records, and magazines were frequent infusions of a "high cotton" culture that would arrive in our mailbox from the North. We received the daily mail with great flourish and anticipation. Anticipation because safe escapes lay inside these printed words. Through these printed materials, my mother found a way to dialogue with other minds about ideas.

One day, a very large, heavy, black hardcover book appeared. Inside this particular book was an old-style cartographer's map of the New World—North and South America with Mexico and Central America in between. Some priest who had traveled with the Spaniards through Mexico had written it.

This time, it took her longer than a month to read the book, but she had finally finished it. I watched her as she closed the heavy book with a tired thud. She paused, shivered, and made a face that read distasteful. "The Spanish are inhumane," she concluded dryly, factually. And then, she went on with her life. I don't believe she ever mentioned this book again. This was strange behavior. My mother almost never dismissed anything. I believe my amazing persistence comes from her steeled will to almost never give up. I had rarely seen her withdraw with such certain finality.

"Who, then, are the Spanish?" I remember thinking. "And what makes them inhumane?" I was undaunted by the book's size. I was too full of curiosity about my mother's response. So, later, I picked up her roundly discarded book to learn what had happened inside to defeat my mother.

It was all there, in this priest's diary. In it, a tragedy unfolded through a written record of a bloody trail left by the Spanish conquistadors: the mass murders done to helpless people on little to no pretext; the horrid spread of syphilis and tuberculosis on those remaining; all about the giving nature and innocence of the indigenous people; about how, after killing the men, they raped the women and then slaughtered them along with the children.

My mother had a lovely, delicate handwriting. Her lettering had well-formed curves. Her sentences were written in almost straight, perfect lines, as if she followed an invisible ruler on a blank page. While reading a book she would argue with its printed thoughts, fiercely underlining ideas she either loved or

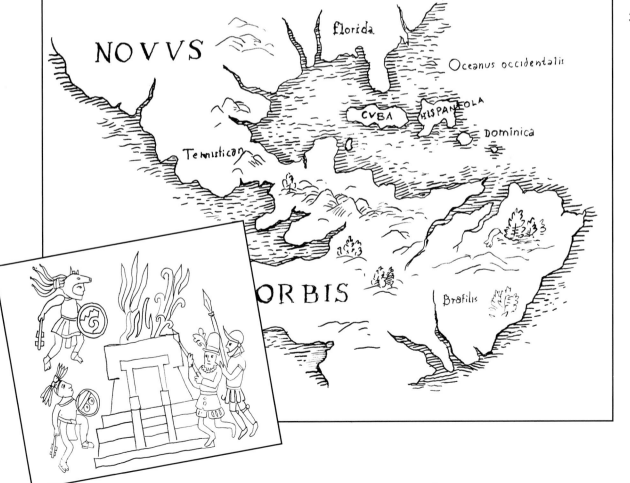

hated right on the page. Her thoughts were written sideways and in the empty spaces at the tops and bottoms of pages. I took great pleasure in reading books after she'd finished them. It was as though she and I could touch each other around someone else's ideas. Her notes appeared in the beginning of the priest's report, but as the story grew more horrific, her scribblings grew sparse. Soon there were no notes from her at all.

Around the same time, Joseph Mankiewicz's 1954 film, *The Barefoot Contessa,* allowed me my first visual glimpse that I can recall of Spain. Ava Gardner, whose actual background was that of a southern white woman of desperately poor origins, with her exotic dark looks, drop-dead-gorgeous body, and a distinct cleft in her chin, was this film's star. Her real-life past was appropriate for her portrayal of this Contessa who, like her, was a famous movie queen who had risen from Spanish slums. Even as a star, this Contessa liked to keep her bare feet in the dirt. I was about eleven years old when I first saw the film with my father. What little I did remember of the experience was that I loved the idea of bare feet, that Humphrey Bogart was her friend, and that Spain, her country, had a tradition of something mysterious, passionate, and red. That something was characterized by clicking castanets, singing voices that sounded in deep pain, dramatic guitar strumming, and rhythmic dancing in tune with the stomping feet, and it was called flamenco.

Ava Gardner. Now, here was a different kind of a woman. Forget the teasing of a Marilyn Monroe or a Dorothy Dandridge. Ava was potent, sensual, and independent. In real life, she floored even Frank Sinatra. Ava was tough like Joan Crawford in *Johnny Guitar,* Barbara Stanwyck in *All I Desire,* and Bette Davis in *All About Eve.* These women were exceptionally beautiful and sexual to the point of possessing unheard-of loose morals. They were strong, feisty, and powerful enough to dominate the males who dared to love them. Clearly, these were women in control. They lived by an internal gyroscope, rather than by society's rules. What would happen to our society if all women acted like them? What this meant in the movies was that these women were somehow—in the end—going to be punished for being free spirits. I knew enough as a moviegoer by then to know that by any such film's final frame, this kind of strong woman always ended up badly.

Not too long after seeing *The Barefoot Contessa,* I was confronted by Nell Grovey, the newly adult daughter of my mother's friend. She had seen me in the movie theater lobby that night. "Why on earth," she demanded to know from me, "would your father take you to see THAT film?" The hostility in her voice implied that my father was either insensitive or not protective.

"Why not?" I quickly shot back.

When I was irritated, the insolent edge in my voice never quite left me, no matter how many times my parents attempted to slap it out of me. My retort was so harsh that the force of it took Nell aback. I could also tell she wanted to hit me, but then she was not my parent and we both knew it. Her eyes narrowed. Her unyielding stare boring straight into my eyes dared me.

"Soooo . . . what was that movie about?" She tensed, waiting for my answer. Flinching, I wavered. It didn't take much time for me to realize that I had absolutely no idea what the film was about. Quickly, scenes flashed before me—the colorful landscapes, Ava's barefoot dancing, and the staccato music. And there was the gentleness that caretaker Humphrey Bogart gave to a very independent and therefore-in-peril Ava Gardner. My impressions were all that I could piece together. Ah yes, there was a wedding night and a funeral. And in the end, she was destroyed. But what did it all add up to? What ever did it all mean?

In my confusion, I looked down at the floor. "Well?" she twisted her knife-sharpened words deeper into my helpless silence. In this uncomfortable quiet I felt overwhelmed with shame—shame because I really didn't know.

Nell's mean-spirited question forced me to realize that movies were supposed to be about something. Yet, I couldn't fathom the "meaning" that seemed to come naturally to adults. I was still a child, and I was angry with myself for that fact. To this day, I am still charged with finding the content and meaning in film. But for now, my time was up, and Nell didn't let me forget it. Still glaring at me, she formed a triumphant smile over her clenched teeth. "That's why," she hissed at me, "your father had no right to take you to that film."

It took until 1962, almost twelve years, for me to lose that shame. By this time, I was an English literature student at Boston University, and I had made up my mind to become a writer. So I wrote everything: essays, short stories, poems . . . I told everyone I knew that I was going to be a writer. Yet, I had absolutely no idea how this would happen. Other than two poets—Vivian Ayers Allen and Gwendolyn Brooks—at the time, I knew of no other Negro women writers.

In 1962, young African American women were as invisible to the world surrounding them as was a gentle chill of the first autumn wind. My best friend in college was Karen Belgrade, a working-class Jewish girl. We both loved the written word and had majored in literature.

Karen was my first intellectual colleague. We'd spend hours discussing our ideas as we prepared our class papers. Only in recent years has she admitted to me that my papers were, in some cases, better than hers. She confessed to me that in our classes together she would be embarrassed when we got our grades back on our papers. She was amazed that I would get C's and D's and she would consistently get A's. Her shame came from knowing that I was somehow being punished for being Black. Her confession didn't surprise me. Early in my college career, I had become inured to racism. Almost daily I am somehow reminded that I am Black, female, poor, of absolutely no value, and therefore completely useless in a white, male-dominated world. Even now, I use the chill inside my hardness to get through every single day of my life.

However, every once in a while I would get an encouraging sign. One day in May 1962, Bonnie Jones, a fellow Black student, introduced me to an emerging young writer she knew. A few days later, William Melvin Kelley told me that he was not personally impressed with me. I was too young, shy, and tentative. But out of courtesy to Bonnie, he did ask to read something that I had written. I gave him a short story I'd just finished. When he returned my story to me, he told me, "You are a writer." And then he disappeared. I never spoke to or saw him again. But he'd added several handwritten pages of his notes to my story.

On these extra pages he'd given me his feedback in bright red ink. This was the first time anyone had ever taken me seriously as an artist. Eagerly, I read his comments over and over. When I finally looked up, it was late that night. And so William Melvin Kelley's affirmation of my work's value became a written mantra for me. Those pages from him were a bold, red-lettered shield that I would pull out to read whenever I was dismissed, ignored, or rejected or felt doubt. That summer of 1962, I remember going on the bus to Mexico City from Houston, Texas, to study Spanish. I took my story with me. While riding on the bus, I remember pulling it out at odd times—with the first morning light or late at night, squinting from the dull overhead light as the bus strained up a mountain road.

One day in Mexico City I saw in the paper that *The Barefoot Contessa* was playing. My shame surfaced. What *was* that film about? So I got up the courage to see *Contessa* for the second time. This time it had Spanish subtitles. Now I was a young adult, about Nell's age when she confronted me about my first viewing of *Contessa*.

Sitting in the movie house, I was surprised to see that *Contessa* held up remarkably well over the years. That's what good film is about, I remember thinking. It is a well-crafted story with terrific acting. This time the story was about a free spirit of a woman who ends up marrying her Prince Charming. Instead of being a frog, he, to her distress, turns out to have no penis ("it was lost in the war," Rossano Brazzi solemnly tells Ava on their wedding night). Her punishment? She'd finally met a decent man who could love and cherish her. The kicker was that he was a eunuch. He could not satisfy her raging and well-experienced libido in bed. Finally, I thought, I understood the meaning of *The Barefoot Contessa*. The real lesson I got much later. It was that, as a woman, I'd better not be too sexual, too independent, and too powerful or I would come to a tragic end similar to Ava's in *The Barefoot Contessa*.

Spain is the country that is at the beginning of my own story as a filmmaker. So in December 1984, when the Spanish government invited me to screen my film

Varnette's World: A Study of a Young Artist at the Bilbao International Short Film Festival, I jumped at the opportunity. It was my first trip to Europe. Traveling from the airport into town, I quickly caught a glimpse of a hanging effigy. It was so real-looking that I audibly gasped. The people on the bus reassured me that it was a figure stuffed with straw.

That very day Bilbao was full of the first large protests I'd seen since the 1960s. There were massive labor union protests, shootings, killings, and bombings going on during my entire stay in Spain's Basque country. I was in the heart of Spain's contradictions.

In the days that followed, I ate fresh sardines and those thin, yellow-skinned pomegranates that were as sweet as sugar. I walked through Bilbao's old quarter, lightly touching its gray stone buildings. I met filmmakers from all over the world at late-night screenings and in smoke-filled bars. I fed my eyes with richly colored paintings of every era and stumbled upon surreal contemporary photographs found in Bilbao's many museums and galleries. These were pre–Frank Gehry's Guggenheim Museum days. We, the festival guests, were summoned to city hall to witness a remarkable pomp-and-circumstance ceremony honoring us. I soon discovered that behind all these proud traditions, Bilbao in 1984 was fast fading into a genteel poverty. Its past as an economic miracle harbored a wildly successful commercial heritage that fed Spain's coffers. No wonder the Spanish tolerated the Basques. This was due to its 1970s supertanker manufacturing boom that went bust when the Japanese mastered the art of shipbuilding.

In 1984, Bilbao's claim to fame, after the city was finally brought to its financial knees, was that it now was home to one of the largest heroin-addict populations in Europe. They were hidden in the back streets of the city. I walked through its well-groomed and civilly inhabited parks on Sunday afternoons. I reveled in the placid domesticity of whole families, from elders to babies, buttressed with baby carriages and well-behaved dogs on leashes. Listening to the droning voice of my slightly vindictive guide, I was informed that I should not be lulled to sleep by what I saw before me. That most of the seemingly upright gentlemen, fathers and sons so cheerfully at their families' sides, spent their nights desperately combing the heroin-filled city streets in search of the prostitutes—male and female—whose presence promised to satisfy their masculine desires. Angrily, my guide spat out that it was all the fault of the repressive Catholic Church.

By now I knew about Spain's religious oppression through the works of its former sons, well-known artists like Pablo Picasso, Francisco de Goya, Salvador Dalí, and filmmaker Luis Buñuel. They too railed against the tyrannical power of the church. And they did so with this strangely perverse sense of humor similar to that employed by American Blacks. The Spanish maintained a "laughing to keep from crying" kind of humor. This bittersweet, blues-kind-of funny made me, a Black person, feel right at home in this strange country.

Fifteen years later, during the very last days of the twentieth century, I watched the film *All About My Mother*. Spanish filmmaker Pedro Almodóvar also is a child of his country's contradictions. He uses film much the same way that I approach writing this memoir. He understands cinema's influence on the roles that we play. We both are at work deciphering what is reality and what is image in the behaviors we adopt as our own.

Huma, one of Almodóvar's central characters, desires to be *All About Eve*'s Bette Davis. Sitting next to his mother, Esteban watches *All About Eve* on television. A tragic young figure, he is an aspiring writer. While watching the film, he decides to title his book *All About My Mother*, in tribute to her. According to the filmmaker, the title is a tribute to Bette Davis, Romy Schneider, all women, all men who act like women, and, finally, to his own mother. Perhaps Almodóvar is right; it really does take a village of women and men who act like women to mother every child.

I also realize that the writer and director of both *All About Eve* and *The Barefoot Contessa* is the same person, Joseph L. Mankiewicz. He also wrote and directed

No Way Out, another unforgettable film that my whole family admired. The Mankiewicz family is a formidable theatrical and motion-picture family lasting from late-1920s silent films to at least the 1980s. This family name represents the films of two brothers—Herman (*Duck Soup*, *Citizen Kane*) and Joseph (*The Philadelphia Story*, *The Ghost and Mrs. Muir*, *No Way Out*, *All About Eve*, *Guys and Dolls*, *Suddenly, Last Summer*, and *King: A Filmed Record . . . Montgomery to Memphis*). Joseph had a son, Tom, who was also a writer and director (*Diamonds Are Forever*, *Mother, Jugs & Speed*, *Superman I* and *II*, *Ladyhawke*, and *Dragnet*). How odd, I think, that the dynasty of these three faceless men, as writers, directors, and producers, has contributed so much toward creating the unforgettable images of strong women that Almodóvar and I hold up to such high esteem.

Joan Crawford, Bette Davis, and Ava Gardner instilled that independence that I still cling to so strongly. The late Audre Lorde said it best in her essay "Uses of the Erotic: The Erotic as Power":

> For as we begin to recognize our deepest feelings, we begin to give up, of necessity, being satisfied with suffering and self-negation, and with the numbness which so often seems like their only alternative in our society. Our acts against oppression become integral with self, motivated and empowered from within.

It is January 21, 2000. Today I celebrate both the entrance of the twenty-first century and my mother's centennial birthday. After my morning routine, I settle in to read a new book that I've just gotten in the mail. *Struggles for Representation* is a history of African American documentary film and video makers. It contains a comprehensive interview of mine. In it, I detail my documentary film work from its beginning to the 1992 work that I did for the late Marlon Riggs's *Black Is . . . Black Ain't*.

As I rise to greet the dawn, I remember my ancestral spirits. I make sure to light two candles—one for this new century and one for my mother.

Struggles for Representation

African American Documentary Film and Video

EDITED BY
Phyllis R. Klotman
AND
Janet K. Cutler

Indiana University Press

BLOOMINGTON AND INDIANAPOLIS

INTERVIEWS

Over the course of the last five years co-editors Phyllis Klotman and Janet Cutler conducted interviews with many documentary film/video-makers who have played a vital role in shaping the direction of African American documentary film and video. While the interviews evolved in different ways in response to the film/videomakers' specific interests and concerns, the same core questions were posed to each of the documentarians. All were asked, for example, to comment on the place of documentary work in their careers, to offer a personal perspective on the nature and function of documentary filmmaking, and to describe the production circumstances and funding environment in which they worked.

The interviews with film/videomakers have been used in two ways. They have served as an important resource tool for the scholar/authors, providing a source for quoted material within the chapters. In addition, the interviews have been excerpted in the following appendix to the book. These excerpts are necessarily fragmentary, having been taken from much longer interview material. Not official artists' statements, they nonetheless provide insight into the careers of very different individuals with diverse experiences and views of the forces that shaped their work in documentary. Full transcripts of the interviews are available for study at the Black Film Center/Archive at Indiana University.

CARROLL PARROTT BLUE

My background is in still photography. I managed to do a summer workshop at MIT guided by Minor White back around 1967. And I started doing street photography during that time. I had seen the work of Roy DeCarava beforehand. His approach to photography was a guiding light for me in terms of what could be done around making images of African American people. He practiced a Black aesthetic—a way of viewing Blacks with pride—that I've incorporated. In 1967, I started walking the Boston streets, taking photographs and keeping what I had seen in Roy's work in the back of my mind.

My documentary photography ended up being published in a wonderful book series called *The Black Photographers Annual*. There were four volumes published. I was very proud to be in volumes three and four. Joe Crawford was one of the original organizers. He took money that he made from an engineering job and poured the money into publishing these books. The series used Black photographers from everywhere. It featured historic sections highlighting pioneers from the early part of this century—P. H. Polk, official photographer for Tuskegee Institute; Harlem's James Van Der Zee; Addison Scurlock, Howard University's official photographer; and Hamilton Smith, from Boston. So you had a sense of the longevity of this tradition's aesthetic. It also included the work of the Kamoinge ("Group Effort") Workshop. Roy DeCarava co-founded this group in New York in the '60s. Kamoinge was part of the public protest against the Metropolitan Museum of Art's "Harlem on My Mind" 1969 exhibition. The group disapproved of the art this museum brought to us as a people. The exhibition contradicted what our aesthetic really was. I am still firmly entrenched in this Black aesthetic. These books honor a positive, beautiful image of the Black people in terms of family, in terms of work, in terms of entertainment and pleasure.

I went to Boston University from 1960 to 1964, graduating in English Literature. I specialized in the English Renaissance period. I wanted to write. Yet, I ended up moving to Los Angeles after graduating and becoming a probation officer. Working on this job, I kept wondering how I was going to do something creative with my life. Soon I quit writing. And I pondered how I was going to get back into it. It was then that I made a decision to go into still photography. I demoted myself from being a probation officer to become a night attendant at Central Juvenile Hall. I worked there from ten at night to six in the morning. Then from nine to five daily, I went to Los Angeles Trade–Technical College, where I majored in still photography. That was my beginning. In Los Angeles at the time, there was another photographer who came from the same tradition as Roy DeCarava. His name was Leonard Taylor. He made incredibly beautiful images. Leonard and Roy were the most influential in terms of helping me to develop my own style and personal expression. After publishing my photographs in *The Black Photographers Annual*, I made a trip back to New York and was introduced to Roy. After he looked at my portfolio, he asked me to go and photograph a smile. That was my hardest assignment.

In L.A. I also met Robert Nakamura, a Japanese American photographer and filmmaker. Bob had just graduated from UCLA Film School. He, with other UCLA Asian American filmmakers, had started a media arts organization called Visual Communications. Today this is the premiere Asian American media arts center. He said, "Well, you're doing photography so you might as well be doing film. Why don't you do film and photography together?" By this time I was working for Professor Harold Zirin, the NASA solar weatherman, at the California Institute of Technology's Solar Astronomy Laboratory. I was a darkroom technician. They would film the sun every day. They threw me into this lab and had me print and process both 16mm and 35mm film. And so I got a chance to work with a contact printer and optical printing in the development of 16mm and 35mm film. I got a chance to see how film worked on a technical level. Around this time, Bob asked me if I would be interested in going to UCLA Film School. So I went to UCLA Film School with this base as a still photographer and a film lab technician. I ended up with an East Coast education from Boston University from 1960 to 1964 and a West Coast education from UCLA from 1976 to 1980.

At UCLA I was influenced by a lot of the Black student filmmakers: Haile Gerima, Larry Clark, Charles Burnett, Ben Caldwell, John Reir, Pam Jones, Billy Woodberry—all who had come in before me. Now my class had several very good Black students as well—Julie Dash, Sharon Larkin, Barbara McCullough, Bernard Nichols and me. We came in together around 1976. Some other classmates were Ramon Melendez (*Stand and Deliver*); Alex Cox (*Repo Man*); Michael Miner (*Robocop*); and Neal Jimenez (*The River's Edge* and *Waterdance*). During this time I was also influenced by the work of Topper Carew's *Say Brother,* of Ellis Haizlip's *Soul!,* of William Greaves's *Black Journal* and New York–style filmmakers such as St. Clair Bourne, Stan Lathan, Gil Noble, Charles Hobson, and Kathleen Collins. Johnny Simmons, then a USC film student, introduced me to Carlton Moss. Carlton Moss introduced me to Frances Williams. Both major film pioneers, Frances and Carlton were the most important mentors for me in this early independent Black film community.

Meanwhile, Robert Nakamura had come back to teach at UCLA Film School. He asked me to be his graduate teaching assistant. During my first teaching experience, my students included Melvonna Ballinger and John Esaki. Bob was really instrumental in encouraging me to combine still photography and documentary filmmaking with teaching. During this time I continued working with Visual Communications. Through them I learned about the idea of taking people's archival photographs and using them to tell stories. I also worked on Bob's film, the first Asian American feature film, *Hito Hata.* And so I was being influenced by African American still photographers and filmmakers while working with Asian American filmmakers as they built an Asian American media community by making documentary and later, feature films.

45

The first film I made at UCLA in 1976 was a Super–8 film called *Two Women.* I had worked on other films and had done smaller things by myself, but this was the first film that I did that I sent out to film festivals after finishing it. Johnny Simmons, who has turned into a wonderful cinematographer and very fine artist, worked with me on this film. The film was a story of a young girl who was eighteen years old and my aunt, Mrs. Lillie Skannal, an older woman who was almost in her eighties. Both women talked about their approach to life. The older woman spoke of her need to turn to a God, or something spiritual to guide her. And the young girl talked about how she used her own will. Before, I had been doing portraiture, still photographs of people so now I translated that style of working into film. *Two Women* was very good for me because I won second place in the 1976 Virgin Islands Film Festival and first place in the 1977 Los Angeles International Film Festival. It was also as a sample portfolio piece used to secure a grant from the American Film Institute to make my next film, *Varnette's World: A Study of a Young Artist.*

Varnette's World won a Gold Hugo, the top award at the 1979 Chicago International Film Festival. It got a lot of play in Europe—everybody was asking for UCLA Black filmmakers' work on the festival circuit. And it turned out that Mark Weiss was producing a local show about independent filmmakers on New York City's PBS station, WNET-TV. He used my film for that program. David Loxton and Kathy Klein saw it and asked if it could be picked up for national broadcast on their program. That's how *Varnette's World* was shown on groundbreaking WNET-TV's series, *Non-Fiction Television.* When I came up with the idea to do a film on Roy DeCarava, I turned to David, who had previously done a film on photographer Henri Cartier Bresson. Immediately he understood my goals and was sympathetic towards what I wanted to do. That's how I got the chance to make *Conversations with Roy DeCarava.*

I went through a lot of trouble to make it to a national broadcast of *Conversations.* David Loxton took my film proposal with Jesus Trevino's proposal to the Corporation for Public Broadcasting and said, "These people deserve money, give it to them with the minority producers set-asides funds." So we got money to make our films. After I finished the film, one PBS executive hated it and blocked it from national prime time broadcast. So I became aware of the "soft feed" system. We made dubs of the video, sent it to several programming people at various stations to get it on air. Although *Conversations* won first place, the Blue Ribbon, at the 1980 American Film Festival, it was still a difficult film to get validated. Today, it's considered a classic. Also, I was able to experiment with some of the formal elements in this film.

Film sound has constantly intrigued me. Especially because as an African American my culture's music is so rich and varied. I like to design sound in film to create dynamic and dramatic atmospheres. In *Conversations with Roy DeCarava,* there's a scene where Roy goes to a subway. As he moves through the subway, I show his subway photographs with the sound of the subway car coming and leaving the station. The design is used as a way of building tension as Roy begins to talk about being a Black photographer encountering prejudice in the 1960 advertising world. The sound emphasizes what that emotional stress and pressure meant to him. The sound, like his life, reached a certain high point. I use this approach to sound the same way in *Varnette's World* and in *Nigerian Art: Kindred Spirits.* Sound is a separate means of telling a story. As a matter of fact, Walter Murch, who got an Academy Award for doing the sound design of *Apocalypse Now,* is my primary sound teacher. He says sound goes straight to the subconscious because your conscious brain can't filter pure sound out. You hear a cry . . . .or, a loud noise. Boom! It goes straight through your brain just as it is, without your thoughts being able to stop it.

Conversations* was made during a very heady period for independent documentaries. We're talking between the early '70s and mid-'80s. Films like *Men's Lives, Rosie the Riveter, Babies and Banners, Seeing Red,* and *Harlan County, U.S.A.* dominated. In 1981–83, I worked for Jane Fonda on three of her feature films—*Rollover, On Golden Pond,* and *Nine to Five.* I also worked on her film for television, *The Dollmaker.* So I got a sense of what Hollywood is like. After this Hollywood experience I made a conscious decision to make personal films out of documentaries.

In the late '80s, I trained with Henry Hampton. I worked on *Eyes on the Prize, Part II.* This was on the *Malcolm X* story and the *Harold Washington* story. Some of the other Black producers on that series included Louis Massiah, Judy Richardson, Sam Pollard, Jackie Shearer. I also trained under Adrian Malone, who did *Cosmos* and *The Ascent of Man,* while Adrian was the executive producer at Smithsonian World. I made *Nigerian Art: Kindred Spirits* under his direction.

Michele Parkerson and I are pretty much contemporaries in terms of what we are doing. Constantly, I look at newer documentary filmmakers. One that I've been really just touched by, beyond belief, is the genius Marlon Riggs. Recently I looked at another avant-garde filmmaker, Tony Cokes, who did *Fade to Black.* I see that many documentary filmmakers are moving more into video, avant-garde, and synthesizing all of the materials into personal expressions. It's almost like jazz. Improvisation, polyrhythms, strange ways of editing and cutting, using

47

strips, moving text—that sort of thing. So I think that technology has a lot to do with how we develop as filmmakers. I have also been influenced by the Black Audio Collective in England. They are working on how to use sound, visuals, and theory in ways that are different, encapsulating all of the stuff I'm talking about.

My biographical life story contains the way I understand the world. I was born on August 23, 1943, in Houston, Texas. I went to elementary school, junior high school, and high school right there in Houston. I remember we had this library contest at Jack Yates High School. The principal said that whoever read the most books would win. I won hands down because I was a kid that read all of the time. So the librarian took the list of books I had read and she said, "Everything on your list is a biography." And up until that time I didn't realize how fascinated I am—even today—with people's lives. Biographies inform me of what my society is about. So that's really what I am doing with documentary film and video. It's not so much me detailing a person's biography. It's me using documentary to get a handle on what my society is by reflecting a person's life on film. How do people get through this society successfully? How do they maintain humanity in a society that doesn't want us to be humane? So that's the essence of what I'm doing. I'm using documentary to comprehend who we are and to leave tracks for people to see and say, "Oh, this is how that person did it. Well, maybe I can do it as well."

My target audience is everybody, or whoever wants to check my work out. Timothy Leary once said, "There are only two kinds of people in the world. There are those who want to evolve and those who don't. And both kinds are at war with each other." I'm with the group that wants to evolve.

JANUARY 1992
LOS ANGELES, CALIFORNIA

IN THE CENTER OF HOUSTON, TEXAS

INDEPENDENCE HEIGHTS
WILL BE INCORPORATED

Colored Municipality Elected Mayor and Two Commissioners at Election Saturday.

Harris county will in the near future have a "colored municipality" in all sense of the word. Independence Heights, a suburb of Houston, with a population of nearly 600 negroes, on Saturday voted almost unanimously in favor of incorporating, only two votes being cast against incorporation.

The commission form of government was adopted by the vote of the citizens at the election held Saturday. A total of 34 votes were polled and G. O. Burgess, candidate for mayor, received 33 votes while his opponent, James P. Parks, received one vote. Two commissioners were elected. H. M. McCullough and S. C. Lamothe. They were not opposed. Independence Heights contains nearly two square miles of territory and the entire population consists of negroes with the exception of three white families.

It is expected that the legal requirements will be fulfilled in a short time and the officers will take the oath of office as soon as possible.

First Negro Town in Texas Is Formed: Officials Colored

The proposition to incorporate Independence Heights carried at the polls yesterday by a vote of 32 to 2. The new city is unique in that its residents, with the possible exception of two or three families are all colored and its officers are all colored. G. O. Burgess, well known colored attorney, was chosen mayor and A. M. McCullough and S. C. Lamothe commissioners.

Independence Heights is located north of Sunset Heights and has a population of between 400 and 600. The negro residents there have always been law abiding and most of them own their homes. They have always conducted themselves in a manner such as to win the respect of white citizens residing adjacent to them and one of the governing factors in the decision to incorporate was a desire on their part to control disorderly elements from the outside.

The new city is further unique in that, according to reports it will be the only incorporated town in Texas in which both city and school officials are practically all negroes.

In the Upper Room with Jesus
Sitting at his blessed feet
Daily there my sin confessing
Begging for his mercy sweet.

Trusting in his grace and power
Seeking there his love and prayer
It is there I feel the spirit
As I sit with him there.
—"In the Upper Room,"
L.E.Campbell

Chapter III **Houston**

My mother was a race woman. Being a race man or woman in the 1950s meant you had dedicated your life to uplifting the Negro race. Your decision also meant that you had consciously endangered yourself. Your surrounding environment would always be hostile and perhaps violent because of your commitment.

One of the safest ways to survive was to form groups of like-minded people and work together. This joint effort provided protection. Someone had to organize these groups and mobilize them toward an action that would effect social, political, and economic change. And so my mother's natural next step after becoming a race woman was to become a community organizer. Primarily she worked through Houston's Negro women's clubs.

While browsing in a bookstore a few years ago, I discovered a remarkable book that gave me insight into the enormous impact of my mother's volunteer work. Ruthe Weingarten's book, *Black Texas Women: 150 Years of Trial and Triumph,* is the first comprehensive history of Black Texas women who toiled like my mother all over the state for over a century. As I rushed through the index of the names of women listed from Houston, I was upset to see her name was missing in the book.

What I did learn was that my mother's seemingly isolated activities reflected a pattern that was part of a historical loss of memory, both nationally and in Texas. This book mirrors my mother's public life completely. It focuses on the Black women's club movement and its contribution to the state's workforce, education, culture, religion, politics, civil rights, and community building. Conversely, my mother's life adds one more piece to the 150-year puzzle of how Black women in Texas came together to create a better life for all Texans. My mother was more like a worker bee or a soldier ant. Historically, she is faceless.

Today, as I write from a vantage point of a certain maturity, I am stunned by how brave, feisty, and relentless my mother was. She worked courageously and tirelessly to right the world's horrible wrongs. Now I place her extraordinary efforts alongside those of Mary McLeod Bethune, Dorothy Height, Marian Anderson, Coretta Scott King, Fannie Lou Hamer, Rosa Parks, Daisy Bates, and Houston's own Christie Adair. All of these women were supported by workers like Mollie Carroll Parrott.

It disturbs me that my mother, my heroine, is invisible to historical record and that her remarkable contributions to Texas life go unmentioned. The Houston women named are the ones I saw stand on the shoulders of my mother's work. I think it is because the book references only the women who made the newspapers or some other public record. These papers became historical records, and so the people written about inside them also became historical record. Very little is written in public records about my mother.

Remember now, I am talking about the South in the 1950s. These were the days when we were "colored," when any white person could publicly humiliate and denigrate any Negro and get away scot-free through the privilege of public, legal, and social sanction. The days when Black men and women were being killed for the simple act of attempting to register to vote, even though their reasons for wanting to vote were perfectly rational. As American citizens, they paid taxes, and so they wanted to have the right to vote that goes with the money they contributed. By having the vote, they could take part in determining who would best represent their interests in public office.

My parents held still-fresh memories of the times when southern lynchings were widespread. They remembered when the peculiar American phenomenon of lynchings occurred almost daily. At one time, Texas had the third highest number of lynchings in the nation. Today Texas still ranks high in deaths resulting from hate crimes and capital punishment, also known as a modern, legalized form of lynching.

One morning over breakfast, my parents discussed one particularly brutal lynching. I remember I was very young, just starting elementary school, but the images that formed in my imagination from their conversation burned deep into my brain cells. To this day, I recall that conversation so vividly that it is almost as if I were still hearing their words for the first time.

I never knew exactly why this particular man was lynched, but the crime he was accused of must have been terrible because the angry white mob surrounding him sought to extract extreme pain from him. My parents spoke of a nude, bound, trembling, and frightened man being led through a crowd that kicked, spat, and beat on him until he reached a stagelike platform facing them. Here a noose was placed around his neck. Then, to the crowd's delight, the man's penis was cut with a blunt hunting knife. The man almost blacked out from the pain. He was forced by the laughing crowd to eat his severed bloody member. Whole. Chewing, crushing, smashing his flesh to bits with his teeth and swallowing until it was all gone.

When he finished eating himself, he was hung to his death. Then his body was doused with kerosene. His corpse was lit and allowed to burn to a crisp. Meanwhile, the mob, in a festive party mood, feasted on barbecue, Rainbo bread, Lone Star beer, and Red soda pop.

Daily, my mother and father woke up to this kind of world—a world that my mother had resolve to change. The tragedy in my mother's struggle is that, in the end, she could not triumph. Instead, she left this battle for equality to us, the living. Even though slavery officially ended in this country in 1865, its racist violence, perpetrated through well-placed hate crimes and government-sanctioned capital punishment, continues to this day.

Jasper, Texas, is a small East Texas timber town of 7,800. With 40 percent of the population Black, it is an integrated community, headed by a Black mayor. Ordinarily, one would not think of this place when imagining hate crimes. Yet, on June 7, 1998, a Saturday night, James Byrd Jr. was walking down a country road from his niece's bridal shower when three white men in a pickup pulled alongside him. Byrd accepted a ride from them, but instead of taking him home, they drove him to an isolated area outside Jasper where they beat him up and spray-painted him. Then they bound his ankles to the end of a twenty-eight-foot-long logging chain attached to the pickup's bumper. For almost three miles they dragged Byrd down Jasper's winding back country roads to his death.

On the following Sunday morning, churchgoers walking these roads discovered Byrd's mangled torso near an African American cemetery. Remains of James Byrd Jr. were strewn everywhere. There were at least seventy-five places on Huff Creek Road where his belongings—bits of his clothes, his keys, and his dentures—were found. Byrd's head, neck, and right arm were located about a mile away from his decapitated body. The men killed James Byrd Jr. simply because he was Black.

And this East Texas, white-supremacist lesson continues past Byrd's 1998 death and the fact that the murderers were given the death sentence. A year later, in 1999, the headstone on Byrd's grave was defaced and the nameplate removed. In March 2000, a Ku Klux Klan Imperial Wizard was photographed next to Byrd's headstone with a sticker that he'd placed on the headstone. It read: "A Ku Klux Klansman was here." The photograph was published in the April 2000 issue of *Details*, the now defunct Condé Nast magazine once described as a lifestyle magazine for Generation X readers.

54

Daily as a young child I observed my mother immersed in grassroots activism. She worked so hard to end the power generated by the fear, violence, and oppression that underlines all racism. Her urgency bordered on mild obsession. And her drive somehow blinded her to the fact that I was also there. I was her child and in her charge as well. At this time, she was fifty-one years old and I was seven. And because I was so young, I didn't understand. All I remember is that I too was scared most of the time. I too woke up to a confusing world. I was swimming in isolation, searching for a friendly shore where I could rest in the warmth and security of a sheltering cove.

I turned to music, which was everywhere—spirituals in the churches, rhythm and blues and gospel music on the radio, pop music on TV, or raw country blues coming from the corner juke joints I'd pass walking the streets. Songs like Mahalia Jackson's "In the Upper Room" became my refuge.

Fortunately, my physical surroundings were exceptionally stable. I lived in the same house and neighborhood until I left for college. My parents were married to each other until death separated them. We lived in a quiet and quite safe part of town. Residential houses were interspersed with "shot-gun" rental houses. Unless the children in these rentals lived next to me, I didn't know them. My house

56

faced a dead-end street. At the end of this street was Blackshear Elementary School, my second school after my first attempt in Mrs. Harrison's kindergarten classes. The Houston Negro Hospital, where I was born, was across the street from Blackshear. When the birth pains came in five-minute intervals, my mother walked from her home to the hospital to have me there. Across the way from the hospital was Kelley's Drugstore, down the street was Rettig's Ice Cream Parlor, and across from that was the office of Dr. Minor, our family doctor. In those days, doctors made home visits. Two blocks on the other side of my house was Jack Yates High School. I had to pass Mr. Gilmore's candy store and Mr. Jackson's gas station and auto repair shop to get to this school. My Aunt Lila and Uncle James Carroll lived across from Jack Yates. Uncle James designed and built my parents' home, his own home, and many other homes and businesses for Houston's Blacks from the 1930s through the end of the 1950s. He was a self-taught architect and building contractor. Mr. and Mrs. Kemp's Cleaners was catty-corner to their home. Down the street from the cleaners was Dr. Richard White's ophthalmology office. Mrs. Hattie Mae White, his wife, was the first Black in Houston to run for and win a seat on the school board. My mother worked tirelessly on her campaign.

Straight past Dr. White's place was Emancipation Park. For a while, this was the only park in Houston open to Negroes. This park was created in the late 1800s solely through the efforts of Houston's concerned Black citizens. Jack Yates High and Blackshear Elementary were named after two of those leaders. Across from the park on the south side was the famous El Dorado Ballroom. It stood on Dowling and Elgin Streets, the Black business part of Third Ward. In the 1930s and 1940s, this ballroom thrived during the big-band heydays. Duke Ellington, Count Basie, Louis Armstrong—all these famous bands would play at lavish social affairs at the grand El Dorado. In the 1950s, it was the home of rhythm and blues: B.B. King, Della Reese, Little Richard, and LaVerne Baker were among its headliners. Across the park on the east was another Rettig's Ice Cream Parlor. Next to it was the Park Theater. Four main churches were perched on corners some blocks away. My parents went to St. John's Baptist Church on Dowling Street. Small businesses dotted the area, including two Black taxicab stands and some eateries, corner stores, and the Mason's Hall. Food stores owned by Chinese, Italians, and Jews were sprinkled throughout the neighborhood. Most everything we needed lay within a walking radius of our home. However, at age seven, I felt terribly alone.

My own mother became so unreachable to me that I used to think she might as well be living on Mars. Both she and my father were seldom at home. Later, as an adult, I discovered that she and my father were also negotiating the terms of a rapidly disintegrating relationship. They had decided to turn their union into a marriage of convenience. And home was not a family haven. We all sought to escape being there. When my mother was home, she was constantly embroiled in multiple arguments with various family, friends, and colleagues. While she angrily spoke into the telephone, I would hear her side of these fights.

Words were her forte. "Why hit a person," my mother used to say with much confidence, "when you can do more damage with what you say?" My mother relished using words as weapons to wound the soul, crush the spirit. Even at such a young age I registered the satisfaction in her eyes as she watched me shrivel while grinding me down with a vicious barrage of her well-appointed words.

There was more that lay behind her meanness. She was under extreme stress. One day I came home to find her hysterical. Her doctor's report was positive. She had cancer and she lost a breast to it. Apart from going through the trauma of breast cancer, my mother was also menopausal. And there was never enough money. Her husband, her aging, the illnesses, and the fact that she had to provide for our family and take care of me, a very young child—all took its toll on her.

Her emotions ran from puzzling opposites to sometimes predictable extremes. She was given to bursting into anguished crying, pleading to me for forgiveness. These outbursts were sandwiched in between amazingly volatile temper tantrums that would sometimes lead to me getting beatings. I was the kind of child who talked back. One day, in retort to some accusation, I gave lip. Her eyes fired up. Immediately, she grabbed my throat. It all happened so quickly. She was choking me while hitting my head against the wall. The force in her movements was so great that my head left a hole in the wall. I didn't talk back for a long time after that incident.

Daddy had slowly turned his presence at home into silent, ghostlike appearances very late at night and very early in the morning. He would not eat dinner with us. He cooked his own breakfast, leaving before we awoke. He lived upstairs, sleeping in a separate bed from my mother. He seemed to function like a boarder, one who paid weekly rent, rather than as a family member.

Determined to spy on him, my mother began to insist that he baby-sit me when she had night meetings to attend. This was how I began to go to the movies with my father a minimum of two nights every week. Then, from time to time, I went by myself to the Saturday matinees with cartoons and adventure serials designed for children. Movies began to be an integral part of my life.

My mother and father had entirely different approaches to how they viewed films. My father didn't go to movies to look at them; he went to movies to hide inside them. He used films to distract himself from his problems. He did not discriminate between what was good and what was mediocre. So when I was with him, I saw everything that came during the 1950s from Hollywood to Houston's five or six Negro theaters. We seldom saw first-run films. This was because we couldn't go to white theaters. And why was that?

Well, Houston was a strange place. It was one of the most segregated cities in the South. There is a historical reason for this. Most people attributed the cause to Houston's 1917 Camp Logan incident. Camp Logan was Houston's first and last military base.

Black soldiers from the Twenty-fourth Infantry Regiment were assigned guard duty during the camp's construction. Much to white Houston's dismay, these men were not predictably meek Negroes. They were well-seasoned professional soldiers, and they had created a distinguished past for themselves.

In 1869, based on Black soldiers' valor and loyalty during the Civil War, Congress created four colored regiments: the Ninth and Tenth Cavalries and the Twenty-fourth and the Twenty-fifth Infantries. The Twenty-fourth is the oldest segregated unit in the U.S. military. Originally, the men who made up the Twenty-fourth Infantry fought in the Civil War. The unit lasted until it was officially disbanded in 1954, after the Korean War. The men of the Twenty-fourth Infantry were proud of their tradition as military pioneers and excellent soldiers.

Their first official assignment in 1869 in Texas and the Indian Territories lasted thirty years. At the time, even their Native American enemies honored them. The Plains Indians consider the buffalo sacred. Out of respect, they bestowed on the Black soldiers the title of "Buffalo Soldiers." In 1898, during the Spanish-American War in Cuba, the Twenty-fourth fought with distinction in the Santiago Campaign and alongside Theodore Roosevelt at San Juan Hill. Because of the success of these military campaigns, Roosevelt became a national hero and the president of the United States. But when he returned to the United States, he made the

2036—NINETEEN NATIONALITIES IN THE NEW ARMY REPRESENTING ALL EUROPEAN RACES.
CAMP LOGAN, TEXAS

60

political decision to disparage the Black military contributions in the war in order to distance himself in his voters' eyes from African Americans. Between 1898 and 1915, the Twenty-fourth helped quell the Philippine Revolution. In 1916, they crossed the border with General John Pershing's Mexican Punitive Expedition in pursuit of Pancho Villa. Shortly after, in July 1917, they arrived in Houston, Texas, to pull guard duty during the construction of Camp Logan.

By this time, World War I had begun, and a few of the men had begun to look critically at their situation. Rejection, discrimination, contempt, and shabby treatment characterized the Black military existence. In 1868, after a year-long campaign against the Cheyenne, a dismayed Major John Bigelow described his men's situation as one in which "the colored men did all the fighting—sustained nearly all the casualties, and the white troops received the commendations." These soldiers first considered the enemy and then their employers, the United States military. Their enemy was colored; their employers were not. Although on opposing sides of the battlefield, both the soldiers and their enemies were fighting whites who were racist toward both foes. The soldiers' participation in the killing began to make less good sense.

The Black soldiers empathized with, befriended, and married their enemy. A few men even fought with this so-called enemy, first defecting in the Indian wars, then in Cuba, and later in the Philippines. In the Philippines, David Fagan was one Black U.S. soldier who taught the rebels how to fight his former army. When he began winning battles, he became a legend. The rebels rewarded him by naming him an officer in their army. The United States reacted by sending the Black

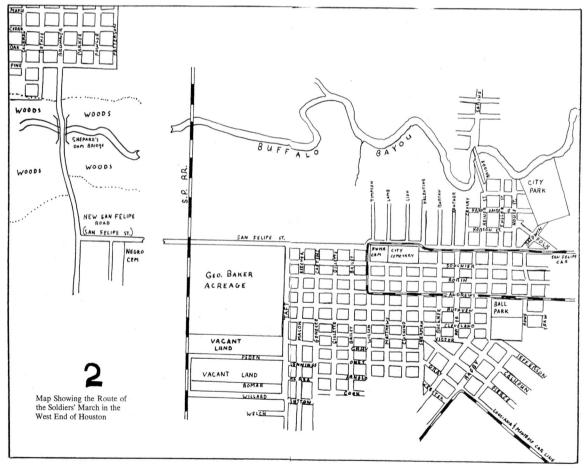

2

Map Showing the Route of
the Soldiers' March in the
West End of Houston

units back home, where some of the Twenty-fourth Infantry Regiment ended up with General John Pershing in Mexico in 1916.

In July 1917, fresh from pursuing Pancho Villa, a 140-plus contingent of these men reported for guard duty during the construction of new camp in Houston, Texas. And in those days, Houston's whites were used to calling all Blacks "niggers." In turn, Houston's Blacks stayed "in their place." So Houston whites were not ready for these proud men.

Immediately, trouble started. At first, there were strong exchanges of cursing between the soldiers and local whites. These Black soldiers gave the whites back what they got. Then the men found themselves objects of abuse, insults, and beatings by Houston police and civilians. They were not the kind to roll over. Bitter street fights broke out when the soldiers continued to refuse to back down over any provocation, no matter how slight, by the whites.

In less than a month the Houston police, City Hall, and the all-white National Guard squared off against the all-Black Twenty-fourth regiment. Houston's white population resolved to break the very backs of these "niggers." The tensions intensified and exploded on August 23, 1917. In a furtive police chase of a Black male crap-shooting suspect, police wrongly entered the house of Mrs. Sara Travers, a respectable Black woman. Failing to find the suspect, one policeman slapped and arrested the woman, then forced her, partly clad, out into the street. In the uproar, Private Alonzo Edwards, a Black soldier in the crowd of onlookers, offered to pay her fine in exchange for her release. He too was beaten and arrested. In the words of one of the policemen: "I hit him until his heart got right. He was a good nigger when I got through with him."

Later, when Corporal Charles Baltimore, a Black military policeman performing his official duty, approached these same officers to inquire about Private Edwards's whereabouts, he was also beaten and arrested. In those days, Black people were not supposed to question *any* white under *any* circumstances.

Corporal Baltimore was a very popular soldier. Rapidly, the rumor flew through camp that the city policemen had beaten the two men to death. Hearing this, the Negro soldiers killed the white soldier guarding the arms and secured most of the base's guns, rifles, and ammunition.

Among the soldiers back at the camp, there was one highly respected leader, Sergeant Vida Henry, an eighteen-year veteran. He was a strong, fearless man who was known by reputation to take no prisoners in any battle.

Much later it was discovered that both soldiers were still alive. But by then it was too late. Sergeant Henry was leading the march into town, with the men shouting the slogan "On to the police station!" Over 140 armed and angry Black soldiers hurried into town, slaughtering anyone in their path who seemed to be a white official. With the killings, the march turned into a major revolt. Hordes of white men, upon hearing of the massacre, broke into gun shops, taking every available loaded weapon. Many whites mobbed the police headquarters, where they were hastily sworn in as deputies and given guns. These angry whites massed to attack the rebellious soldiers who were by this time moving through Houston's Fourth Ward, a Black part of town.

There the whites blocked off the area. Desperate, the soldiers regrouped in an empty ball field. They were surrounded. They had killed between seventeen and twenty whites, thirteen of them policemen. Their choice was elegantly simple. They could live long enough to be killed or they could die right then and there by their own hand. The core of loyal soldiers who had followed Sergeant Henry's lead that night chose to live. Henry was the only one to refuse. Regretfully, the group left him. As they walked into the night's darkness, one shot rang out. The sound of it pierced the men's hearts as they ran from the sounds of angry white voices moving closer.

At daybreak Sergeant Vida Henry was found cold, with the gun in his mouth and the back of his head blown to thick and bloody bits. Chunks of his brain had fallen heavy beside his crumpled body. Rather than be taken, he had committed suicide.

Four months later, on November 30, 1917, 13 of 118 court-martialed men were sentenced to death. Subsequently, 19 of the soldiers were hung and 86 were jailed, some of whom were sentenced to life imprisonment. This trial remains the biggest and longest court martial in U.S. military history. It is also the largest murder trial held to date in the United States. Its impact permanently changed both the military and the city of Houston.

WAR DEPARTMENT,
WASHINGTON.

August 28, 1917.

Dear Mr. President:

I have just received your note of the 27th inclosing a very informing telegram to you from Mr. Eagle with regard to the cause of the outbreak at Houston.

I am having a careful investigation of that whole situation made and have sent the Inspector General of the Army there to insure its thoroughness and fairness. All told, I think the people of Houston are to be warmly praised and congratulated for their fine behavior under these trying circumstances. Undoubtedly, some part of their moderation can be attributed to the presence of the Illinois National Guard who seemed to have behaved with great composure and effectiveness; but when all the allowance is made which is properly due to this restraining cause, these people still deserve credit for having remained calm, refrained from any sort of attack upon the colored people of their own community and generally not to have permitted an East St. Louis riot to arise out of a very provoking and tragic situation.

Respectfully,

The President

Largest Murder Trial in the History of the United States.
Scene during Court Martial of 64 members of 24th Infantry U.S.A.
on trial for mutiny and murder of 17 people at Houston Tex. Aug 23, 1917
Trial held in Gift Chapel, Ft Sam Houston
Trial Started --- Nov 1, 1917- Brig Genl. George K. Hunter, Presiding.
Col J.A. Hull - Judge Advocate.   Counsel for Defense.
Maj D U. Sulphin, Asst.   Maj. Harry S. Grier.
        Prisoners guarded by 19th Infantry Co. "C" Capt. Carl J. Adler

66

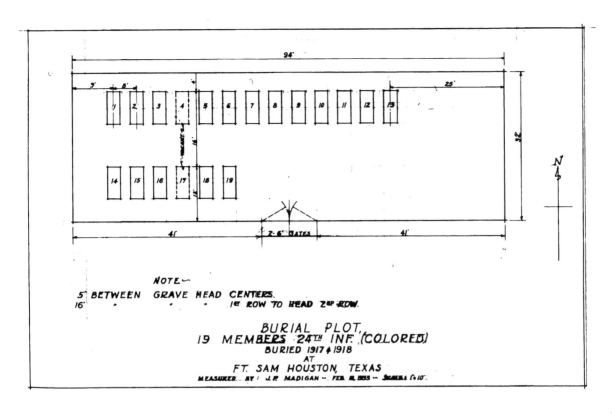

NOTE ~
5' BETWEEN GRAVE HEAD CENTERS.
16'   "   "   " 1st ROW TO HEAD 2nd ROW.

BURIAL PLOT,
19 MEMBERS 24TH INF. (COLORED)
BURIED 1917 & 1918
AT
FT. SAM HOUSTON, TEXAS
MEASURED BY: J.P. MADIGAN ~ FEB. 8, 1935 ~ SCALE 1"=10'.

In this plot of Ground are buried 18 members of the 24th U.S. Infantry Hanged near this site for mutiny at Houston Texas Aug. 23rd 1917

On December 11, 1917, the day after the death sentence was read, thirteen men were awakened just before dawn. All of this—the trial, the hanging, and the burial—were done secretly. According to historian Robert V. Haynes's book *A Night of Violence: The Houston Riot of 1917,* it all ended in a secluded wooded area of scrubby mesquite trees. The men died along the bank of a narrow meandering creek choked with dense underbrush. This was a desolate, lonely spot on the banks of Salado Creek in Fort Sam Houston, some four miles east of San Antonio, Texas. The flickering light of bonfires illuminated a hastily built large wooden scaffold that held thirteen gallows hung above two large trapdoors on a twenty-four-by-eighteen-foot platform situated twelve feet above the ground. The bleak landscape appeared as streaks of daylight streamed through a blanketlike gray sky.

It was still and quiet. Spontaneously, a low guttural drone came from the doomed men's chests. The only eyewitness to write a description of the execution was a young white draftee, who wrote that he heard the men "droning a hymn, very low and soft." The only words he could make out were "I'm coming home, I'm coming home." In a sea of white men, there was one Black minister, there to give last rites. And yet, to the end, these Black soldiers never broke.

The force of these Black men's defiant voices singing a spiritual startled the white onlookers. Then suddenly, it was again quiet. The nooses passed over the men's heads, quickly landing on their necks. In the heavy stillness that followed, the circles of rope tightened. The weight of the men's falling bodies made the strong cord squeeze up, snapping their necks. Their heads drooped sideways like fat, old wilted tulips, too heavy for their slender stems. It was an ugly death, made all the more terrible by the slow, agonizing pain, the bodily fluids oozing out. Tremors continued to rack the now lifeless bodies that swayed in the cold early morning air. The accumulations of many early morning frosts had made the ground's grass cover soggy and brown. The trees were stark and barren. It was, after all, winter in America.

HEADQUARTERS SOUTHERN DEPARTMENT
OFFICE OF THE DEPARTMENT INSPECTOR
FORT SAM HOUSTON, TEXAS

September 13, 1917.

FROM: Colonel G. C. Gross, Cavalry, A.I.G.

TO: Commanding General, Southern Department.

SUBJECT: Investigation of trouble at Houston, Texas, between Third Battalion,
24th Infantry, and citizens of Houston, August 23, 1917.

CONCLUSIONS

10.   That the tendency of the negro soldier, with fire arms in his possession, unless
he is properly handled by officers who know the race is to become arrogant, overbearing,
abusive and a menace to the community in which he happens to be stationed.

11.   That so long as the people of Houston and of the State of Texas maintain their
present attitude towards the negro, troubles more or less aggravated and similar to the
affair at Houston, are likely to occur as any time negro troops are stationed within the
boundaries of the state.

Fort Sam Houston, Tex.
Dec. 11, 1917

Dear Mother & Father,

When this letter reaches you I will be beyond the veil of sorrow. I will be in heaven with the angels. Mother don't worry over your son because it is heavens gain look not upon my body as one that must fill a watery grave but one that is asleep it in Jesus.

I fear not death, Did not Jesus ask death "Where art thy sting" Don't regret my seat in heaven by mourning over me. I now can imagine seeing my dear Grandmother and Grandfather and the dear girl Miss Bessie Henderson that I once love in this world standing at the river of Jordan beckoning to me to come, and O! Mother should they be sensitive of my coming don't you think that they are anxious for tomorrow morning to come when I will come unto them. I am sentence to be hanged for the trouble that happen in Houston Texas altho I am not guilty of the crime that I am accused of but Mother it is God's will that I go now and in this way and Mother I am going to look for you and the family if possible I will meet you at the river. Come unto me all ye that are heavy laden and I will give the rest. Bless his holy name. This is the happiest day I met with since Jesus spoke peace to my soul in Brookstone church from my promise to God I have strayed away but I am with him now Send Mr. Harris a copy of this letter. I am your

Your son T. C. Hawkins
Fort Sam Houston
San Antonio
Texas

P.S. Show this to Rev. Shaw

Rev. Shaw I am with Jesus and I will look for you in that great morning

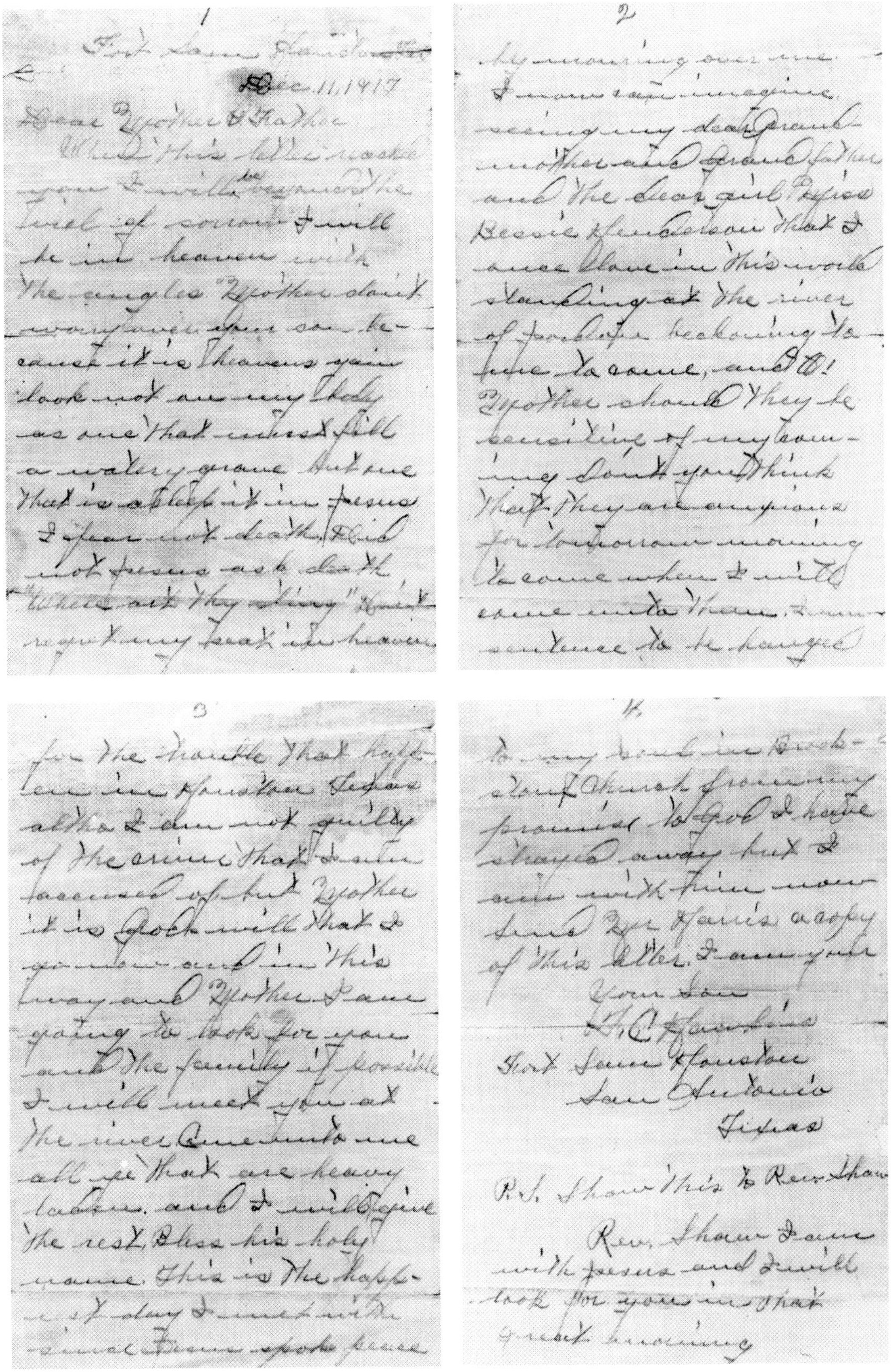

Fort Sam Houston

Dec. 11, 1917

Dear Mother & Father

When this letter reaches you I will be gone. The trial of course I will be in heaven with the angles. Mother don't worry over me because it is heavens gain look not on my body as one that must fill a watery grave but one that is asleep in Jesus I fear not death did not Jesus taste death "Where art thy sting" I expect to meet you in heaven

by morning over one I now can imagine seeing my dear grand mother and Grand father and the dear girl Prof Bessie Henderson that I once knew in this world standing at the river of prolife beckoning to me to come, and O! Mother should they be sensitive of my coming Don't you think that they are anxious for tomorrow morning to come when I will come unto them, my sentence is to be hanged

for the trouble that happen in Houston Texas altho I am not guilty of the crime that I am accused of but Mother it is Gods will that I go now and in this way and Mother I am going to look for you and the family if possible I will meet you at the river Come unto me all ye that are heavy laden and I will give the rest. Bless his holy name. This is the happiest day I met with since Jesus spoke peace

to my soul in Brook Stone Church from my promise to God I have strayed away but I am with him now Send Bro Harris a copy of this letter. I am your
Your Son
L.C. Hawkins
Fort Sam Houston
San Antonio
Texas

P.S. Show this to Rev. Shaw

Rev. Shaw I am with Jesus and I will look for you in that great morning

AN ACADEMY TRIBUTE TO

SIDNEY

Presented by
The Academy
of Motion
Picture Arts
and Sciences
and the
Academy
Foundation

Thursday,
June 18,
1998
at 8 p.m.

The
Samuel
Goldwyn
Theater

POITIER

A Tribute to
SIDNEY POITIER

PROGRAM

- Opening Film Excerpt -

LILIES OF THE FIELD (1963) - with Sidney Poitier, Lilly Skala and Lisa Mann. Directed and produced by Ralph Nelson; written by James Poe. Rainbow/United Artists. *Academy Award™ for: Actor (Poitier). Nominations for: Best Picture, Supporting Actress (Skala), Writing (Adapted Screenplay), B & W Cinematography.*

- Welcome from Academy President Robert Rehme -

- Opening remarks by Program Host Peter Rainer -

FILM EXCERPTS

NO WAY OUT (1950) - with Sidney Poitier, Richard Widmark and Linda Darnell. Directed by Joseph L. Mankiewicz; produced by Darryl F. Zanuck; written by Mankiewicz, Lesser Samuels. 20th Century Fox. *Academy Award™ Nomination: Writing (Story & Screenplay).*

BLACKBOARD JUNGLE (1955) - with Sidney Poitier, Glenn Ford, Paul Mazursky and Vic Morrow. Written and directed by Richard Brooks; produced by Pandro S. Berman. M-G-M. *Academy Award™ Nominations: Writing (Screenplay), B&W Cinematography, B&W Art Direction, Film Editing.*

THE DEFIANT ONES (1958) - with Sidney Poitier, Tony Curtis, Theodore Bikel, Cara Williams and Claude Akins. Directed and produced by Stanley Kramer; written by Nedrick Young, Harold Jacob Smith. United Artists. *Academy Award™ for: Writing (Original Story & Screenplay), B&W Cinematography. Nominations: Best Picture, Directing, Actor (Curtis, Poitier), Supporting Actor (Bikel), Supporting Actress (Williams), Film Editing.*

- Remarks by Richard Roundtree -

A RAISIN IN THE SUN (1961) - with Sidney Poitier, Claudia McNeil, Ruby Dee, Diana Sands, Louis Gossett, Jr. and Ivan Dixon. Directed by Daniel Petrie; produced by David Susskind and Phillip Rose; written by Lorraine Hansberry. Columbia.

After the blood bath was quelled, and the sting of the event's import whitewashed into oblivion, Houston's city officials permanently removed the base, banned any Black soldier's future access to firearms, and sharply segregated all of Houston's municipal facilities, eliminating any hint of mixed-race use. For close to fifty years, everything public in Houston remained racially separate—restrooms, churches, schools, beaches, parks, theaters, public transportation. Only in movie houses and the city auditorium were Blacks allowed the right to sit upstairs, isolated in what was called "the chicken roost." City officials couldn't imagine that any Blacks would be attending the symphonies and ballet concerts, but my mother and I did. We would sit up there, alone. And so in Houston, Texas, from 1917 to the 1970s there were also separate movie theaters for Blacks, some of which Blacks owned. As a child, I attended these theaters alone and with my parents.

> This was in 1950, and it was the first time my parents had ever seen a movie. But near the end of the movie Richard Widmark pistol whips me in the basement of some house. He's beating the crap out of me with the pistol, and my mother jumps up in the theater and yells, "Hit him back, Sidney! Hit him back! You never did nothing to him!" She's for real, completely in the moment. "Hit him back, Sidney! Hit him back!" That was my mother.
> —Sidney Poitier, *The Measure of a Man: A Spiritual Autobiography*

I followed my father's lead. The movies became my escape. While my father used film to forget, my mother, on the other hand, used film to cultivate and refine her aesthetic taste. *Life* and *Time* magazines were her bibles to culture and news. She depended wholly upon them to guide her aesthetic choices. She avidly viewed what she could of the films, art, and books they recommended, her tastes leaning to those with social and political content. She chose her films carefully. She loved films that were beautifully crafted, so when she and I went to the movies, I was assured a top-quality film experience.

One day in 1950 my mother insisted that my father and I go with her to see one film together. I suspect she must have found out about this film in *Time* magazine. The film, *No Way Out,* was the first major vehicle for the rising young star Sidney Poitier. Other than one-time dignified screen appearances of Canada Lee and James Edwards, there were almost no images available to us of talented, strong, intelligent Black actors or actresses on the silver screen. In this film, Sidney was close to being a complete person. He was sensitive, he was angry, he was smart, he spoke articulately, and he even had a love interest. In short, he was a rare creation of Black imagery in U.S. cinematic history: he was a human being. Richard Widmark, I remember, called Sidney Poitier a "nigger" in the film. In a later sequence, Linda Darnell pestered Sidney: "Why do you let him treat you this way?" She demanded that Sidney explain why Richard Widmark was getting away with so much. Even I, at six years old, remember being very disgusted with Ms. Darnell. "You're so stupid," I remember thinking, "Don't you know it's because he's a Negro?"

Forty-eight years later, in the summer of 1998, I sat in the audience at the Academy of Motion Picture Arts and Sciences. The event was Sidney Poitier's fifty-year retrospective of his film career. I watched that clip of Linda Darnell's still-stupid query. Apart from being Sidney Poitier's first starring role, *No Way Out* was a groundbreaking documentation of the race relations of that period. Stanley Kramer, the once-energetic director of that film, rolled on the stage in a wheelchair. Mr. Kramer seemed to forget where he was and could not control his body movements well. Sidney Poitier's face was now stabilized by deep grooves of well-set lines, and his skin was strangely etched by maturity. Finally, I saw his countenance lined with age. This man had managed to look young for so long.

Oddly, the entire retrospective of Sidney's films chronicled the obsolescence of the liberal style and approach first fostered by directors and producers like Stanley Kramer. He and Stanley Kramer are from a Hollywood that is now part of a curious history, marked by an attempt by a group of people to question this country's racist views. *No Way Out* was made near the end of a succession of such high-minded films as *Home of the Brave, In This Our Life, Intruder in the Dust, Broken Arrow, A Medal for Benny, Pinky,* and *Gentleman's Agreement.*

Later, when I tell a late-1970s activist where I was, he dismisses Poitier as "that outdated Uncle Tom." I keep my peace. It's hard to explain to a younger, angry person that Sidney's work in those days stood out as a beacon, a rallying cry of what Black actors and actresses could become in a public space. This young man wasn't there with me to hear Diahann Carroll tell the audience that Sidney Poitier taught her—and generations of actors and actresses—dignity. He didn't understand Poitier as a link that prepared an insensitive white audience for change. Nor did he realize the impact of Poitier's screen personae on the contemporary, far more respectful representation of Blacks in film in the work of today's Black filmmakers. I am saddened by this loss of a public memory, erased by such a short passage of time.

I can remember that for one brief moment on that night in 1950 my parents and I watched Sidney Poitier come alive on screen. He transformed himself before us into a proud and courageous Black doctor. A real doctor. Watching the film, we experienced a Poitier and a Kramer in the prime of their creative lives. They were struggling to transform the fears and the ugliness in our lives into our hopes for a better future. They were a part of a Hollywood that sought to use film to help change the world.

But such inspired moments were not enough for our family. As my father continued to slip away from the marriage, I became the target for my mother's pain and frustration. Filled with loss, anger, and a deepening depression, my mother glared in my direction and decided that I was her main problem. If it weren't for the responsibility of me, a child she felt too old to parent, she reasoned that she would be happy. Sometimes my presence was, to her, a colossal drag. Anything I did was liable to set her off. I lived in fear of her hot-and-cold mood changes. At times she would physically beat and verbally abuse me. Within minutes she would be weeping deep, uncontrollable sobs. And later she would be screaming at me, at the top of her voice. She used carefully selected and dangerous words, words that drove vivid, sharp pain into my heart, hurtful words. Angrily, she would tell me that "neither she nor my father wanted me," "that I was in her way," "that I was a total burden to her," and "that I should never have been born." And, finally, there would be her pleading demands that I console her with a warmth, care, and tenderness that I found particularly hard to provide, given that seconds before she might have been choking, slapping, or shaking me violently.

I was trapped.

All my time was spent either in a classroom, at church, or in my parents' home, where I ping-ponged between my mother's frighteningly erratic behavior and the emptiness of my father's strange, unexplained absences. Or, I was stuck at one of my mother's meetings.

The meetings. At seven, I was convinced that my mother belonged to every kind of organization on the planet Earth. In addition to teaching full-time, she was

on the board of the Negro YWCA, cofounder of the Garden Club, and a member of the Texas Negro Democratic Party, the NAACP, the 1906 Club, the Ladies Auxiliary of the Dr. Charles A. George Dental Society, many church groups (she even cofounded a church, Wheeler Avenue Baptist Church), various school committees, the PTA, and other teachers' groups, along with numerous interfaith organizations, interracial organizations, the Book of the Month Club, the Girl Scouts, and Jack and Jill. It felt to me as if every day of every week my mother had at least one meeting that she had to attend.

In those days, daycare hadn't been invented. And for poor, yet professional Black women, employing baby-sitters was a largely untested concept. My mother was overwhelmed by her civic obligations. She tried many ways to balance how she managed me, a small child, but her most consistent resolution was to take me to her meetings. There she'd assign me to a corner, leave me to my own resources, and hope that my solutions were silent ones. On the fringes of those meetings, I taught myself to have imaginary friends, to daydream, to observe cracks in the walls, to conjure up pathways on floors, and to devise patterns on ceilings that I would turn into animals, angels, and monsters.

And I listened.

For twelve to fifteen years I overheard what, in effect, were high-level training seminars disguised as meetings. These women's interactions taught me leadership training, political activism, community organizing, and how to run local and national political campaigns. In addition, these women's clubs were part of a state-wide federation of Black women's clubs.

This federation was part of a national resource of grassroots political power in the Black community. The club movement blossomed when Black women organized the civil rights movement. National icons like Rosa Parks, Dorothy Height, and Daisy Bates came out of this Black women's movement. For instance, during the late 1940s and 1950s, the NAACP's largest membership base was situated in the state of Texas. And I was there, playing in the corners of those meetings when national leaders like Mary McLeod Bethune, Adam Clayton Powell Jr., and Thurgood Marshall would come to town to caucus with these women. I observed them all as they gave brilliant, fiery speeches to rally a poor, frightened, southern Black community to fight against injustice. I watched them all huddle in private small groups after the large meetings designed to help Houston adjust after national events like the historical 1954 *Brown vs. Board of Education* Supreme Court decision. In this way, they worked to shape Texas' political, educational, and economic systems to support its African Americans.

I especially liked attending the meetings held at the Blue Triangle YWCA. Here I enjoyed much more physical latitude. My mother also relaxed then because

OPENING PROGRAM

12th Annual Session of
GULF STATE DENTAL ASSOCIATION

St. John Baptist Church
2100 Gray at Bastrop
Tuesday night, June 14, 1949
8:15 P. M.

Negro National Anthem .... Audience
Invocation .... Rev. E. R. Boone
Music .... St. John Baptist Church
(Male Chorus)
Welcome Address, Behalf of Houston .... Councilman Phil Hamburger
Welcome Address, Behalf of Negro Citizens .... Roscoe A .Cavitt,
Secretary, Houston Negro Chamber of Commerce
Welcome Address .... Dr. A. E. Bowie
Houston Medical Forum
Welcome Address, Behalf of the Ladies Auxiliary of the Houston
Medical Forum .... Mrs. Howard W. Williams
Pleasant Hill Baptist Church
Music ...... Charles A. George Dental Society, Dr. C. T. Ewell
Welcome Address .... Charles A. George Dental Society
Welcome Address, Behalf of Ladies Auxiliary of the Chas. A. George
Dental Society .... Mrs. C. A. Phillips
Response, Behalf of Gulf State Dental Society .... Dr. W. V. Hurd
San Antonio, Texas
Response, Behalf of Ladies Auxiliary .... Mrs. B. H. Ingram
Texarkana, Texas
Music .... Nathaniel Dett Glee Club
Introduction of Speaker .... Dr. J. E. Codwell
Address .... Dr. R. O'Hara Lanier
President, Texas State University
Music .... Wesley Chapel Choir
Introduction of State President ...... Dr. L. M. Mitchell, Austin, Texas
Remarks and Introduction of State Officers .... Dr. J. W. Davis,
President, Gulf State Dental Association
Music .... Fourth Missionary Baptist Church
Benediction .... Rev. N. C. Crain
Dr. A. J. Maddox, Master of Ceremonies

PROGRAM

Ladies Auxiliary to the
Gulf State Dental Association
June 14, 15, 16, 1949
DODSON ELEMENTARY SCHOOL

Tuesday, June 14, 1949

10:00 a.m. Meeting called to order .... Mrs. C. A. Phillips, Local President
Selection .... Mixed Chorus
Jack Yates High School
Prayer .... Mrs. S. I. Dixon
Welcome to Houston .... Mrs. W. I. Howard
Response .... Mrs. L. L. Smith
Dental Health (10 minute talk) .... Mrs. London
Dental Hygenist, Houston Public Schools
Business .... Mrs. Shirley Ingram
President, Gulf State Dental Association Auxiliary

Wednesday, June 15, 1949

10:00 a.m.   Selection .... Mixed Chorus
Wheatley High School
Prayer .... Mrs. S. I. Dixon
Panel Discussion — "What the Auxiliary Can Do To Make The
Community Dental Conscious" .... Mesdames C. E. Jeter, W. T. Burke,
H. E. Haywood, and C. Ewell
Business .... Mrs. Shirley Ingram, President, Presiding
Annual Address .... Mrs. Shirley Ingram, President
Luncheon
Election
Reports

SOCIAL PROGRAM

Tuesday, June 14, 4 to 6 p.m. — Reception

Mrs. F. D. Parrott — 3520 Delano Street

8:30 p.m. — Public Program

St. John Baptist Church

10:30 p.m. Soirie

Mrs. J. W. Davis — 2914 Nagle

2:00 p.m. Wednesday, June 15, 1949

Luncheon

9:00 p.m. — Dance

Texas State University Auditorium

12:30 Thursday, Luncheon

Groovey Grill

she felt this building was safe. So I could wander out of the meetings into a variety of empty rooms. And when the sun was out, I could even play outside on the surrounding grounds.

One of my favorite rooms was a huge multipurpose room with a row of windows covering its outside wall, overlooking the street. A wonderful golden light from the evening sunset would beam through the window shades to paint the rooms inside. The solid white walls would capture the light and throw it back into the room's center. I swear that this room retained a special glow, and to this day I still believe it was magical. Once there was a public fair at the Y. There were lots of games and clowns, a rented Ferris wheel, and one pony that went around the block. And there were plenty of homemade pies, cakes, cookies, popcorn, cotton candy, and soda pop.

During this event, my favorite room was filled with booths and floor games for the children to play for prizes. On this particular evening, just as I entered the room, a secret voice started telling me where to go and what to play. The voice didn't talk directly to me, like in a conversation. It was more as if I sensed what to do. I didn't question. I just did everything the voice told me to do. Soon, I was winning up a blue streak—toys, dolls, stuffed animals, candy—until Mrs. Ramsey went out to tell Mrs. Barnard, our next-door neighbor, to please come get me and take me to my mother because they were running out of prizes and the other children were getting pretty mad, whispering to the adults that my presence was jinxing the games. But being kicked out didn't bother me. By then I was totally convinced that this room was my very special secret place, that it was designated for me alone. Secure in my knowledge that the room would return to me after this fair had ended, I was content to just share it with everybody.

And, in fact, not too long after the fair, something really special did happen to me in that room. I clearly remember the very beginning. I was sitting on the empty floor in the room, playing with my imaginary electric train. I had dreamed up a track going through a lovely village with a river flowing between the town and a range of snow-capped mountains. One mountain had a tunnel cut into its side through which the train sped. Just as my dream train and I were turning a bend, heading toward a suspension bridge leading across a river, the room's double doors burst open.

A man holding a small ladder, some buckets, paints, and brushes rushed in quickly, like a fresh, early-spring breeze shaking off the winter chill. It was Mr. John Biggers. I knew who he was because two years before John and Hazel Biggers had stayed at my parents' house. They had just arrived in Houston and didn't have a home. They used our home as a place to room until they got settled.

They had come from Hampton Institute. One of the few times I ever saw my father get dewy-eyed was when he described Hampton's history and how proud he and other Blacks were of the school. He told me that Hampton Institute was one of the finest colored colleges in the United States. "Baby," he said, with a faraway look in his eyes, "you got to admire what they have done at Hampton. They have uplifted the race."

John Biggers had come to Houston fresh from studying with Viktor Lowenfeld, a renowned Jewish artist who had migrated from Hitler's Germany to Hampton. During the early 1930s, nearly 1,200 European Jewish intellectuals and artists ousted from Hitler's Germany came to America in search of work. While stars like Albert Einstein found work relatively easily, other lesser-known academics faced unemployment because of the Great Depression and this country's anti-Semitism. Black administrators seized on the opportunity to invite them to teach at their schools. The documentary *From Swastika to Jim Crow* describes these unusual 1940s and 1950s Black-Jewish professor-student alliances in southern, historically Black colleges that were based on a common bond of oppression. Thus, through Viktor Lowenfeld's teachings, influences from German Expressionism and other European avant-garde movements found their way into Biggers's art. Biggers, in turn, has passed on his knowledge to generations of other emerging Black artists.

In 1949, Mr. Biggers came to Houston to create an art department at Texas Southern University. This new school, TSU, was built within walking distance of my home in Houston's Third Ward.

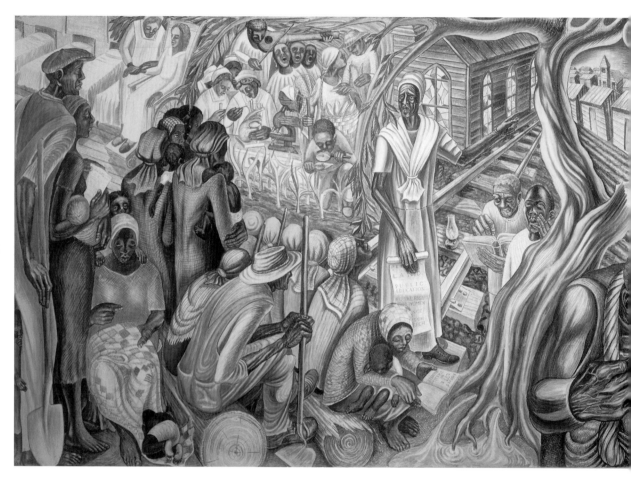

Houston is divided into wards that resemble districts in other cities. The Third, Fourth, and Fifth Wards were the areas where Houston's Blacks settled. TSU's presence helped to turn some of Third Ward from its working-class roots into a middle-class enclave for Black intellectuals—professors, scientists, engineers, lawyers, pharmacists, artists, and writers—who came from all over the country and settled into creating a college-town atmosphere around TSU's boundaries. Young professors like Nobel Prize winner Toni Morrison taught here. This new group of professionals also had the money to buy into the white section of town that bordered our home. Once TSU was built, other Black educators, doctors, and postal workers also settled there. In a short time, Third Ward had become the city's economic and cultural hub for Blacks. Along with the artists Joseph Mack and Carroll Simms, John Biggers built TSU's art department from the ground up. In addition to creating an art program, these artists-scholars also brought to Houston the notion of art as a vital part of community life and of artists as valuable community members.

In 1951, when he burst into "my" room, John Biggers was the chair of a fledgling art department that most people wouldn't have called a real art program at all. At the time, there were no sinks for ceramics. Drawing classes had no paper or crayons. Sculpture classes had no clay. Instead, these artists-educators faced an administration that was convinced that TSU had no earthly need for visual art, a discipline that promised no known career or financial success to its students upon graduation.

John Biggers was a muralist who was creatively on the move. Influenced by the Mexican muralists, European avant-garde artists, and German Expressionists, his work was rapidly evolving into new, uncharted creative territory. Taking over "my" room at the Y, he moved about it like a man on a mission. Briefly acknowledging my presence, he began to prime the walls with a really white paint. I settled in to watch him. I ended up observing him at work for an entire year. During this time, he painted a mural and named it *The Contribution of Negro Women to American Life and Education.*

Today this mural by John Biggers is acclaimed as historically groundbreaking in its technique. "God works in mysterious ways," my mother would always say when up against any of life's inexplicable moments. Recalling the confluence of events that led to me having one of the world's great artists teach me for one year when I was seven years old, I think my mother had it right. During that year, we all fell into a fairly regular routine. At the end of the school day, Mr. Biggers, my mother, and I would arrive and sometimes leave the Y at the same time. While my mother was attending her meetings, I would go into my room for a free, custom-crafted university art seminar with Mr. Biggers. I was, oddly enough, aptly prepared to learn from this fledgling master artist. I'd spent time before this "class" learning, in grown-up, fairly sophisticated meetings, how to listen, observe, and imagine.

First, Mr. Biggers imparted to me essential history lessons about the Black woman's role in building the United States of America. As he painted, he would tell me stories about Harriet Tubman, Sojourner Truth, and Phyllis Wheatley, the second woman in the United States to publish a book. He and I talked about slavery, the struggles of Black people, the courage of Black women, and how these women before me had made contributions to better our people and enrich all of American society. The finished mural was such a powerful, watershed accomplishment for this artist. Its execution and subsequent written analysis earned Mr. Biggers a Ph.D. from Pennsylvania State University and a promotion at TSU to full professor in 1954.

Through Dr. Biggers, I observed an artist start and complete a major work of art right before my eyes. The very fact that he completed the mural taught me that artists can accomplish many important things. They can conceptualize, produce, and finish what they have started. They can grow and evolve from the art-making process. I also learned that art making and teaching can be synonymous and that everyone has creative potential—even me, as a seven-year-old child. I am still taken by his ability to think of me, a very young person, as important enough to listen to and to teach.

But the best lesson I learned from Dr. Biggers was that all Black women, including me, are beautiful and valuable. During the time he was painting this mural he was also under siege. His challenge came from the women board members who were meeting there at the Y in the room right next to him. These women were very angry that he wasn't painting "pretty Negro women." They wanted to see light-skinned women with Nordic features like a Lena Horne or a Dorothy Dandridge. These women objected to Biggers's interpretations in his mural of raw-boned, large Black women with strong Negroid features, features deemed ugly and repulsive to white Western standards. They also didn't like it that he highlighted slavery, a period regarded by the women as being "too dark." As a child, I never knew of this battle. I only learned about it in 1996 when I stumbled upon a Biggers fifty-year retrospective at the prestigious Wadsworth Athenaeum in Hartford, Connecticut. In the exhibition catalogue, I discovered that the mural that I watched grow before my eyes from 1951 to 1952 was now acclaimed as a pathbreaking work of art by one of America's master artists.

Forty years before, when I was very young, when that door to my magic room was closed, it silenced the disgusted, angry board members' voices of protest. I suspect my mother, who urged her offspring to give her light-skinned grandchildren, may have been one of those leading the way. In the sanctum of Dr. Biggers's "art class," as the last rays of the setting sun painted our faces golden, he and I were alone. He would extol for me the beauty and the strength of Harriet Tubman, whose skull had

been smashed in by a white slave master's brick. "The wound," he would whisper to me, "left her open to fainting spells, unseen voices, and mysterious visions." While painting with his back to me, he would continue, "Undaunted, she was still determined. She successfully transported numerous slaves north, to freedom. And in doing so, she was a tremendous success at what she did."

When my mother spoke with admiration about Lena Horne's physical beauty, I would compare Ms. Horne's photograph to my face in the bathroom mirror. Even then I knew that I would never measure up. Yet my photograph of Henrietta Parrott, my paternal grandmother, looked remarkably like Harriet Tubman. And I looked more like my grandmother than like Lena Horne. I saw myself as part of my grandmother's lineage. As such, I began to believe that I too could be strong, courageous, and therefore beautiful.

Dr. Biggers taught me that every woman's beauty comes from within, that the outer face is only a reflection of the humanitarian deeds a woman does. He taught me that a woman leaves her deeds as her legacy to her life and society. As he turned to dip his brush into a dusky paint, his art making taught me that I was

valuable, important, and beautiful just as I am. And that I had a role to play just as powerful as the ones being played by the grand, towering, feminine figures in his mural.

Houston, Texas, was a state of mind. As a child growing up there, my mind was unfettered by categories. And so the myriad lessons that my mother, John Biggers, my family, and my community taught me have all finally settled into a cohesive way of life for me. All the concepts behind the noble words have finally gathered, meshed, fused, blended, and united into a single expression for me. I call it living a life. Houston, on the other hand, left my mother with the fears and nightmares of its special brand of racism. The sting of it haunted her until her death. Yet, through her community activism, she helped to change Houston. By exposing me to what she felt was the best in our merger culture, she also managed to awaken my own sense of beauty that lay dormant inside me.

INSIDE HOUSTON

Texas can-do builds a city of raucous amusements and astonishing art

BY VANCE MUSE

It's an exhilarating sight, this gleaming Oz rising improbably from a Gulf Coast marshland, this city of contradictions—futuristic and old-fashioned, ramshackle and refined. A free-wheeling boomtown, Houston is the boastful originator of Texas can-do and know-how that first put a man on the moon and an air-conditioned dome over a sports stadium. It is also an arts center that has lavishly housed its museums, symphony, opera, theater, and ballet companies. In population Houston is now the nation's fourth largest city, gaining on the triumvirate of New York, Los Angeles, and Chicago with an increasingly international mix of people and cultures, accent on the Latin and Asian. And though it continues to expand—the construction cranes around town are too numerous to count—Houston is at last turning some attention to its delicate 19th-century core, bringing entire blocks back to life. Having survived a brief but sobering economic shakedown at the beginning of the decade, Houston is growing into its complicated, cosmopolitan self.

You don't so much arrive in this sprawling city, which lacks a definite, magnetic center, as you circulate through and around it in a dizzying freeway swirl, catching glimpses of skyline, acres of pine-scented parks and greenbelts, outrageous amounts of concrete clutter, and billboard braggadocio: "Welcome to Space City! 'Houston'—First Word Spoken

Born on a bayou, clockwise from top left: The downtown skyline, from a freeway perspective; Vaquero, by artist Luis Jiménez, riding high; Solero, a tapas bar, has brought new flavor to old Market Square; midcentury finds at As Is; a downtown mural recalls market days of early Houston; Renzo Piano's louvered roof for the Menil Collection. Center above: Art installations all in a row at Project Row Houses. Center below: The silvery Contemporary Arts Museum.

GERALD MOORHEAD FAIA

Interlude #1 **A Memory**

A Memory

I hate you.
My mother screams her secret
smack into my face.
We never acknowledge her words.
Or the pain that we both now
know rests in my heart.

I am six years old.
I realize I am alone.
I sit very quietly.
I will myself to live until I die.

Thoughtfully, she watches my stillness.
I stare at the sound of her words.
Finally, it is she who is surprised.

Quite unexpectedly, I uncover her fear
of me now growing in her eyes.

I spend the rest of my life teaching
myself how to be human in a world
hostile to my very breath.

A Teacher's Prayer

Dear God of all teaching
Give me an open mind to day
That I may see, may feel
The need of each little child
That comes my way.

Help me to love all children
So that I may be aware
Of their fears, their desire, and broken spirits
Of their attitudes, their hurts and glee
That I may meet each condition with
Faith and loving care

When the school day is over
Grant that I may look back and see
In the six golden hours that have past
My little ones happy, and their souls
One step nearer Thee
Dear God I pray.

Mollie Carroll Parratt

Chapter IV **Detroit**

After my mother's funeral in 1976, I found a rich treasure of personal and family letters in her study. There were also carefully stored boxes full of her written reports. She had diligently detailed each event and catalogued each one according to date. She seemed to keep everything—I think to leave behind her very own personal record of who she was. To my astonishment, I discovered she had a long history of fighting with her coworkers. She had recorded every argument, no matter how trite or mundane. Alongside her detailed synopsis of each incident, she had outlined her countering rationale for each personal affront or humiliating slight. She forgot nothing. She even used her written reports to continue all the arguments. On paper, she made sure to win every battle, because the last words were always hers. Words may well have been her only real weapon.

Her study: I remember waking up sometimes very early at the break of day to find her reading and writing at her desk. When her two brothers, James and Fred Carroll, built her home, she made sure the house had a study—a room of her own. I found the stored boxes here, underneath her desk. She sometimes called this room the library. It was lined with customized bookcases that surrounded a desk facing a window that overlooked the backyard. The walls were a natural brown color. The even rays of a large fluorescent lamp covered the desk, which had lots of space for writing and reading. The wall closet held a portable typewriter mounted on a small table with wheels. From the reports, it appears that it was a succession of particularly nasty fights with her coworkers at the Eighth Avenue Elementary

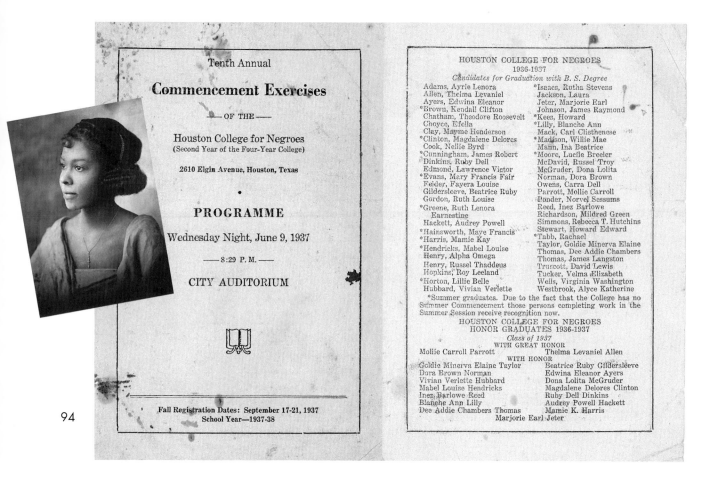

School located in the Houston Heights that had motivated her to seek change. She wanted a new working environment, so she made up her mind to go back to Detroit's Wayne State University to get a master's degree in special education.

She chose this specialty not because of any personal interest but because it paid more money. Money was always a problem for us. I believe that as a result of her master's degree, she became Houston's only Black teacher of legally blind students. In effect, she had carved out a specialization niche for herself. Since no one else was doing what she was, she became virtually independent of most of the politics of Blackshear Elementary, her new school.

On May 16, 1946, a few years before she arrived at Wayne State, there had been a legal decision regarding Texas Blacks' access to equal graduate education in *Sweatt v. Painter*, the historic lawsuit filed by Heman Marion Sweatt. He was one of Houston's few Black postmen, and he wanted to be a lawyer. At the time, there were no universities in Texas granting graduate degrees to Blacks, and the white ones were off-limits. According to my parents, Sweatt's victory in the June 1950 Supreme Court decision brought about many changes. For one, his win helped

COMMENTS OF THE TEACHER

FIRST SEMESTER

1. I am pleased with Carroll Ann's progress. Her Citizenship habits are improving daily.
2. Improving
3. I am happy Carroll Ann's Citizenship habits improved I have enjoyed working with her.

SECOND SEMESTER

1. Carroll Ann is doing very good work.
2.
3.

SIGNATURE OF PARENT OR GUARDIAN

First Semester — Fred D. Parrott, Sr.
Fred D. Parrott
Fred D. Parrott, Sr.

Second Semester — Mrs. Parrott
Fred D. Parrott

School Year 19 51 19 52

Fall Semester: Carroll A Parrott is promoted to the L 4th grade.
retained in
Ella Mae Henderson Teacher

Spring Semester: Carroll A Parrott is promoted to the H4 grade.
retained in
Ella L. Mitchell Teacher

HOUSTON PUBLIC SCHOOLS

HOUSTON, TEXAS

Elementary Grades

REPORT CARD

19 51 19 52

NAME Parrott, Carroll Ann

GRADE 34-3

SCHOOL Blackshear

TEACHER Ella Mae H. Smith & C. Mitchell

PRINCIPAL J. R. Cunningham

TO PARENTS:

You are cordially invited to visit the school and to acquaint yourself with all phases of your child's school life. If conferences are desired, the principal and teachers will arrange appointment at a convenient time.

Please sign your name in the space provided on the back of this card and return the card promptly to the school.

WILLIAM E. MORELAND,
Superintendent of Schools

establish Texas Southern University. Also, every Black educator who wanted a graduate degree could now apply to the state of Texas for financial assistance to be able to study in any university above the Mason-Dixon line. My mother was awarded one of those competitive scholarships, and that opportunity changed her life. I learned another political lesson, which was that my mother's decision to create a unique career position for herself was the result of one person's political agitation. Although Heman Sweatt and the NAACP filed a suit that ultimately went before and won in the Supreme Court, my community's perception of Sweatt's activism was that all of us benefited. The widespread view of this victory's impact was never lost on me. Nor were the consequences. Through pre-civil-rights-movement situations like this, I learned how important it is to fight for our civil rights in the courts. Later, during the Clarence Thomas and Anita Hill debates and in the 2000 presidential election, I also learned that in a democracy it is equally important to fight for courts that are peopled by judges who are fair and just.

Every June for four summers from 1950 to 1954, in pursuit of her graduate education, my mother would leave Houston for Detroit, taking me with her. And

every year in late August she would return home. Watching her successfully complete her work and actually graduate after those four years of toil, I learned other lessons—that no matter your age you could always dream, turn that dream into an action plan, start and then successfully finish whatever it takes to reach your goal.

The first summer we went to Detroit, we arrived by train. I loved traveling by train and sleeping to the fluid sound of the train's wheels turning on the tracks. Yesterday's train stations still hold for me a special kind of promise inside their walls. And the first time I actually felt that promise was when I was seven years old, arriving at Detroit's central train station on a sweltering hot June day in 1950.

I stood there, facing the huge waiting room, spellbound. I observed the magnificence of everything unfolding before my eyes. While watching all the people bustling back and forth, I drank in the buzzing sounds and even felt how the sunlight coming down from the huge roof skylight broke into sharp white streams that sliced into the shadows below. These were the days when train stations were overcrowded, straining to direct the massive energies of all kinds of people coming and going.

Right away, my harried mother hailed a redcap. Instantly, a man appeared and started helping us with our luggage. In those days, Black porters and redcaps showered single Black women traveling with children with special courtesies. We were their mothers and siblings or their wives and children, so they took very good care of us.

Almost before he started to load our luggage, my mother set about inquiring about her cousin Millard Carroll. Did he know Millard Carroll, who also worked there as a redcap? Somehow, over the years, she had lost touch with her northern relative, but she just knew he was probably still in town. Her line of inquiry helped us to meet a host of other Black station employees. Later we discovered that Millard worked a different time shift and that this was his day off.

While this was happening, I was standing there thinking "this is what the North looks like." This is where, I had heard, Negroes and whites could drink out of the very same water fountain, eat in the same restaurant, use the same bathrooms, go to the same movies. But for now, because Cousin Millard was not at work and not at the telephone number that the supervisor's office gave us, we had no place to sleep that night.

We never took the train again. As a teacher, my mother got paid only nine months out of the year. As a result, trains were too expensive for her to do each time. In subsequent years, we drove to Detroit. Mother loved seeing new places. I suspect that she used driving as an excuse to satisfy her desire to investigate. In another time and place, my mother could easily have been an explorer. She used our times on the road to discover America. On our way to Detroit, we would find ourselves visiting Mammoth Cave in Kentucky or going to Cleveland to see the Great Lakes or to Chicago to eat the South Side's best barbecued hot links. On returning to Houston from Detroit, we'd find ourselves visiting my mother's best friend in Los Angeles or our family members in Oakland. During the three summers from 1951 to 1954, we meandered through the United States. While my mother drove, I learned to read road maps and, by observation, how to drive. I also learned how to survive as a Black person on the road in 1950s America.

Our on-the-road adventures started the minute we paused at that Detroit train station. The fact that we did not have a place to stay in a big and strange city sobered even me. We finally made it to the station's curb with our luggage. "Excuse me," my mother spoke with what I sensed was a hollow authority as she turned to address the Black taxicab wrangler. She started asking the question that would become central to our successful survival during our travels for the next four years. The man politely strained to hear her. She was too embarrassed to speak louder. Hesitantly she queried, "Where is the Negro part of town?"

By the time the sun was turning red-orange and nearing the horizon, we had a place to stay. But this minor miracle was the result of the genius of my mother, who was one of the most resourceful people I've ever met. She could find a place to stay anywhere in the world.

Our new lodging sat on a side street that ran into Detroit's main thoroughfare, Woodward Avenue. I remember Woodward as being the widest avenue I'd ever seen, with tracks going down its middle. These rails carried smoothly running forest green trolley cars with clang-clang warning bells.

We rented a room from Mrs. Hayes, a single parent with two little boys younger than I was. She was a gruff, paper-bag-brown-skinned woman who almost always wore a scarf wrapped turbanlike around her head.

We lived in one bedroom of a two-bedroom apartment located in a run-down, unpainted, brown wood fourplex with a screechy, torn front screen door. The whole street had this worn-down, dusky brown look. Front yards were made up of firmly packed dirt surrounded by cracked gray-brown concrete. Even the shrubs, trees, and few plants were dried out, barren from lack of care.

A few houses down from ours was the liveliest place on the block. It was a makeshift bar with a blinking pink-red neon light that would begin to shine right after the sun went down. As night fell and the place filled with people, honky-tonk music from the jukebox would waft out the windows, onto the street, and up the wall into my place.

I would watch all the activity from our upstairs bedroom window. Looking into the bar's windows, I'd see heads close together, bodies slow dancing, and hear hearty laughter pierce the smoky atmosphere. From time to time over the music lulls, as the liquor began to warm the bellies, angry fires that lurked inside would flare up. Mean words would be shouted. Fights would quickly follow. Bodies would suddenly spill out the bar's screen door. Men, wounded by fists or knife stabs, were pushed outdoors. Anger, I quickly learned, used any excuse to burst free. While my mother studied for her classes, I would watch the street quickly fill up with curiosity seekers. When the cops pulled up, everyone would scatter. What I saw in that street always saddened me.

My mother finally talked Mrs. Hayes into baby-sitting me during the day for extra pay. Usually, I would play outside with her two sons. One day, in the alley behind the house, I fell down while running. As I landed, I felt a pile of broken glass below me. Instantly, shards of it got inside my knee. I went blind with a pain that lasted all day.

That night, when my mother came home, she immediately called a doctor. In 1950, doctors still made house calls. This one came to the house sloppy drunk. I remember the strong smell on his breath and how badly he stumbled into the room. He then proceeded to diagnose me as having polio, which immediately sent my mother into a justified terror.

That summer, Big Mama Thornton had a hit called "Hound Dog." I remember hearing it in Detroit, listening from Mrs. Hayes's bedroom window. The roughness in Big Mama's deep voice would grab hold of the words and push them low to the ground, like a dog baying to the full moon. I loved the backbeat, how the rhythm of that song would jerk start and stop so quickly:

...Cryin' all the time.
Well, you ain't never caught a rabbit
and you ain't no friend of mine.

I listened on the bed as that juke joint next to us played down-home southern blues. Devil's music, some church ladies would call it. No matter. Its rhythms and patterns were woven into the very fabric of our lives. We couldn't escape it. It was deeply embedded in the gospel songs at the holiest of our churches; it was in the core of the blues in the most sin ridden of our bars. Aretha, who was my age, was singing it in Reverend C. L. Franklin's church, in her father's children's choir, on Sunday mornings. Meanwhile, across town on Saturday nights a young Berry Gordy was searching through Detroit bars like the one on my street for those unforgettable voices that would later build his empire based on that emerging Motor City sound: Motown.

Mother slammed our bedroom door hard, breaking my reverie. The doctor had gone. We were alone. She stared at me with a meanness that scared me.

"You!" Furiously pacing from one side of the room to the other, she began her assault. "How dare you do this to me!"

I was confused. *What* had I done to her?

"Here I am with no money, and you make me spend what little I have on some drunk, no-good doctor!"

Sitting upright in the bed, with my sore knee bandaged, I followed her with frightened eyes as her movements ricocheted side to side from one wall to its opposite.

"I just threw away my hard-earned money on that...that...drunk!"

I thought she must be hurt. I didn't mean to hurt her.

"All because of your, your...carelessness...your thoughtlessness."

Racing through my thoughts, I recalled that I was just playing. And that I didn't mean to fall.

"If it weren't for you, none of this would have happened!"

She's wrong, I reassured myself. I didn't plan any of this at all.

"If it weren't for you, I'd have enough money to make it through this godforsaken summer...now just look at me. Just look at me!'

My mother stopped pacing. She turned, intent on glaring me down. But now there were tears welling up in her eyes. They spilled down over her cheeks. She started to cry, at first silently and then in wrenching sobs. Her breathing grew so deep that she stopped walking, and she stood there shaking violently, overcome with sadness.

"I'm sorry, Mommy. I didn't mean to hurt you."

Here I go again, begging her forgiveness for something I did not do. But saying I was sorry always worked. She would stop saying mean things about me.

The music down the street paused. In the lull, the bar's muffled voices and my mother's sudden silence made the empty air between us heavy. I could feel myself grow hurt inside. What was I supposed to be sorry about? That we were far from home? That my mother had no money? That I was alive?

Some days I can still remember the slow, lush, velvet quality that warmed Johnny Ace's voice: *"Forever, my darling our love will be true… Always and forever I'll love just you…"* That bittersweetness lingering inside the base of Johnny Ace's throat has stayed on to haunt my heart even to this day.

My mother had very little money, she was frightened, and she was stressed beyond belief over her graduate studies. Her own body was betraying her. She was overweight, and her breasts now sagged. Her hips had grown thick and flabby. She was battling full-fledged menopause. And the rumors she was hearing from home did not help. Now that she was in Detroit, my father was openly taking up with other women, bedding his mistresses in my mother's house. He also worried her with his fears that now that she was better educated then he, she would leave him because he was out of her intellectual league. Did her impending master's degree make her unattractive to him? She was confounded, alone, and prone to screaming fits of anger and violence. Her behavior became increasingly predictable. After her spells lost their intensity, she would be full of a cloying remorse that felt, to me, insincere and manipulative. There was no one there but me. And I had become her target. In her mind, I was part of this vast conspiracy designed to bring her to her doom. She was a Black woman. How could she win? She never knew Black women to win.

Soon after my knee started healing, we moved. Her family rescued us. Cousin Millard and Excel, his wife, took us in. We moved to a well-kept street that had beautiful green trees lining its sides, and sidewalks that opened on to well-tended grass lawns and brightly assorted flower beds. Millard and Excel's house was well maintained and located in a peaceful, predictable environment. Stanford Avenue sported shiny, washed, carefully cared-for cars (big cars designed for families, like Hudsons, Oldsmobiles, and Lincolns) that were proudly parked out on street curbs in front of the houses.

On Sundays, after church and baked-chicken dinners, we would ride through Detroit's streets. We'd drive by really fancy homes of the Black elite or into Dearborn

100

to peek behind the gates of the mansions of the wealthy industrialists. Weekdays, the television cared for me. There was *Kukla, Fran and Ollie, Howdy Doody, Lash of the West, Hopalong Cassidy, Beulah,* and my absolute favorite, *Amos 'n' Andy.*

We had heard rumors that *Amos 'n' Andy* would be taken off the air. "Why?" I lamented. And no one else in the house really knew why. We all thought everyone on the show was very funny, although my mother did think they set a bad example: buffoons, stereotypes, simplistic portrayals of the Negro race. But then when Kingfish, Andy, or Calhoun would say something amazingly funny, she too would break down and laugh. These actors were something else. They were really very funny.

It wasn't until the photographer Roy DeCarava explained to me in 1980 that the *Amos 'n' Andy* boycott was a national effort by progressive Negro artists to raise our awareness of how we African Americans were portrayed in media that I finally understood. Our contemporary anti-stereotype protests had their genesis in movements like these that had begun in the 1940s and 1950s.

And so, very quickly, 6610 Stanford Avenue became our new summer home. On those pleasant sun-filled summer mornings, after finishing my assigned chores, I would run out to survey my new world in the North from the top of my cousin Millard's porch.

When I stood at the top of the stairs, I would look to my left and then to my right. Two blocks down on my right, there was a corner drugstore, Black owned, I believe. At least everyone who worked in there was Black. There was a long soda fountain. On Saturdays, with my weekly allowance of a quarter, I would buy a chocolate malted milk shake and drink it real slow while reading a prized new comic book—*Archie, Superman, Mr. and Mrs. Jiggs, Love Confessions,* and *Brenda Starr*—from the beginning to the end and then back again.

If I decided to go down the porch stairs to my left, then a few houses over from us lived my very best Detroit friend, Emma. Emma, Teddy, her baby brother, and her mother and father lived in a house that looked very much like everyone else's. But we could play together only in the streets or in my house. So we would play jacks together or walk around, exploring our block, while we imagined that we were going to faraway lands. I never could understand why my mother had sternly warned me: "Don't go into her house. Stay outside. Never go inside."

Emma's parents were very gentle and respectful, speaking to us children in soft, patient voices. One day, as I knocked on the screen door, I found the front door open. I peered inside. The living room was neat, clean, and well appointed.

Emma's mother appeared and invited me in. Curiosity helped me ignore my mother's prior admonishment. The living-room walls were covered with book-shelves filled with all kinds of books. On one side of the room was a writing desk with a notebook open to handwritten pages and a pen lying across it. The sofa and large chair on the other side of the room both had floor-sized reading lamps next to them. A book lay open and turned upside down on the chair.

There was no television. And the radio was off. This living room seemed to serve a purpose that didn't require noise. It seemed to be a place used for writing and reading. The air in here hung expectantly, like that in a library. Thinking back now, I realize this was the home of the first Black intellectuals I had ever seen. Words—those handwritten and those in books—were at the center of this room's focus. No one seemed to be loud, drunk, or fighting in here. Why, then, was I forbidden to come inside?

When we returned to Detroit the following summer of 1953, Emma, my playmate, was happy to see me. But things had changed drastically. Millard and Excel had a new roomer. He was my cousin, Kenneth Zachary Marshall, a very handsome, young, dark-chocolate-colored Black man with a heart-melting smile. He was also a bachelor with a flair for dressing very well. He would spend what seemed to me like hours polishing and shining his shoes. I remember that because I used to watch him from across the hall. And I fell in love with him. We were all proud of him. He was our "Cousin KZ," who worked for Army Intelligence. Not too many Negroes could claim to have a grand job like his. We were all pleased at his accomplishment. He was sent to Detroit to spy on that terrible Communist Party, and his work started with Emma's parents.

This was in the early 1950s, during what we now call the McCarthy period. Emma's father and mother were Communists. "Just imagine," my mother would marvel, "they're Negroes, poor, *and* Communists." And then she would shake her head back and forth in absolute wonder.

We were all sitting around the dinner table. Cousin KZ and his job were the center of attention. He had a day job that no one took seriously. But then his other job was something else. His real job was to watch Emma's parents' every move. He attended meetings that they went to at night. Cousin KZ was a spy for the military, like Herbert Philbrick, who was the star of that FBI television program *I Led Three Lives*. On TV, I learned that these dirty Red Commies were bad enough to be spied on. They all wanted to destroy America and all that we stood for. When I asked Cousin KZ what the Reds were like, all he ever told me was that the food was very good at their meetings. Then he told me not to say anything about this outside of this house, and that by keeping my mouth shut I was doing my duty as a loyal American citizen. I was very proud of keeping his secret.

Emma and I never talked about Communism. We just played. We were, after all, young children. But Excel and my mother were afraid. They never said anything to me about it, but very soon I too became oddly distanced from Emma. I found it difficult to continue playing with her. Eventually, I stopped going to see her. I was always too busy. In return, Emma's visits became less frequent. And so we drifted apart that summer. The following summer I discovered a new family living in her house. Millard said that one day they moved. I never knew what happened to her.

For much of the rest of my life, Cousin KZ would appear and disappear as he moved throughout the country on various clandestine assignments. Sometimes the military would send him outside the country to live. He said it was to take him out of circulation so that people would forget his face. One day, in 1958, he suddenly appeared on our doorstep in Houston. He'd just been in Little Rock, Arkansas, where angry white people stood outside Little Rock High School jeering at the brave Negro students who dared to attend. I asked him why he was there. He proudly told me that the government was always everywhere there was trouble brewing.

Always everywhere. This time, however, when he spoke to me about this notion of an everlasting, universal presence, there was something now vaguely chilling about the idea to me. Here was the United States government, invisible yet always present, in crowds, blending in with unaware citizens. Here were its operatives, always everywhere watching, listening, recording, reporting. Why, then, weren't they doing something about those jeering crowds of Little Rock whites? I watched Evelyn Ecford walking alone in that vicious mob. Why didn't they come out and help her? Even Louis Armstrong got in trouble for raising his voice against what was happening. He too wanted government intervention. And as popular as he was at the time, even he was punished for speaking out.

Four years later, in the summer of 1962, an unusual chain of events forced me to revisit Cousin KZ's words. I was in Mexico City, and while walking across the campus of the Universidad Nacional Autónoma de México, I ran into a large public meeting. As I watched a disturbing newsreel, I saw American planes bomb Havana. Later, I read in the Mexico City newspapers that the U.S. military was in Panama, amassing a huge retaliatory military force. All signs pointed to the fact that my country was preparing to attack Cuba.

When I returned home in September and told people, they all thought that I was crazy. No one here had heard any of this information. And so they laughed at my story's implausibility. Worst of all, I had no written proof, so my concerns were dismissed. When the Bay of Pigs happened shortly thereafter, I became increasingly suspicious. Not only were "they" always everywhere, "they" also controlled any information that we have.

From 1967 to the late 1970s, I was in this country's streets photographing all kinds of public happenings—rock concerts, Black Panther rallies, antiwar demonstrations, and events in People's Park. I never forgot KZ's words—that they are there . . . "always everywhere."

I know because I was out there, in those streets filled with protesters. As a photographer, I was watching what was unfolding in my country from behind a 35 mm still camera's viewfinder. Ultimately, undeniably accurate information about COINTELPRO, the FBI's Counter-Intelligence Program, surfaced. Amazingly effective, it, like the 1950s House Un-American Activities Committee (HUAC) and the McCarthy hearings, silenced this country's protest movements. In the 1970s, I became increasingly skeptical about the beneficial nature of the U.S. government's role in the lives of its private citizens whenever those citizens dared to challenge injustice. First, it was Paul Robeson speaking out against this country's racism. Next, Louis Armstrong rallying against what happened at Little Rock. Then, in the 1960s, it was Eartha Kitt protesting the Vietnam War. If you spoke out, I was learning, you were punished, no matter how famous you were. There was no safety net when you spoke your truth.

Over the years, my fears that my country would move toward a loss of civil liberties and a repressive police state have heightened with each new assassination (Malcolm X, Martin Luther King Jr., John and Robert Kennedy, George Jackson, and Fred Hampton, among others), national election (especially the 2000 presidential election), shootout or bombing (Waco, Ruby Ridge, Oklahoma City, the World Trade Center, and the Pentagon).

Around the mid-1970s I finally lost contact with Cousin KZ.

DR. FRED D. PARROTT
419 1-2 MILAM STREET
SUITE 5
HOUSTON 2, TEXAS

Honey! Honey!

I just can't find my
baby no where. I called
Saturday night, couldn't get
you, in fact I couldn't get
any one. So the first thing
Sunday morning I just
knew you were there, I
called, Mr Carroll answered
after a long time, and then here
he come telling me that you
left Friday evening going
some where, Oh! I just
wanted to hear the sweetest
girl voice in the world,
I had such a bad week
Hay fever, I really had a
time, I called Dr Forde

105

August 8, 1951

Honey! Honey!

I just can't find my baby no where. I called Saturday night. Couldn't get you, in fact, I couldn't get any one. So the first thing Sunday morning I just knew you were there. I called. Mr. Carroll answered after a long time. And then here he come telling me that you left Friday evening going some where. Oh! I just wanted to hear the sweetest girl voice in the world. I had such a bad week. Hay fever. I really had a time. I called Dr. Forde Saturday. He came telling me that is what I have. I said you ought to know something that is good for it. So he sent me lots some things over, and the junk really did me good. Ha! Ha! I feel better today than I have felt for a long time.

Honey! I am so glad that the time isn't long before I can see you. I am so lonesome for you all until I am all most nuts. Just 2 more week and I will have my own Celeste in my arms.

I hope you all had a good trip. I have got to go now.

Just love! love! and more love.

Dad

I am sure you are out of money.

I sure want to see you <u>baby</u>. I am trying to get Fred D. Parrott to come and go to school here and make up those marks.

Love Darling

PHONE CH. 5228

DR. FRED D. PARROTT
419 1-2 MILAM STREET
SUITE 5
HOUSTON 2, TEXAS

Saturday, he came telling me
that is what I have had, I say
said you ought to know
some thing that is good
for it. So he sen it me
lots some things over,
and the junks really did
me good ha, ha, I feel
better to day then I have
felt for a long time.
Honny! I am so glad
that the time isn't long
before I can see you,
I am so lonesome for
you all until I am
all most nuts, Just
2 more weeks and I

PHONE CH. 5228

DR. FRED D. PARROTT
419 1-2 MILAM STREET
SUITE 5
HOUSTON 2, TEXAS

will have my own
Celeste in my arms.
I hope you all had
a good trip, get to go
I have got to go
now
Just love' love'
and more love,

Dad

I am sure you are out
of money,
I sure want to see you
baby, I am trying to get
Fred D, Parrott to come and
Joe to school here, and move
up there mama, love' darling

From
Fred D. Parrott D.D.S.
419½ Milam St
Houston, Texas.

via Air mail Special

HOUSTON, TEX
AUG 9 1951

Mrs Fred D
6610 Stanford
Detroit 10 Mich.

VIA AIR MAIL
SPECIAL DELIVERY

POSTAGE DUE 3 CENTS

6610 Stanford
Detroit 10, Michigan
June 21,1953

Dad:

Why din't you write me this week end? Do you know that when one goes
away from home she is so anxious to get a letter from home and nothing
else satisfies like a letter from home. Then when a woman leaves a sweet
good doing man like you you know she wants to hear from him. Now is that
enough to let you know that you must write me each week and you must
do the writing yourself for if you let the girl do it I will be too mad.
I even don't want her to address my letters. I like to see your writing
Seeing your hand writing does something to me , like it use to when I was
a girl. You remember when you drew that heart? Well I still like that
kind of letter. You know I want to be made to feel good even if I can't
measure up to what I did then I am like Neadom I just like to pat it.

I start to work Monday, and I will be going like mad until Au gust
first. The brakes on the car are out. There is nothing there. I step
on the brakes Saturday and there was nothing so I will have to go by bus
to school until I can get then fixed. You will have to send me money
for that immediately. I do not know what it will be. The man will come a
and pull it in for I am afraid to drive it on these streets without any
brakes. Millard said that he does not know what the trouble is. He h
has named several things that might be contributing causes. He thought
it best to let the Pontiac people do the work. You need also to send
my allowance. I had to pay my tuition and today I am about broke. You
can't have your babies here without money you know.

Who is doing the preaching at our church now a day? I have thought
so much about that. What is all the news? Have you moved yet?
How is Fred? I hope he will make it through until I get back home.

I am enclosing a check for Fred's money. I thought I might get to
use it until you got over the schock of sending us up here but no that
wont happen for he is sending for his money as of today, so I am sending
you this check, please get the money out of my account and send it to him
immediately.   Please get the Dean's name of Baylor and send it to him.
I hope something can be done to get him in Med. school since nothing
else will satisfy him. Do ask around about the motel construction business
I guess you think we are asking so much of you but you are our big srtong
Daddy and we feel that it is nothing you can't do for us.

We are so sorry that we didn't send you a Father's Day gift but
our money is so short that we just couldn't at this time.

Please let me hear from you immediately because I hate to ride this
bus. Then too, I am having to take Carroll Ann with me for Excell is
doing days work three days a week so I thought it best to take the
baby with me . I do not like leaving her around with any and every body.
This seems to be going to be a hard year for me. That is the way things
always are when you are about to get to the top of the mountainxx
mountain top. I am going to fight like mad though. I hope it will not
be too much of a financial load for you,

Please let me hear from you immediately.

Love and kisses,

Sweetheart

Chapter V **Niagara Falls**

Way before you see anything, the sound takes over. And as you move closer, you realize this sound is endless. Very soon you can see for yourself that this thundering roar is the constant sound of tons of falling water. There before you is the incredible view of the falls. The power of Niagara Falls is that it is huge, massive, and while you are in its presence, it feels like forever.

I was eleven years old in August 1954 when I first saw Niagara Falls. Its natural power and energy certainly got my attention. The volume of that perpetual sound remains steadfast in my memory. Concrete was everywhere. The walls surrounding this natural phenomenon were thick, deep, man-made slabs of gray, weatherworn concrete. I stood holding the metal rails and looked way down at the whirling waters below. The sound enveloped me with its strength. When the wind blew, I felt soft sprays or wisps of water touch my face and arms even from where I stood. This all impressed me because I was very far away. Down below I saw tiny tour boats steer past the vortexes and whirlpools that plumbed the depths at the bottom of these falls. My mother and I stood there for what seemed like eternity.

She continued reading aloud the descriptions from the tour book. I was particularly impressed that even women had gotten inside wooden barrels at the top of the falls to successfully tumble over the falls and live to tell the world about their adventures.

My mother chose to take us there to celebrate her graduation. She was fifty-four years old when she received a master's degree in special education from Wayne

State University. I can't recall how many times my mother actually rewarded herself for her accomplishments, but this was the one time that she gave herself a gift for having completed a major feat. She was the first in her family to graduate with a master's degree!

One day she simply said, "Let's go to Niagara Falls!" We arrived in Niagara Falls from Detroit by bus. I never knew why she chose this place as her special destination. I imagine that as a staunch NAACP member perhaps she knew about the Niagara movement that came out of a meeting convened there by W. E. B. DuBois in 1905. Challenging Booker T. Washington's nonconfrontational tactics, twenty-nine Black leaders met in Niagara Falls to demand Black citizenship rights. This meeting was a catalyst for the formation five years later of the National Association for the Advancement of Colored People (the NAACP).

Even when she told me where we were going, I didn't have even the vaguest notion of what Niagara Falls was like. Yet, I was excited for three reasons. One, this would be my first trip to a foreign country. Two, I would see something new. And three, more important than anything else, Marilyn Monroe.

From almost the beginning of the time that my father started taking me to the movies, I was captivated by those larger-than-life images of beautiful people before me on that silver screen. By now I had graduated from comic books to movie magazines—*Silver Screen, Photoplay, Modern Screen.* Every month I would buy these magazines and cut out the large full-page color photographs of stars like John Derek, Tab Hunter, Audrey Hepburn, and Vera Miles. Lovingly, I'd make special places for them in my now overflowing collection of scrapbooks. I had even started to write to the stars, savoring the return-mail rewards of 5x7 or 8x10 glossy black-and-white photographs, sometimes with engraved signatures written at angles on the right-hand corners of the photographs. I was an avid reader of Louella Parsons, Hedda Hopper, and Walter Winchell. And I sought to know everything about the stars—their real names, their histories, their courtships, marriages, divorces, and scandals. I was Elizabeth Taylor rescuing Montgomery Clift from his auto accident; Debbie Reynolds defending my man, Eddie Fisher, from Elizabeth Taylor; and the distraught Janet Leigh as Tony Curtis walked out the door forever. And how dare Rock Hudson get married to some mousy-looking woman named Phyllis who wasn't even a movie star?

Why on God's green earth was a little Black girl living in Texas in the 1950s so preoccupied with the lives of a group of young, factory-made, pretty white people? Especially since, for the most part, these were ego-driven men and women from dubious backgrounds who were overeager for crowd adulation, money, and material rewards? Richard Dyer is the only film studies scholar who seems to have adequately explained the rationale of the siren song emanating from Hollywood's star phenomenon. Being a star was the closest thing this country had to royalty.

And the platinum-blonde woman with the slinky eyes filled with innocence and desire, the coy baby voice, and the curvy body covered by skin-tight dresses seemed to be the only one at the top of the royal heap. Thus, I bravely, foolishly dreamed of becoming Hollywood's next Marilyn Monroe.

Connecting Niagara Falls and Marilyn Monroe made all the sense in the world to me. She had made *Niagara*, the movie, here. My goal was to go to all the places in the movie so that I could act out each of Marilyn's scenes. So at the Falls, my pink full-skirted dress became Monroe's outrageously red dress tugging at my behind and fully armored, curvy breasts, with the cleavage correctly positioned over the draped, revealing top. My white patent leather Sunday flat shoes became slinky high heels that gracefully allowed me to slither past the admiring tourists.

So I got off the bus as I imagined Marilyn would. Never mind that my mother didn't have enough money to rent the slick raincoats so we could walk down the stairs next to the falls like SHE had done. I could make up those particular scenes in my daydreams while my mother and I ate breakfast at some cheap, nondescript coffee shop. During the day, as I hurried to keep up with my mother's long strides, I would secretly practice moving my hips side to side in—I assumed—some sexually provocative manner. And at night before going to bed, I would lock the bathroom door and secretly practice my facial moves. It took hours to learn how to turn my head ever so slowly to the right and tilt my head ever so slightly up as I—simultaneously—raised my left eyebrow seductively. My brown nappy hair, brown skin, pug nose, thick lips, flat chest, huge hips and thighs were inconsequential roadblocks.

Right now, I was in Niagara Falls, just like she had been. The fact that I was here was confirmation enough from the gods that I had the power to transform myself into Marilyn Monroe, with a body sexy enough to flow all over Niagara Falls!

Only there was one African American woman already ahead of me. And this one was more determined than I to achieve Marilyn's crowning glory. She was the talented Dorothy Dandridge, and she was already in Hollywood STARRING in *Carmen Jones*. Masterfully, she dominated the screen in that Dowling Street theater where I sat watching her in a role that would make her Hollywood's first bona fide Negro star. Ms. Dandridge's sultry portrayal of Carmen won her an Academy Award nomination. Her success helped move me away from Monroe and closer to wanting to be a beautiful Black woman.

According to the film scholar Donald Bogle, Monroe and Dandridge, as aspiring actresses, were friendly to each other. Remove the color thing and they were sisters under the skin. Bogle even goes so far as to hint that they might have unwittingly shared the same lover, the suave, debonair, and legendary jazz musician Phil Moore

Sr. Struggles with prescription drugs, alcohol, and depression hounded both women. Dorothy and Marilyn died untimely, tragic deaths. Tragic because their potential talent was rendered impotent with the onset of aging. They, like my mother, were defined by young bodies and wrinkle-free, dewy-skinned faces.

Dandridge's tragic courage to be a pioneer in Hollywood was one of many small victories that culminated in the 1960s belief that "Black Is Beautiful." And over the years, my gradual acceptance of who I am would be echoed in my second and third films. Twenty-five years later I would make films on Black women who were

complete opposites of Marilyn's image. I made my first films, *Two Women* and *Varnette's World: A Study of a Young Artist,* to exalt the images of a variety of Black women, as Dr. Biggers, the artist, had taught me.

Both of these films were crafted under the watchful eye of two remarkable people, Carlton Moss and Frances Williams. The cinematographer John Simmons was a film student at the University of Southern California when he introduced me to Carlton Moss. Carlton, one of the pioneer Black filmmakers, had been Johnny's professor at Fisk University. In addition to being a filmmaker, Carlton was a scholar, historian, writer, and script doctor. His first film, *The Negro Soldier,* was made under the umbrella of director Frank Capra's *Why We Fight* film series, a group of classic World War II documentaries. Capra oversaw U.S. government propaganda-filmmaking efforts during World War II and had hired Carlton Moss as a writer.

Carlton took me, an aspiring filmmaker, under his wing to mentor me. Understanding that as a Black woman I had to know things that he couldn't teach me, he soon introduced me to Frances Williams. Frances was a remarkable woman. She was a skilled actress, a fabulous dramatic arts teacher, and a notorious gossip. And could she dish the dirt! She volunteered to teach me acting. Clumsy, stiff, and entirely uninterested—except in her delicious gossip—I was probably one of her lesser acting students. In the 1930s, she studied with Russia's Sergei

Eisenstein, and she also told me that, in 1943, she was the first Black woman to attend the University of Southern California's Film School.

Just as the Houston artists John Biggers and Vivian Ayers Allen inspired me as a very young child, Carlton Moss and Frances Williams were my cinema tutors in my quest to become a filmmaker. For years, Carlton Moss had served as a script doctor to the liberal Hollywood elite. He had worked with luminary directors like Frank Capra, Stanley Kramer, Elia Kazan, and Carl Foreman. In honor of Carlton Moss, Foreman, in his now classic film *Home of the Brave*, gave the dignified Black character, as played by actor James Edwards, the name of "Mossy."

Carlton and Frances were part of the African American group of the Hollywood blacklistees. As Blacks, they probably suffered the worst of the economic hardship. I also met some of the white members through Becca Wilson, a fellow UCLA Film School student. Her father was the writer Michael Wilson and her uncle, the producer Paul Jarrico. Her aunt, Sylvia Jarrico, was the partner of the Black actor William Marshall. They, in turn, introduced me to others. This remarkable group taught me about the McCarthy era from the invaluable point of view of those who felt directly the immediate, personal impact of the Hollywood blacklist. I was fortunate enough to hear both Black and white versions of what it meant to live through the McCarthy blacklist era.

Along with *Niagara* and *Carmen Jones*, there was yet another film made in 1954. This classic, *Salt of the Earth*, had an even greater impact on me. Union financed, it was made by Silver City, New Mexico, Latino residents and blacklisted Hollywood filmmakers. The film was a controversial story of a successful mine strike as told by primarily Latino mine workers in New Mexico. Because of its progressive politics, it was one of the few American-made films actually banned by this country's government and the Hollywood establishment.

The film's leading lady was a Mexican actress named Rosaura Revueltas. In time, she has come to replace Marilyn Monroe and Dorothy Dandridge as the best representative of the kind of womanhood I now admire. Revueltas, an artist and activist, was an amazingly talented and brave actress. The blacklist was so solid that after making this film, she was never able to work again in films anywhere in the world. She was brave, because she knew this would happen ahead of time, before the film's production started.

I first saw the film in 1979 at a conference with all of the film's then living participants present. It was a rare honor to hear about the making of this film from the people who were actually involved. Michael Wilson, Paul Jarrico, Clinton Jencks, and Frances Williams—people that I knew—had all worked on this film, though Frances's work was uncredited. When Frances described to me what it was like for her, as a Negro, to work on *Salt of the Earth*, I could understand the racist, classist, and sexist slights and oversights meted out to her by progressive

yet privileged-class whites. These slights happened while both groups, white and Black, were under siege by the HUAC.

It was sobering to hear a peculiar kind of bitterness hanging in the voice of Frances Williams as she told me how she "made" newscaster Chet Huntley, by teaching him voice articulation and stage presentation skills. And how once he'd "arrived," he'd forgotten her. Or to hear Carlton Moss speak with resignation about the uncredited script-doctor work he did on Elia Kazan's *Pinky,* and what it meant for him to learn about Kazan turning "friendly" witness to the HUAC. Fear was running rampant in the 1950s, and Kazan contributed to it with his testimony. What Kazan said helped to destroy the careers of many of his peers. Carlton was not alone. In his testimony at one House Un-American Activities hearing, the baseball hero Jackie Robinson personally attacked Paul Robeson. Other Blacks who made tremendous contributions to our nation's cultural life, such as W.E.B. DuBois, James Edwards, Canada Lee, and William Marshall, also suffered.

The trouble is that many times our history is presented in ways that permit us to forget how closely our present actions and reactions are connected to our past. So in 1998, I watched the Academy Awards on television with mixed feelings of both anger and sadness as many of my heroes and heroines—Martin Scorsese, Robert De Niro, Warren Beatty, Celeste Holm, and Debbie Allen—honored Elia Kazan.

That night the Academy gave Elia Kazan a special Lifetime Achievement Award. *Variety*'s Amy Archerd reported that a third of the audience sat in silence, with arms folded, protesting Kazan's past actions. Others present gave Kazan the traditional standing ovation. I knew two people actively involved on opposite sides of the two arguments. There was Debbie Allen, the daughter of my childhood mentor, the poet Vivian Ayers Allen. We grew up together as children in Houston, Texas. She joined the ones who stood and energetically applauded Kazan's tribute.

Meanwhile, across the street from the event and behind police lines, I knew that Becca Wilson, my former film school colleague, stood with another crowd of protesters who faced the building where the ceremony was in progress. She and others carried signs in protest of Kazan's honorary award and in tribute to her family and friends scarred by Kazan's testimony in the same blacklist period that elevated those who named names at others' expense.

I don't believe many people fully understood the entire story—of just how damaging those years were to issues of an enriched creative expression, the stemming of authority in the industry's labor unions, and the blunting of diversity by restricting the talents of American artists like Paul Robeson, Carlton Moss, Frances Williams, Canada Lee, and William Marshall. All of these concerns fit into this seemingly minor protest. Tragically, it was seeded so far in the past that it appeared trivial to those ignorant of its historical context. The audience applause was for an unapologetic Kazan. With no visible sense of remorse for his part in the destruction of so many of his talented peers, he resolutely faced a divided Academy audience.

It was my mother who first took me to see Kazan's *On the Waterfront*. I watched Marlon Brando mouth those legendary words, "I could have been a contender." In the film, Rod Steiger and Marlon Brando are brothers. One brother has betrayed the other. They speak to each other about this disloyalty during a night scene in the back of a car. As an actor, Brando does a magnificent job of infusing a sympathetic quality to a character who I later learn was Kazan's metaphor for his own testimony. His role was also what the blacklisted group labeled as a portrayal of a snitch, a turncoat.

This film's writing and acting are but two of the elements at work here. There's much more present. It can be seen in the sharp, white light that moves across Brando's and Steiger's faces at oblique angles, solidifying this scene's harshness. This "something more" lay concealed in the visual design created by the film's cinematographer, Boris Kaufman. It was his camera work that helped to make *On the Waterfront* real. His eye provided the visuals that gave life to the grimy Hoboken,

New Jersey, waterfront atmosphere, and by doing so, Kaufman added a dimension of realism to the actors' dramatizations.

Boris Kaufman's talents matured out of a remarkable confluence of cinematic contributions from many different countries. Boris was the youngest of three Kaufman brothers that also included Denis and Mikhail. All three were trained in the new Soviet cinema emerging from the 1917 Russian Revolution. The most famous of this talented trio was the Russian avant-garde and documentary filmmaker Denis Kaufman, or Dziga Vertov. Denis had renamed himself the equivalent of a "spinning top" during the revolution days. As Dziga Vertov, he was one of the world's major founders of documentary film. His wide-ranging influences have impacted the development of cinema soundscapes, the 1930s *March of Time* newsreels, and the 1960s Cinéma Vérité documentary movement.

In his books *Media Marathon: A Twentieth-Century Memoir* and *Media Lost and Found,* the historian Erik Barnouw touchingly relates how Mikhail Kaufman taught his younger brother Boris cinematography, sight unseen. Boris Kaufman left Russia in 1917 as a young man. As adults, Mikhail and Boris never saw each other again. Boris first emigrated to France and worked as a cameraman on surrealist director Jean Vigo's films. This impressive list of classics includes *À Propos de Nice, Zéro de Conduite,* and *L'Atalante.* He then moved to Canada and worked at the John Grierson–inspired National Film Board of Canada. In the 1950s and 1960s, Boris Kaufman was a U.S. citizen and a major American cinematographer on such films as *Splendor in the Grass, Baby Doll,* and *12 Angry Men.* For many of those years, Mikhail continued to teach Boris cinematography through the mail.

The irony is that Kazan won his *On the Waterfront* Academy Awards through the contributions of, among others, a Communist-trained Boris Kaufman. Kaufman created a cinematic marriage between Soviet Kino Pravda principles; the 1920s avant-garde "city symphony films" from Russia, Germany, and France; the 1930s French surrealist movement; and the later development of classic Hollywood cinema in the 1950s. His mature work is best viewed in the 1965 Sidney Lumet film *The Pawnbroker.*

Sunday evening, March 21, 1998: The Seventy-first Academy Awards. Inside a tribute; outside a protest. Brief, odd juxtapositions—Art and Commerce, Censorship and Resistance.

Pinky. Carlton Moss. *No Way Out.* Roy DeCarava. *Amos 'n' Andy.* John Biggers. *Niagara.* Vivian Ayers Allen. *Carmen Jones.* Clinton Jencks. *Salt of the Earth.* Frances Williams. *On the Waterfront.* Boris Kaufman. *The Pawnbroker.*

These images and the people who make them are like my country. Sometimes they are sad with greed, and sometimes they are brave with courage.

Interlude #2 **Soap and Cereal**

The first step towards lightening

The White Man's Burden

is through teaching the virtues of cleanliness.

Pears' Soap

is a potent factor in brightening the dark corners of the earth as civilization advances, while amongst the cultured of all nations it holds the highest place—it is the ideal toilet soap.

The more things change
the more they stay the same.
—Alphonse Karr, *Les Guêpes*

I sat in the bathtub furiously scrubbing my underarms with a scratchy plastic bath brush. Turning on the tap's scalding hot water, I rinsed off the suds. Then I lifted my arm up to my face and sniffed at my armpit. Although faint, the odor was still there. I sighed.

Suddenly my eyes hurt. When I squinted, tears rushed out. In seconds I was crying my heart out, sobbing out of sheer frustration. I had done everything that I knew to do, and still, nothing had worked. The Ivory soap floated past my water-shriveled fingers, leaving behind a thin white film on the top of the bath water. I wanted to smash that soap cake into bits.

"Did you say I've got a lot to learn..."

I was also listening to the De Castro Sisters singing "Teach Me Tonight." Their song was playing over and over again in the bedroom. I had adjusted the record arm to replay beforehand, because I loved listening to that song. I didn't know it then, but it would take another thirty years before I'd hear a better version. That would be Al Jarreau's 1980s rendition. At the time, however, all the words did was to make me feel all the more defeated.

"Well, don't think I'm trying not to learn..."

It was around 1956 and I was thirteen years old. Literally and figuratively, I was in hot water. Both my parents were angry with me. "It was all your fault," they told me.

I was moving into puberty. The hormonal changes were exploding all over my body. Only there was nothing very dramatic about it. No, the change was ugly and embarrassing: I smelled bad. Very bad. All the time. Every one of my body openings—other than my ears and hands—emitted some kind of foul, terrible odor. My feet, crotch, armpits, and mouth. Everywhere had a remarkably different, yet horrific stench. My lack of control was beyond belief.

My underarms were the absolute worst of all. There, the smell in my body had a field day. It would impose itself in a profusion of my sweat. This sweat ran out of me into the cloth under my arms. My blouses and dresses had ragged-edged, discolored outlines drenched in odors so strong that no amount of washing, detergent changes, or dry cleanings would help. Rendered useless by smell, my outfits had to be dumped. In a valiant attempt to save the new clothes, my mother stocked up on underarm pads. But once on me, they too failed. The pads actually transmitted the smell to the clothes rather than blocking it. Sighing, we all went back to the drawing board.

Determined not to give in, both my parents went on separate buying sprees, bringing back various and sundry soaps, deodorants, pharmacy chemicals, even baking soda, vinegar, and other kitchen remedies. And two to three times daily I'd slip into school restrooms to perform sponge baths. I'd try new deodorants every week, sometimes combining two together in hopes that double strength would work. It didn't. Then came the assaults of enhanced smells—toilet waters, colognes, dusting powers, perfumes, douche preparations, and mouthwashes. But once my body chemistry mingled with these fragrances, I began to smell even worse. Other than some of these so-called cleaners hindering the odor, not one of these products made a bit of a difference to my raging hormones wreaking havoc all over my body.

Overnight, it seemed to me, my body turned me into the family pariah. And now they had given up on me. My parents were mad at me. They started blaming me. They were visibly ashamed at what I had become.

I had failed them. I had failed the whole family. Worst of all, my mother insisted that I had failed the entire Negro race. "You smell just like some old roustabout," she would sometimes sniff. "How could you embarrass me like this?" she implored on other occasions.

I didn't understand it myself. Why couldn't I clean myself well enough to be acceptable? I actually lay awake nights mentally flagellating myself for letting my body betray me.

And then, one day, the smell went away. Poof! Just like that. Ultimately, my own body chemistry reset itself to adjust to my newfound womanhood.

Somewhere, some time later, I learned that every story like this emerges from a historical context. So when I started writing this book, I recalled this painful story and looked to history for some answers. My father was born in 1899 and my mother in 1900.

While researching my parents' births, I located two soap advertisements from 1899 that illuminate the cultural origins of my parents' shame. An October 1899 Pears' Soap ad promises that humankind would miraculously take "the first step towards lightening the White Man's Burden" by purchasing its product. Later that year, in a December 1899 Pears' ad, a crisply dressed white girl admonishes a dusky-clothed Black girl. The white child's assumption is that the soap will render the Black child clean and white. This ad assures us that "all sorts of stores sell it—all sorts of people use it." These ads infer that Blacks are dirty, nasty, smelly, and inferior, and that the whites are not because they use soap. Thus, the ads dismiss something I learned the hard way by personal experience: that soaps do not always rid the body of its smell.

These ads implied that their products could clean away smell and race. Perhaps my parents didn't believe, as maybe the whites did, the race part. I know they did believe that the soaps they bought could create a smell-free body. And that they believed that Blacks were perceived to be smelly. I know, because when my body continued to smell, my parents denigrated me. What's worse is that in my little saga, I was blamed while the soap got off scot-free.

Though the story I tell here is primarily about my mother and me, it is also about our cultural history and us. It is also about economics: my parents came into the world during a time and in a place that had too many goods and too few buyers. Faced with this dilemma at the beginning of the twentieth century, manufacturers needed to create a demand for unwanted goods, so they joined forces with colleagues in a new, emerging industry called advertising. Unwittingly, this producer-salesman alliance fostered a brand-new relationship between culture and economy. During the same time, scientists and inventors were busily creating cameras, photography, film, telephones, telegraphs, music records, and phonographs. Much later, radio, television, and digital technologies appeared. Creative artists like movie stars were always present as beautiful role models. These artistic, business, and advertising forces aligned with the up-and-coming communications technologies like movies and radio. All worked in unplanned coalitions to transform this country into a mass-consumption, mass-mediated society. And this consortium unwittingly conspired to send all of us in search of "the American Dream," a dream that claims that any need can be purchased.

In many ways, my family's values about cleanliness illustrate the commercial influence of the marketing of soap, cereal, and song. It describes what happens when market-driven values get in the way of human relationships. In striving to keep up with what they are told is important, people inadvertently hurt each other. So in this book, I attempt to make real the impact that mass media has on my life. In the end, I became a photographer, filmmaker, and writer to directly challenge some of these influences.

I am my interaction with all the people I've known. At the core of my story is my relationship with the most influential person in my life, my mother. And so this book is a mother-daughter story.

127

In this memory of my past, I am also the ideas and ideologies that shape my society. To their credit and to my good fortune, my parents did not buy the pitch in "the American Dream" hook, line, and sinker. They cared about values and people. They worked for a better world for everyone. In so doing, they created just enough of a space for me to succeed past their accomplishments. Because of them, I now have the liberty to tell my version of our story in order to lay claim to our existence.

Researching, remembering, and then writing this memoir has helped me to encounter the strange, wonderful, and self-liberating experience of the direct power of storytelling: it empowers me to finally know and say who I decide I am.

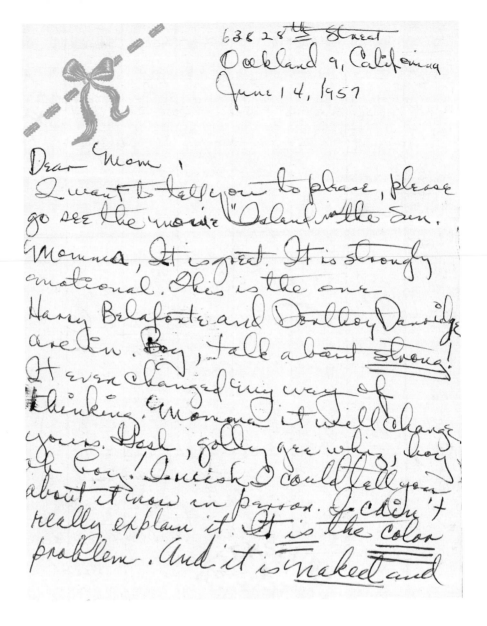

638 28th Street
Oakland 9, California
June 14, 1957

Dear Mom,

I want to tell you to please, please go see the movie "Island in the Sun." Momma, It is great. It is strongly emotional. This is the one Harry Belafonte and Dorthoy Danridge are in. Boy, talk about <u>strong!</u> It even changed my way of thinking. Momma it will change yours. Gosh, golly gee whiz, boy oh boy! I wish I could tell you about it now in person. I cain't really explain it. It <u>is</u> the <u>color</u> problem. And it is <u>naked</u> and <u>raw</u> with its pure real facts. Like—well intermarriage, and you know how I said that I would never marry a white man? Well, now, I just really don't know. Basically, a man is a man—white, black, green, blue, yellow, etc. Those parts well they just seem _real_. (and they were _real_!) Me, in a mixed, (white & colored) theater made it even worst. Momma, even up here where just about everything is equal, I was _quiet_ even a white boy next to me after the show turned to me and said "That will give you something to sleep on— its just that doggoned powerful." And gee everyone agreed. The place was filled. From top to bottom. I cried some, but you know I am so very emotional. It's not like any other racial picture I've ever seen. The negroes don't kiss the whites but the show gives you a feeling that they might have kissed. Harry Belafonte, I think you will admire. Mostly in 3 scenes. They are to difficult to explain, but they are (1) at the first party, (2) at the meeting (3) at the end. Basically, the story is based on an island. There are 3 main charts of people. First a white family, 2nd Harry and the white girl who loves him, 3rd Dorthoy & a white boy who are in love and marry. Harry is truly the star. And at the end he has to decide between his people and this white woman. He chooses his people and the woman wants to know why—One of the reasons he says "Is because of the night you'll forget, and call me a nigger." Under your circumstances you won't get the same quiet, different feeling because of so many spook nergoes. And they will maybe laugh at truly emotional scenes. Mostly at the time Harry faces this white man and blesses him out. Just go! And enjoy it. It will move you quietly but emotionally.

   Boy! Whew!
Send me: Aunt Birdie's address, Aunt Emma's address, A letter from you, Money from somewhere (smile)

Love to all mosty Lassie,
Mom   Daddy
X X X   X X X
Kisses to you & Daddy

. . . into the world. The boys out here are much more mature than Houston boys. But they just aren't cute. There aren't any Frenchmen out here. They are just as black until they are purple. Oh in Island in the Sun the boy that Dorthy fell in love with, they suntanned him until he's about Dorthoy's color. But they don't kiss— Instead give the appearance of being kissed. Harry Belafonte is the best—he should be nominated for a "Oscar." Oh here is why he marry that white gal. She incidentally is pregnant. What do you think?

into the world. The boys out here are much more mature than Houston boys. but they just aren't cute. There aren't any Frenchmen out here. They are just as black until they are purple. Oh in Island in the Sun the boy that Dorthy fell in love with, they sun tanned him untill he's about Dorthy's color. But they don't kiss — Instead give the appearence of being kissed. Harry Belafonte is the best — he should be nominated for a "Oscar" Oh here is why he marry that white gal. She incidentally is pregnant.

Harry Belafonte, explaining in Ebony magazine his mixed marriage to dancer Julie Robinson: *"I believe in integration and work for it with my heart and soul. But I did not marry Julie to further the cause. I married her because I was in love with her."*

→ What do you think?

132

The bitter paradox of the Black performer—using your art to entertain your oppressor—is nowhere so evident as it is among musicians, perhaps because it is so difficult to maintain detachment while singing or playing your heart out.

—Darlene Clark Hine and Kathleen Thompson, *A Shining Thread of Hope: The History of Black Women in America*

Chapter VI **My Harry**

Surely the only explanation was that I was in love. Because, I seriously reasoned to myself, if his hair was as nappy as it was, then why did I still think he was cute? Well, it was true that he was light skinned, with a sharp, thin nose and high cheekbones. So he looked almost white even though his skin was caramel colored. But then, here I was, making excuses for his hair, so maybe it really was love.

Here comes the bongo roll.

Then his sexy, husky voice: *"Day-O, day-ay-ay-o…Daylight come and me wan' go home…"* His song was everywhere. He was undeniably popular. Why, all America loved Harry Belafonte. So certainly it just had to be all right for me to love him too.

I was immersed in the middle of the long, hot summer of 1957. Joanne Woodward was my new idol. She was a lot more interesting than Marilyn Monroe. Besides, she had it all over Marilyn. Joanne had Paul Newman. It was my first summer away from home. I was in Oakland and Berkeley, California, staying in and around the houses of my father's siblings and their spouses—Aunt Edna and Uncle Chris; Aunt Lillie Bell and Uncle Gilbert; Aunt Henrietta; and Aunt Eola and Uncle Alex.

Uncle Alex worked in the construction industry. He bought a new Cadillac every year. Although behind Uncle Alex's back, my parents and I derided the stereotype of "Negroes and Cadillacs," all of us were proud to ride around with him in his newest luxury liner whenever we came to town. All my aunts had been

"Rosie the Riveters" during World War II. And all of them were still working for the navy in the shipyards.

Harry Belafonte. All the young Negro men were wearing cut-below-the-knee white pants, colorfully printed Caribbean shirts tied at the waist, and big, round straw hats. And in downtown San Francisco, there were even some white boys dressed calypso style. Just like him.

My Harry. I fell in love with his face. His husky voice. His too perfectly sexy body. His shirts that opened up to show off his hairy chest. But there was his hair. Why did his hair *have* to be so kinky? Why didn't he wear a stocking cap so that it would lay down? Or use a hint of a conk?

Most everyone in my immediate family despised truly Black-looking Negroes: black skin so dry it was rusty looking; nappy, uncontrollable hair; broad noses; thick lips; wide and big, soft hips and buttocks flopping over the sides of tiny chairs; big, long, rusty feet—these features horrified all of us beyond description. Yet that's what my father's people looked like. It's what I looked like. And so I had made a God-given pledge to make some white-looking babies. I really tried my very best to attach myself to the light-skinned—almost white—Louisiana Gheechie boys. But alas, I was a brown-skinned, nappy-haired girl with full lips and a behind that was too embarrassingly big. Besides, I was going to remain a virgin until I married. So having no use for me, these fair-skinned knights rejected me.

Just imagine my additional confusion when my body became inexplicably drawn to my super-black-skinned cousin Robert Lloyd Hoffman. Why, Robert Lloyd was as black as my patent leather shoes. But he was the real thing and not a secret daydream like Harry. Robert Lloyd was a living, breathing man. And he was unmistakably alive and in the flesh. He had laughing eyes and a heart-stopping grin that ended in dimples on a decidedly handsome baby face that made me melt inside every time I saw him. And that was as much as possible. When Robert Lloyd was around, I would situate myself in places in the room that would allow my eyes free access to look at all of him, from that cute face to all up and down his fine, elegant frame.

It was my body that quickly taught me that color and genetic build didn't have a thing to do with how I felt next to some man, no matter how African black, if I had the hots for him. The color of black became a no-man's-land where my emerging values began to war with those of my family. My parents, my family, and some of my friends despised my hair, my lips, my pug nose, my backside, and my very skin tone.

I spent a great deal of time that summer doing my very best to first struggle with and then finally accept the bits and pieces of Harry's Africanness. "He's amazingly handsome," I thought as I gazed upon the perfection of his remarkable face sculpted in obviously white features. "It's okay," I would muse while listening to the hint of anger and always seething passion in his haunting voice.

And then HE had the audacity to betray me.

Harry Belafonte had the nerve to leave his middle-class, educated Negro wife and their beautifully colored children to go and—gasp!—marry a white woman. At first, the press said she was an American Indian. Then later she was Jewish. And then she was a dancer who had studied with the legendary Black dancer Katherine Dunham. Just as if all of that was supposed to make any kind of difference at all to me. She was then, and still is to this day, a white woman.

I was crushed beyond repair.

And so was everyone reading the July 1957 issue of *Ebony* magazine. In 1957, *Ebony* and *Jet* magazines were part of the pulse of Negro America. Filmmaker Stanley Nelson's film *With Swords and Pens* best describes the role of this country's local and national Black press organs. Johnson Publications is a long-standing national empire that publishes both *Ebony* and *Jet*. It is a leading power base for its middle-class and middle-class-aspiring African Americans. And this conservative Black community extracts much from its icons.

To my surprise, Harry Belafonte transcended the crisis that made him the cover story of *Ebony*'s July 1957 issue. He remained a "race" man. He took his position as a leading Black role model very seriously. Even his acting role in *Island in the Sun* directly addressed interracial lovers as a major issue. Later, as I read about Dorothy Dandridge's life, I began to understand how hard it was for any Black actor or actress in the late 1950s. It's remarkable that *Island in the Sun* was even made.

Robert Rossen directed this film. Rossen, like Belafonte, was a self-made man who had risen above poverty and violence. At one time he'd been a boxer. Think of it—a young Jewish man who made his first living as a boxer becoming a famous Hollywood director. His social idealism and political concerns were reflected in his filmmaking and placed him a cut above some of his contemporaries. Wanting to work for change, he'd joined the Communist Party in the 1930s. By World War II, he had become disillusioned, cutting all party ties by 1945. He won an Academy Award as best director for his 1949 film, *All the King's Men* (he produced, directed, and wrote this film). During the "Red Scare era," his political past caught up with him. In 1951 others identified him as a Communist. Called in to testify before the House Un-American Activities Committee, he bravely refused to identify others. He was promptly blacklisted. Two years later, he broke under the pressure and named more than fifty colleagues. His reward was that he was able to work again. Choosing to work in locations other than Hollywood, in 1957 he directed *Island in the Sun* in the Caribbean. His friends described him as a man who died tortured and driven by his own personal demons. He left behind a formidable body of work—*The Strange Love of Martha Ivers, The Treasure of Sierra Madre, Body and Soul, The Hustler,* and *Lilith*—to mark his amazing career.

Yet he arrived on the set of *Island in the Sun* a broken man. While taking a picture with me, Harry Belafonte tells me that *Island in the Sun* was really Darryl Zanuck's brainchild. He faces me to say that "Zanuck did some very important films." I must look unconvinced because he continues, "and some of his films attempted to address racism—why, look at *Gentleman's Agreement, Pinky,* and *Island in the Sun.* Look it up!" I followed Belafonte's instructions. I researched Zanuck. And I discovered that *The Grapes of Wrath, All About Eve,* and *The Man in the Gray Flannel Suit* were also his productions.

Film historians talk about the appearance of "social consciousness" films in the late 1940s and early 1950s. These films were building blocks for a realistic perspective of American life. And they provided respectable work to Black actors and actresses. At his Academy tribute, Sidney Poitier spoke of working for these liberal-thinking men. Starting with *No Way Out*, these men made Poitier's career possible.

And Harry's. However initially maligned by Blacks and whites for his choice to enter into an interracial marriage, Harry Belafonte never seemed to waver in his political beliefs. He has moved beyond just being a race man. Today he is a responsible and widely respected world citizen. He continues to work for African Americans, civil rights, Third World liberation and independence. He is a master artist. The social and political choices he's made in his life are reflected in his art. His art reflects the peace-and-justice work that he's done in his life. In addition, he supports the rise of many fellow artists as well. For close to forty-five years, he has modeled for me how to be both a world-class artist and a global citizen.

Starting with *Bright Road* and *Carmen Jones*, Harry's choice of movie roles has always signaled his serious commitment to uplifting the Black race. I remember sitting in Houston's Park Theater, absorbing the important message in *The World, the Flesh, and the Devil*. I walked out of that movie thinking about the threat of nuclear annihilation. A later film on the same topic, *On the Beach*, also impacted me. Both films were prime influences in shaping my present-day anti–nuclear armament stance.

Yes, in 1971, I did see *Sweet Sweetback's Baadasssss Song* many times. Subsequently, Melvin Van Peebles's book on the making of this film became my filmmaking bible. But it was the 1972 film *Buck and the Preacher* that really challenged me. Here, the acting, the words spoken by Harry Belafonte, Ruby Dee, Sidney Poitier, and yes, even my nemesis, Julie Belafonte, transformed me. Sidney Poitier's directing debut helped convince me that yes, Black people could make films that reflected our dignity. And so, in 1972, I began to dream that even I could make films.

But way before then, in 1967, I had made up my mind to be a still photographer. Billie Holiday and Harry Belafonte played a part in that decision, which took root on a chilly, quiet, kind of peaceful, gray-sky Sunday afternoon. It was on December 8, 1957. Earlier that day I had been to church, so I knew it was too cold to play outside. Instead, I sat my little fourteen-year-old self down, alone, in front of the television set. Fortunately, I was completely unprepared for what lay ahead.

He wears high draped pants, stripes are really yellow...
But when he starts in to love me, he is so fine and mellow...

The haunting sound of Billie Holiday's one-of-a-kind voice mesmerized me as its soothing tone oozed its way into my consciousness...slow moving, like molasses. And her face. I had no idea just what this image of her singing would mean to me until much, much later. Lady Day's presence faded up and on to the very live

CBS television program. Billie had signature songs that belonged only to her. "Strange Fruit" was one. And here she was, singing the flip side of that record, her classic blues song "Fine and Mellow." The program graced by her appearance was aptly titled "The Sound of Jazz." The show's vivid black-and-white cinematography gave me my first view of Billie Holiday. Her backup band included some of jazz's greatest musicians—Mal Waldron, Lester Young, Ben Webster, Coleman Hawkins, Doc Cheatham, Vic Dickenson, Jo Jones, Jim Atlas, and Danny Barker. All the Black sidemen wore these incredible narrow-brim, wonderfully tailored hats on their heads. Some were in suits with ties. They circled the great Billie Holiday like a casual, yet military escort. The Lady sat royally on a high stool. She was unmistakably caught up in the power of the music. And within this circle of greatness surrounding her, she was in total command. Later, I realized she was also teaching me how to enjoy the heritage of our music. As Prez, Ben, and the Hawk blew, she coolly rocked her fragile head back and forth in tune with the heart of the beat. There was her eyebrow knowingly raised there, a slight smile turning up here, and her eyes closed with an icy wisdom of this music's lyrical twists and turns. At the end of each musician's solo, her mellow voice would pick up the tenor of the beat in such a keen yet subtle way that she'd turn the bite of this melody inside out again. I was then and now, forty-three years later, still in total amazement at her melodic phrasing. She was using her part in the music to tell us, her subjects, what it meant to be an independent and free Black woman and, better yet, how she commanded us to treat her, a one-of-a-kind free spirit.

Just treat me right baby, I'll stay home night and day;
but you're so mean to me baby, I know you're going to drive me away...

The camera work in this all-too-short seven-minute interlude of sheer musical genius became an aesthetic touchstone for how I still do my photography to this day. As I sat there with my eyes fixed to my parents' tiny screen, the television studio disappeared. What remained were these very close-up views of the lines, the creases on the drug-and-alcohol-ravaged face of this great lady, and the darkness inside her eyes. The natural light in the studio lovingly cast a contrast between shadow and highlight that peered into the faces of these master jazz musicians busy at work loving the music they were making.

Oh, the better-known still photographers such as Dennis Stock, Frances Wolff, and Gordon Parks made their attempts, but it was only the master photographer Roy DeCarava who best captured these moments in jazz when the musicians and their music embraced. DeCarava caught this love in the silver halide that glistened in his photographs. There was only one other time when I again saw this quality of beauty in Black American music on television. That was on a television program hosted by Harry Belafonte.

Believing the quality of Mr. Belafonte's program was enhanced because he was wise enough to use Roy DeCarava's blown-up photographs as studio set backdrops, I query him. When I ask him about this program's history, he smiles with a justified pride. "Like 'The Sound of Jazz,' this was another CBS production. It was titled 'A Night with Belafonte,' and it won an Emmy." In the late 1950s, when no Blacks had television programs, this was no mean feat. He continues to reminisce, "I took a chance on a young, talented director. My program was his first job. That young man was Norman Jewison." "Oh," I banter back, "Jewison won you that Emmy." Harry laughs out loud, like what I'm saying is absurd. "That was *my* show," he counters. "I hired DeCarava and Jewison. They simply executed my vision."

My first glimpse of television's potential to capture America's Black music was contained in this segment of Lady Day at work. The image I now have of the great Billie Holiday is a tiny mirror fragment unjustly fractured by the reality of America's racism. I saw what it meant to be a free-spirited and creative African American woman, and it frightened me. When I held my vision of Lady Day in my mind's eye, I had to be careful not to cut myself on the thin, needle-sharp edges that held that glimmer of her image in place. Not too much time had passed before I read about her untimely death. I remember that I was not at all surprised. Later, in search of the why, I bought her book, *Lady Sings the Blues,* cowritten by William Duffy. Duffy later wrote another influential book, *Sugar Blues,* with the actress Gloria Swanson.

Harry Belafonte's lifelong contributions as a world artist and film and television producer were important to me—as were Roy DeCarava's dark photographs, Billie Holiday's haggard face as she sang her sweet music, and Duffy's frightening book, coauthored with Billie Holiday. All helped me to understand the insides of those powerful television images as they went about documenting the depth of the sound of the jazz that I experienced that Sunday afternoon. Lady Day's story kept me from using drugs or alcohol, and from tolerating men whose greed would motivate them to use women like me. But it was her voice, its unique, dull-edged sharpness, that cut through the South's mundane atmosphere on that winter-laden afternoon.

In the early 1970s, I discovered that Harry Belafonte was on the United States government's enemy list. In the early 1980s, when I saw *Sometimes I Look at My Life,* a Cuban documentary on his life, I began to understand how important it was for an artist to be a responsible world citizen. And so, it was how Harry Belafonte chose to live his life as an artist, along with that something inside Lady Day's voice, that began to urge me on to find a way to express what was inside me.

Love is like a faucet, it turns off and on.
Sometimes when you think it's on baby, it has turned off and gone.

I have personally interacted with Harry Belafonte on three occasions. I first met him one October night in Houston, Texas, in 1967. Pluria Marshall, then a Houston photographer, had taken me under his wing as an aspiring still photographer. Pluria went on to be a media lobbyist in Washington, D.C. In those days, he was a southern, small-town "colored" photographer specializing in sports and Black high school annuals. Generously, he took pity on me. On that particular night, he took me with him to Houston's Hobby Airport. There, a then defrocked heavyweight champion, Muhammad Ali, loudly greeted Harry Belafonte as he got off the plane. We photographed Harry Belafonte and Muhammad Ali together. Bravely, Muhammad Ali had come out earlier with an anti-Vietnam stance, refusing to serve his military duty. He was punished with the loss of his title and of his right to pursue his livelihood. Jobless and under siege, Muhammad Ali had moved to Houston.

Pluria let me tag along the next day to Houston's infamous Shamrock Hotel. There we were the only two outsiders allowed to attend an incredible meeting between Harry Belafonte, Martin Luther King Jr., Andrew Young, Ralph Abernathy, and Jesse Jackson. I watched them discuss how to prepare Houston's Black community for an obviously unpopular and potentially dangerous anti–Vietnam War concert—with musicians like Aretha Franklin, Curtis Mayfield, and many other famous Black entertainers—set for that evening in the city's Jesse Jones Auditorium. These performers had come out to support Martin Luther King Jr.'s protest against the war.

And there, behind closed doors, away from the press and the public, I was part of a remarkable, historic meeting. Andrew Young even turned to me to ask my opinions of Houston's Black community. This privileged access hastened my decision to become a professional still photographer. Six months later, Martin Luther King Jr. was assassinated in Memphis, Tennessee. The inner cities in the United States burned in protest as Sarah Gamble, a young friend, and I drove across the country to Boston.

In 1987, I called Harry Belafonte at his home for a richly detailed and valuable telephone interview. I was now a television producer for the late Henry Hampton's *Eyes on the Prize, Series II*. Belafonte and I talked for one and one-half hours. He told me about the 1960s and 1970s and the civil rights movement years as he had experienced them. He told me how he met Martin Luther King Jr. He talked in detail about his work with the Southern Christian Leadership Conference (SCLC) students in Mississippi during the summer of 1964, a summer of events so inaccurately portrayed in Alan Parker's film *Mississippi Burning*. He talked about Fannie

Lou Hamer's brief television appearance at the Democratic Convention, about President Johnson's television interruption and upstaging, about what happened after the 1964 Democratic Convention and its debilitating effects on the Student Nonviolent Coordinating Committee (SNCC) students and the Mississippi residents.

"They were all suffering from sheer exhaustion," his voice comes to me over the wires very huskily. "I wanted to lift their spirits." He tells me that he sent the beaten-down, despairing, and just plain exhausted students to meet Sekou Toure in Africa to get a vision of what a Black-run country could look like.

He mused over his relationships with Cuba's Fidel Castro and a then imprisoned Nelson Mandela in South Africa. He remarked on his contributions to worldwide justice. He spoke of his often troubled relationship with Sidney Poitier and other more conservative Black leaders regarding the civil rights movement. Then he told me his 1988 version of his dreams for world liberation and its relationship to his youthful poverty and lack of education.

"What keeps you going?" I ask off the subject, and I do it mainly for myself. I want to learn how to be as strong as he is. "Why do you keep on fighting?" I want to know his secret. "Life," he answers with one word. I finally have enough sense to stay with the silence.

I had already learned most of what I knew about Mr. Belafonte's international and national contributions from *Sometimes I Look at My Life*. In this film, Harry Belafonte—openly and without shame—cries as he speaks about how this country broke Paul Robeson's spirit during the McCarthy era. The film's exploration of Belafonte's life widened my view of the role of an artist. In June 2000, I met the filmmaker, Orlando Rojas, in Havana, Cuba. Rojas tells me that very few people actually saw this film. He was surprised and pleased that his film, one that he thought of as a failure, had managed to be seen and enjoyed by me in 1982 at FILMEX, the now defunct Los Angeles International Film Festival.

At UCLA, Professor Tshome Gabriel's Third World Cinema class opened a door for me. In his class, I learned about East Indian, African, Asian, and Latin American films. While I admired the works of Glauber Rocha, Satyajit Ray, and Ousmane Sembène, it was the Cuban films that inspired me. Starting with *Lucia, One Way or Another, The Last Supper,* and *The Other Francisco*, this magical blend of political underpinnings with dramatic and emotional stories worked together to move me.

In 1984, I made a film titled *Conversations with Roy DeCarava*. In the 1950s, Harry Belafonte had worked with Roy DeCarava, Lillian Hellman, Ossie Davis, Ruby Dee, Paul Robeson, and others to present Black people with pride. Roy explained to me that this group of enlightened artists were the ones to mount the

141

successful drive to shut down the 1950s *Amos 'n' Andy* television series that I had watched with delight as a child in Cousin Millard's house on that tree-lined street in upwardly mobile Detroit.

My third contact with Harry Belafonte was in 1995, when he performed at Escondido's California Center for the Arts. The Center's education director, Leah Goodwin, asked me to facilitate a preconcert audience discussion centered around Harry Belafonte's artistry. I chose to screen Rojas's documentary of Belafonte's life. My audience was made up of die-hard Belafonte fans, many of whom I suspected knew more about Belafonte's life than Belafonte himself. One gray-haired, pot-bellied man brought an original album of Belafonte's calypso songs. He had hoped to get Belafonte to sign it after the concert. I could imagine this man, youthful in the summer of 1957, walking on a downtown San Francisco street with a crew cut covered by a straw hat, moving to the beat of Harry's "The Banana Boat Song."

Of course, I too was excited about meeting Harry Belafonte again. Following a very long wait after the concert, a small group of us met with this great man. Someone had a camera, and we all unabashedly pushed our way forward to take a picture with him.

I knew how important it was for me to capture my long and still unfulfilled dream of standing next to him. After all, nothing in the intervening years had ever diminished my childhood crush on this still quite handsome man. So, patiently, I waited. Suddenly, there he was. Everyone pushed forward. When it was my turn, I walked over to him and took control. "Harry," I whispered, quietly enough that only he and I could hear, "take off your glasses. And smile into the camera. Now here, let me get next to you." To my utter surprise, he obeyed me. Here I was directing this great man who was a friend to some of the world's legendary revolutionary leaders, such as Fidel Castro, Sekou Toure, and Nelson Mandela. Politely and without any hesitation, he was following my instructions!

As our picture-taking session wound down, I looked at him. I mean, I *really* looked at him. What I saw was a very tired seventy-year-old man. His on-stage magnetism had faded. His voice was hoarse and somewhat strained. He had wrinkles on his face and heavy bags under his eyes. His body was aging; he carried himself like an old man. His face mirrored the loss of a youthful matinee idol. Exhausted, his weariness hung on him like a soft, gray shadow.

I pushed out a torrent of questions, rushing to get him to clarify things that were still unclear to me. I wanted to know about *Island in the Sun*, Dorothy Dandridge, South Africa, Cuba, the civil rights movement, life…An anonymous stiff elbow started pushing me out of the way. I had to hurry. I had only seconds before the next small group descended on him. I turned to face him directly, hoping to block the crowd's advance. I reached out and shook his hand. I then

looked directly into his eyes as our hands met. "Thank you," I started, "for your life and your work."

A group of pushy onlookers—Harry's die-hard fans—finally succeeded in overtaking me. His hand escaped mine and he disappeared from my view. How could he understand what I meant? He hears such earnest and adoring declarations all the time. For him, I must have been a blur in a sea of faces compiled from his latest international tour. For me, I was shaking the hand of one of my heroes. As I stood there, thinking about what had just happened, yet another middle-aged matron began to proclaim her long-term admiration for him as well.

"Oh my God," I thought with a slight cringe, "she sounds just like me." And I wondered what kind of past lay in her back story. I'm sure so much of what we, his audience, say to him must, over time, strike him as being trite...

Yet, basking in the glow of this crowd's devotion, Harry became young and animated again. There was a subtle exchange of energy that certainly must be addictive to those who have been named our stars, our icons, the designated keepers of our dreams. Harry Belafonte straightened up from the invisible force of this crowd's energy and began to stand tall. He graced us with his husky, golden laughter. As he regained his stature, that infectious smile of his returned. His eyes sparkled. He was, once again, that fiery and fearless young hulk, that courageous West Indian Black man whose image I had fallen in love with over forty years ago.

It could be that when one is in love one doesn't understand too well. And when Annie, shortly before her death, wants to see Sarah Jane for the last time, her love still prevents her from understanding. It seems to her to be a sin that Sarah Jane should want to be taken for white. The most terrible thing about this scene is that the more Sarah Jane is mean and cruel, the more her mother is poor and pathetic. But in fact, exactly the reverse is true. It is the mother who is brutal, wanting to possess her child because she loves her. And Sarah Jane defends herself against her mother's terrorism, against the terrorism of the world. The cruelty is that we can understand them both, both are right and no one will be able to help them. Unless we change the world. At this point all of us in the cinema cried. Because changing the world is so difficult.

—Rainer Werner Fassbinder, translated by Thomas Elsaesser, "Six Films by Douglas Sirk"

Chapter VII **That Forty-Year-or-So Argument**

It is thick, pervasive, undeniable. My mother and I sit spellbound. The tension glues us to the screen like metal to a magnet. Forty years later, I realize the tension was deliberate.

It lay in her pacing. And in the sweetness of her sad eyes, filling slowly with water. In her ability to will her mourning to shine through her very pupils. And then she pushes that sad energy into her tears—teardrops that turn into rivulets, tiny, thin whispers, streaming down her soft, dusky brown cheeks.

And then there was her oddly precise control of her movements. She had this slow, molasses-like way of turning...hesitating...then walking...how to say it? Away? Away, because within her movement, "Away" became a blossoming realization—on her part and now ours—that she was being cruelly rejected, that there was everything extraordinary about this turndown. She turned her energy outward, helping us better to feel her exquisite, savage pain as she experienced yet another angry, slap-in-the-face and tongue-lashing denial from that bitch of a daughter. Her only daughter. This child, her bitter fruit, who was her only hope to escape her eternal, Negro-bound existence.

Riveted, my mother and I sit there in the dark, with those Technicolor images flickering on our faces, with those painful sounds floating through the air, dancing on the single beam of light from the back of the theater. For this mother and her daughter reflect so much of what we have become, my mother and I. We hardly

1884-14AD

147

know where their story ends and ours begins. It is a strange irony indeed that the film's title is *Imitation of Life*.

We watch the unfolding of not one, but two mother-and-daughter stories in this film. Two single women—one white, one Black, both poverty stricken—join forces to secure the financial futures of their two daughters. The white daughter feels neglected as her mother strives to become a famous actress. After seeing the tremendous struggles of her Black mother, the colored daughter decides to pass for white, forsaking both her race and her mother. In actual screen time, the major mother-and-daughter story belongs to the two white actresses, Lana Turner and Sandra Dee. But who are they kidding? Both of us completely ignore this story's progression. We crave that of the Negroes—Juanita Moore and Susan Kohner.

Even when I screen the film for my Women in Film class forty years later, the logic—that a majority of screen time determines the story's value—still doesn't mesh. Back then, my mother and I—and even now, my students and I—still choose the minor story, the one about the Black mother and daughter, as the center of our obsession.

The secret lies in the acting. This tiny fragment of a story is creatively and cunningly played by Juanita Moore, a Black actress with a fundamentally ethical intelligence. Her powerful performance was probably deliberate on her part, its force perhaps borne out of her desperate need to practice her craft. In the 1950s, respectable roles almost never came to Black actresses. Incredibly, these actresses had to fight to get paid to act. In addition, if they had any sense of dignity, they had to subversively transform the scripted stereotypes—their roles as maids, mammies, and whores—into some semblance of multidimensional human beings. In many cases, it would usually be years before they worked again.

So once working on screen, Juanita Moore held on for dear life simply by possessing the entire film. It helped that she was supported by another female performer, a new white actress also hungry to succeed. She was the young Susan Kohner, yet another studio version of Natalie Wood's role in *Rebel without a Cause*.

From the very first time my mother and I saw this film, we immediately began to use its story to frame the quality of our own interactions in our immediate lives. Today, I realize that I've never quite stopped being on the grand treasure hunt this film's emotions elicited. I still rely on it to uncover the skeletal outlines of our troubled relationship.

Summer 1959, Houston, Texas. Outside the air-conditioned theater, a full blast of the oppressively sweltering heat hit us. We were quiet. We walked on a sidewalk next to a paved street. We turned a corner to a street covered with oyster shells and no sidewalk. Rolling car tires crunched these shells down. A bright sun pierced through the humidity. We found the car. My mother unlocked the door. Her anger resurfaced just as she slammed it shut. We were finally alone. She could talk to me any way she wanted now, with little fear of public embarrassment.

"You!" she spat the words out at me. "You act just like that ungrateful heifer up there on that screen!" Her slamming of the car door is done as a dramatic effect designed to get my full attention. She wanted to wipe that dreamy-eyed look off my face. Now she added fuel to her fire. "You're just as crazy as she is!"

Crazy? Her words rolled off my back. As for me, I felt triumphant. At last I had seen a vision of who I am on the big screen. It mattered little to me that my only version of myself was one of a total bitch. That irrationally furious girl up there was me; she was at last real to me as someone full of my own rage.

My rage was her rage at a mother who refused to at least acknowledge that there was a red-hot meltdown taking place in the center of her daughter's soul. Never mind that Susan Kohner was really a white girl masquerading as a Negro. Her rage was mine. And thus my rage was finally real. It railed at a society that forced my mother to pinch my nose at birth in hopes that it would be slim, not broad. Her actions damaged me, leaving me with permanent sinus problems. Or her shame at my broad lips. Early on, I learned to hold the top lip folded so that it would appear slim. Or me starving myself so that my buttocks would not grow naturally big and wide. How I longed to have a flat behind so that my clothes—the ones designed by white designers for white women's bodies—would fall "right" on my body.

Juanita Moore. Here was a respectable Black mammy who adjusted to the indignities of our world with a dignified "Thank you for letting me work for you, Miss Ann" attitude. Humble, meek, grateful to be the Rock of Gibraltar, to hold together and to protect the cheap, tawdry, materialistic yet spiritually empty, pristine, blonde, blue-eyed world of the elegantly vapid Lana Turner.

Susan Kohner and I challenged everything! We championed our every right to be angry at our mothers' spinelessness; at her mother's acceptance of the white society as the right way; and at my mother's devotion to the consumer culture as the good life.

My mother and I roll the windows down to get the hot, sticky air circulating in the car. I know where she's getting ready to come from. And this time, I am ready for her. By observation, my father had taught me a new technique. Today I decide to try it. As my mother continues screaming at me, I sit quietly by, with my eyes averted, looking down at my feet.

"You're like a brick wall!" she fumes as she watches my eyes turn inward to the protection of my secret thoughts. Her voice gets louder as her accusations grow more absurd. I wait for her temper to spend itself. It always does, sooner or later. My peaceful demeanor is filled with the arrogance of having actually seen myself up there, on the silver screen. I am a feisty young woman enraged and unafraid to speak out against the lack of justice in America. I confront my mother with my knowledge that she does not really love me now and that she never did. Never mind that Susan Kohner does it clumsily for me, or that Juanita Moore stacks the deck by using her artistic command of her intimate knowledge of suffering to win the hearts and minds of the adults in this audience by acting the part of the victim. In the end, even though manipulators like my mother win, in the heart of their victory, she and others like her are left stunned and puzzled.

What I didn't know was that the vision behind this version of *Imitation of Life* came from a Dane who was named Hans Detlef Sierck at birth but later called himself Detlef Sierck during his career in German theater and film. He left Germany when Hitler's rule proved oppressive. Upon his arrival in Hollywood, he reinvented himself a third time to become Douglas Sirk, motion picture director.

As a very young man, he managed to experience the short-lived Bavarian Soviet Republic, perhaps the only revolutionary government of the twentieth century dominated by poets and intellectuals. Its influence left a deeply progressive mark on all who lived through its tenure. His experience with that time changed him forever. Sooner or later, he would always run afoul of everyone who threatened the freedom of his self-expression. Something of Susan Kohner and me grew deep inside him.

He combined his early life experiences with his impeccable aesthetic style and left-leaning political adventures. All of this sophistication served him well in the Hollywood of the 1950s. There, in that time and place, he directed some of the most commercially successful, yet extremely unsettling, melodramas of the time. His hits included *Written on the Wind, The Tarnished Angels, All That Heaven Allows, All I Desire, Magnificent Obsession* (one of my mother's absolute favorites), and *Imitation of Life*. He mastered the ins and outs of the melodrama in women's weepies while making Hollywood's Universal Studios lots of money.

He was very good at walking tightropes and playing both ends against the middle. His films were so constructed that both my mother and I could find adequate representations of our reflections. But my mother's favorite film, *Magnificent Obsession*, his first in a line of silly melodramas that propelled him to director stardom, also helped finally to exhaust him.

Winter 1998. I live in a cottage in downtown La Mesa, California, a small San Diego suburb dotted with slowly decaying buildings fashioned from 1950s architecture. My revisiting of the 1950s through these buildings causes me to remember Houston. My walks through the village provide me with a sense of the familiar, a return to the streets of my childhood. As a Black woman, these streets remain oddly routine, regardless of the gains and losses of the 1960s civil rights movement. But in this year, the angry white man has returned to the forefront of American life. In the worst domestic terrorist act in United States history, he and his friend bomb an Oklahoma City government building. Americans killing Americans. They kill mostly white people like themselves.

My mother is dead now. I miss her terribly. I cannot tell her what I have learned from the lessons that *Imitation of Life* has taught me. The film is a repository of those past stories that modeled how my mother and I should relate to each other. Rather than ignore them as outlandish mockeries built for ridicule, we took them too seriously. Her death intervened too quickly; we both lost the argument.

It has taken me forty years to realize our mistake. She and I built this hurtful relationship that revolved around playing out some theatrical roles we saw on some celluloid strip of plastic. When we fought and she lost, she became the long-suffering Juanita Moore who dies, defying her daughter's independence by having Mahalia Jackson continue the masquerade by singing at her funeral. And I turn into Susan Kohner—repentant, yet riddled with guilt for challenging her authority. She is forever right and I am forever wrong.

Yet, when I won, I pulled out the mighty sword and slew the falsely labeled, feminized version of the dragon I now name Ms. Melodrama. And she would forever lose and I would forever win. Jointly we bought into an improper dream.

Consequently, as an adult, I work to dislodge melodrama's phony hold on my emotions. I have decided to declare dead my guilt and my shame about being the "bad" daughter. I became determined to right all our wrongs. Obsessed and against all odds, I became a filmmaker. Then a film educator. Then a film scholar. Then, when I realized that film was part of the global experience of media, I became a media activist.

As a film educator, I searched for meaning through the annals of film theory. As I uncovered some of cinema's secrets, I dedicated myself to reveal Hollywood's power to destroy women's stories and the stories of people of color in film. In the end, I discovered how visual literacy was really my mother's way of talking back to the screen's logic. These skills become my allies. With them, I slay the paper dragons borne out of the imaginations of those producers, directors, and screenwriters holding down the status quo while using the money they make on their commercial productions to buy ocean-front houses in Malibu, drive Mercedes Benzes, put their children through Ivy League schools. And some of these children return to the entertainment industry as its most privileged class members.

I would learn how to support and admire my efforts and those of other Black women filmmakers—like Euzhan Palcy, Julie Dash, Kasi Lemmons, Jackie Shearer, Michele Parkerson, and many, many others. I would be thankful that so many grassroots media activists before us—like Carlton Moss, Paul Robeson, Ruby Dee, Ossie Davis, Frances Williams, and all the others—did the work necessary to make a way for those of us who follow. And I dream of the day when women can state from childhood that they will pursue media as a career and then go on to work successfully in their chosen fields. And I dream of the day when they will be able to rely on their mothers, who, in turn, will appreciate and support their efforts.

My mother had to protect me from dreaming my dreams. Her experience of the world would not allow her to imagine that my dreams could ever be realized. How could she? Nothing out there could have told her different. Even the stars in this movie didn't fare well, not to mention that Lana Turner was coming off the trauma of witnessing the tragic murder of her boyfriend Johnny Stompanato.

In 1960, Susan Kohner, daughter of Lupita Tovar, the famous Mexican actress, and Paul Kohner, the very powerful Czech-born Hollywood agent, was nominated for an Academy Award as best supporting actress for her performance in *Imitation of Life*. After her marriage to fashion designer John Weitz, she retired from acting.

Juanita Moore, one of the most respected Black character actresses of her period, also received an Academy Award nomination for her work in *Imitation of Life*. Even Sidney Poitier continues to laud her work some forty years later. The very best follow-up part the industry could give her was that of a housekeeper in the 1988 *Tammy Tell Me True*. She continued acting in similar maid-like supporting roles. Then did she just disappear? I wondered what happened to Ms. Moore.

Juanita Moore and Susan Kohner left us something. Juanita Moore left my mother the gift of that film's primal energy, based on her fine acting—a classic interpretation of suffering. And wherever you are, Susan Kohner, thank you. Your portrayal of a character like me gave me the special gifts of finally being able to express an honest anger; to feed an insatiable hunger for self-expression; and to recognize that all of us have been working to make this world a better place.

Douglas Sirk's last Hollywood film, *Imitation of Life*, afforded him his greatest commercial success. But the experience of making this film cut even Douglas Sirk down to a Hollywood version of size. After *Imitation of Life*, he retired, moving to Switzerland. And there he initiated his fourth incarnation, returning to Detlef Sierck, his second name, the one he had given himself in his youth. In his old age, he continued fitful efforts to jump-start his career. He died in 1988. Douglas Sirk left us the gift of a disturbing story that pried open a different kind of dialogue between my mother and me. Sirk's ability to skillfully layer contradictions in his films provided, at the end of the day, a double-edged sword. He cut both ways. Our viewing of his movie forced me and my mother into much unnecessary melodrama. Both of us were justified in our oppositional readings of the film. What did he care? His goal, I suppose, was to satisfy a wide spectrum of his audience. Because we were both right, we fought so fiercely for our separate victories. Yet,

A HARD LESSON FROM HOLLYWOOD'S PAST

After her Oscar nomination for 'Imitation of Life,'

Juanita Moore was never again to find work of equal

stature. At 77 and working again, she's no longer bitter.

By ERIC HARRISON

She speaks without a trace of bitterness, no apparent residue from her long years in Hollywood, toiling in a time and place where dark-skinned actors were lucky to get through a casting agent's door, much less land a non-demeaning part. She talks even of her finest hour, and its inevitable disappointing aftermath, with a wistfulness and calm that belie the emotions she must have felt at the time.

Who even remembers her name today? Juanita Moore. What movies was she in again?

Oh, but there was a time. . . . "I was in New York," she says, her moon-pie face erupting in a smile. "The Apollo Theater marquee had on it: ' "Imitation of Life" starring Juanita Moore.' I thought Lana would have a fit if she saw that."

That would be Lana Turner, the titular star of the film that was one of the biggest moneymakers of 1959 and a postwar masterpiece of subversive, socially conscious cinema. The film is an extravagant Technicolor melodrama, but through its overwrought visual style and structure, director Douglas Sirk managed to comment on both the oft-derided "women's picture" genre and on Hollywood itself. At the same time, the movie dealt movingly with issues of race, class and female independence.

Turner was the star, but the picture belonged to Moore. When Sirk hired Moore ("He said he liked my face"), he told her that the movie, an expensive prestige picture for its time, rested on her shoulders.

" 'If you're not good, the picture is not going to be any good, " she remembers him telling her.

"That was a heck of a weight to place on me."

Up until then, Moore had played mostly small roles, usually servants who provided little more than background for the white stars. In "Imitation of Life," she once again played a maid, but this time the maid was the story's emotional center. As the industrious Annie Johnson, Moore was the pillar of strength and decency for two woman-led families. Amid Turner's glamour and the lavish visuals and show-business glitter that dominate the movie, her steady, dignified presence provided an anchor.

In a later time, "Imitation of

Please see Moore, Page 80

After the Oscar nomination, "I had hopes, but not high hopes," Moore says of acting.

JUANITO HOLANDEZ / For The Times

Life" might've made her a star. She was nominated for a supporting actress Oscar, as was Susan Kohner as her daughter, a light-skinned black girl who brings misery down upon her mother by renouncing her and passing for white.

"My agent told me, 'Juanita, I'm sure you're going to be nominated, but don't have any high hopes.' He told me that right away," Moore recalls.

The advice made sense. "I knew what had happened to Hattie McDaniel," she says. "She won it [for playing a mammy in 'Gone With the Wind'] and what happened? Nothing. Absolutely nothing. Her career went nowhere."

Moore also had been longtime friends with Dorothy Dandridge, the stunning beauty of the '40s and '50s who flirted with stardom but was unable to crack the color barrier. Moore and Dandridge met years earlier at the Cotton Club in New York, when Moore was a chorus girl and Dandridge, no more than 13 or 14 years old then, was a singer. They remained friends until Dandridge died, broke and dejected, in 1965.

Dandridge received a best actress Oscar nomination in 1954 for "Carmen Jones," and she was a top-lining nightclub singer. Still, she could hardly find work, and the fancy hotels at which she sang sometimes wouldn't allow her to stay there.

"I had hopes," Moore allows, "but not high hopes."

She was bitter during those years. "But now I'm not," she says. The bitterness faded with age. According to reference works, Moore is 77, although she won't confirm that and suggests that she is older. Whatever her years, she is of an age when most of her friends from her acting days are dead, an age when most actresses have long since retired. But Moore, after taking a break from acting, in part to nurse her sick husband, is back working before the cameras.

It came about by accident. Her career was never what you would call hot. What black actress in the '50s and '60s, when Moore was in her prime, carried box-office clout? You could count them on one hand and still have digits left over. She continued to work in Hollywood, taking small parts in films, but after "Two-Moon Junction," in 1988, she dropped from sight.

"I just quit for a while," she says. "The kind of movies they were making about 20 years ago. . . ." She shakes her head dismissively, not bothering to fin-

ish her sentence. "And they're right back at it again, making those awful movies." The profanity, the sex and the violence disturb her.

"Maybe I'm old and don't understand, but I can't be a part of that. I don't care to be part of it."

But last year she was lured back into the business, at least tentatively, by an agent who didn't know she'd ever acted but who knew the camera would love her. Sid Levin said they met when one of his clients asked that he consider representing a young aspiring actor.

"The kid came in with his grandmother, and the grandmother was Juanita Moore," recalls Levin, who has an independent agency in Beverly Hills.

"She was in the waiting room, and when I invited her grandson into my office, I asked if she wanted to come in also. . . . Then I looked at her and said, 'You could do great in this business.'

"It was her demeanor, her face, the way she came across, her spirit," he continued. "It was just something about her." Only later did he learn who she was.

Fairly quickly, he got her a small role in the just-released "Disney's The Kid" (she plays a grandmother at a wedding) and a job in a Hallmark commercial. Casting agents, who remember Moore from "Imitation of Life," are always surprised to hear that she is acting, he says, and are eager to see her. She chooses not to go out for many roles, though, preferring to stay home at her Inglewood condo to look after her husband, a retired bus driver whom she married 45 years ago after she stepped in front of his bus and almost got hit.

"You got to be careful, lady," he shouted at the struggling actress. Two weeks later, they met again by accident and started dating.

Growing up in South Los Angeles, Moore was urged to consider an acting career by a teacher at Jefferson High School, "Miss Templeton."

"During that time we didn't have too many choices," Moore says. But Miss Templeton told Moore that she could be whatever she wanted to be. When the Lafayette Players, a black theater company from New York, came to Los Angeles for an extended stay, "I scrambled up enough money to go and see it. It was maybe 50 or 75 cents or something like that. I was enthralled. I had never seen live black actors before. They were here two or three months. They changed productions every two weeks. That was one of my inspirations that told me I

wanted to be an actress."

An actor friend, Joel Fluellen (who later would play Moore's minister in "Imitation of Life") told Moore that she needed to study if she wanted to act. He took her to the Actors' Lab, a group that staged plays in Hollywood.

She found work as an extra in the movies, making $10 or $12 a day. "That's how I met Marlon Brando," she says. "He was doing the movie 'Streetcar Named Desire' [1951] at Warners Bros." They became friends. "A couple times he came out to the chicken shack where I was working and he had chicken. He loved that chicken, yes he did."

Moore started acting in black theaters such as the Ebony Showcase Theater, a South Los Angeles theater founded by Nick Stewart, an actor who appeared on the old "Amos 'n' Andy" television show. Like other African American actors who played stereotypical characters on TV and in the movies, Stewart was a serious actor who cared about his craft.

The Showcase Theater provided black actors a chance to hone their talent and do challenging work. Among other Showcase alumni are Beah Richards, Isabel Sanford and James Edwards, a nearly forgotten actor who busted the Stepin Fetchit stereotype in dignified roles and who is best remembered for his lead role in "Home of the Brave" in 1949.

Among the plays Moore appeared in were James Baldwin's "Amen Corner," which went to Broadway, and Jean-Paul Sartre's "No Exit." The audiences were more white than black, she says, and the plays were chosen without regard to race. "[Stewart] would do what he thought would be entertaining."

On screen, though, the roles generally were neither challenging nor large. And then came "Imitation of Life."

She almost didn't get the part. Only Sirk wanted her. Others associated with the production wanted to hire Pearl Bailey or gospel singer Mahalia Jackson (who stirringly sings "Trouble of the World" in a funeral scene in the movie). "Mahalia said, when I met her, 'Child, I told them I'm no actress. I'm a singer.'"

After landing the part, Moore spent every weekend studying her lines. Sometimes she'd lose weight because of the stress and come to the set Monday noticeably thinner. "When the director would see me he'd say, 'Give her some malted milks, give her something, she's lost weight again.'"

"One day I did 28 takes" of a scene involving her character and Turner's character, she recalls. "Each time it was getting worse. Lana stayed right by me. She was so wonderful. I never did get it. . . . The responsibility was just so much. The next morning when I came back, I was up to it. I said, thank God."

Sirk, she says, "was an angel. He was so helpful. When I came in in the morning, he would sit me down and talk to me."

For many viewers, the radicalism of "Imitation of Life" is obscured by its lush stylization and its blunt use of dated tear-jerker conventions. But Sirk, who directed Bertolt Brecht on stage in Europe, deliberately used the artificiality to keep audiences at an ironic distance. At the same time, though, the warring emotionalism of the material manages to provoke tears.

Not until the '70s did the melodramas of the '40s and '50s and filmmakers such as Sirk begin to earn respect from academicians, especially social theoreticians of a Marxist or feminist bent. The late German filmmaker Rainer Werner Fassbinder, who adored Sirk, loved that nothing in this, his last film, appears natural—"not in the whole movie," he once said. Allison Anders, the independent feminist filmmaker who has excoriated Hollywood for its treatment of women and for ignoring class issues, praises Sirk's movies as "some of the greatest woman-centered stories" ever.

Turner's role in "Imitation of Life," in many ways, seemed pulled from her biography. She brought so many associations to the part of Lora Meredith that Turner was called upon to play herself, as she was popularly perceived to be. Just as Lora's teen daughter gets involved in emotional complications with her mother's boyfriend, Turner's 14-year-old daughter had, only months before filming, fatally stabbed Turner's boyfriend, Johnny Stompanato. Moore recalls that because the controversy made the stu-

dio leery of hiring her, Turner took a percentage of the profits in lieu of salary. "She was very clever," Moore says. Turner briefly had had trouble finding work, but the movie—despite stinging reviews—was so successful it "made her rich again."

Moore did not have the option of receiving a percentage. But Annie was the character the audience came to know and care about. The tears the movie elicits with every viewing are all for Annie. (The best supporting actress award went to Shelley Winters for a role in "The Diary of Anne Frank" that Moore maintains should've been considered the leading role.) She continued acting. But never again did she get a role approaching the size or significance of Annie Johnson.

"I didn't work for a whole year," she says. Part of the problem was that after winning an Oscar nomination, an actor's asking price goes up. Sometimes actors find that no one is willing to pay it. Moore says she met Louise Fletcher, who won an Academy Award for playing Nurse Ratched in "One Flew Over the Cuckoo's Nest" (1975), and Fletcher told her the same thing had happened to her. She went two years without working. "And she *won* the Oscar," Moore says.

The situation for Moore was worse because of the limited number of roles for which black actresses were considered.

"What can you do?" she says. "They're not going to pay me a lot of money for carrying a tray. That's all we did at the time in movies."

Ross Hunter, producer of "Imitation of Life," hired her for her next movie, "Tammy Tell Me True," starring Sandra Dee, who played Turner's daughter in "Imitation of Life."

Moore's role in "The Singing Nun" (1965), starring Debbie Reynolds, was sizable, "but nothing compared to 'Imitation of Life,'" she says. "I never again had a role that big." □

Eric Harrison is a former Times staff writer.

Growing up Weitz

John Weitz, fashion's most elegant designer, raised Hollywood's raunchy new brother act, Chris and Paul, the makers of 'American Pie.' CATHY HORYN ponders the paradox.

Clockwise, from top left: Paul and Chris Weitz in Palm Beach, Fla., ages 10 and 6; Chris and Paul, 1999; John and Susan, New York newlyweds in 1964.

'It was the middle 60's, and I was going back and forth on the train to Richmond, where I am from," says the author Tom Wolfe, recalling the moment he first met John Weitz. "It was a crowded train, and people were walking past. I noticed out of my peripheral vision that this man had stopped in front of me. He looked down and, in this British voice, said, 'Awfully good-looking socks you're wearing.' I thought this was rather cheeky. Then I saw his face and realized it was John Weitz." It turned out that Weitz had designed the socks. "I remember them very well," Wolfe says. "They were a checkerboard design in aubergine and pumpkin."

If John Weitz wasn't the first American designer to make a big name for himself, he was certainly the most dashing — with his aristocratic good looks, impeccable manners and a voice that could lift the ladies of the fashion press right out of their sling-backs. "I'm the modern man's designer," he declared in 1966, and, in a way, he was. He raced cars. He wrote novels and, later, serious studies of Nazism and the evil that had driven his family out of Germany in 1937 and made them refugees.

In other words, Weitz had life beyond fashion. He wasn't at all modest about it, either. His friend James Brady once said that if Weitz "weren't such a damned blowhard, I would be even fonder of him than I am."

But all right. Weitz wasn't one to hide his light under a bushel. In the 60's, he and his glamorous wife, Susan, a former actress who starred with

Cathy Horyn is the fashion critic for The New York Times.

Lana Turner in the 1959 version of "Imitation of Life," were part of the Beautiful People. She's a story in herself. The daughter of the Mexican screen legend Lupita Tovar and the late producer and agent Paul Kohner, Susan and her brother, Pancho, grew up in Bel Air, Calif. Dolores Del Rio was her godmother, and when Susan and her brother were kids, Diego Rivera painted a portrait of them in native Mexican dress.

Wolfe recalls the pleasures of going to the Weitzes' Park Avenue apartment. "It was a classic," he says, "and they had a Chinese chef. I used to sit by the mailbox, waiting for an invitation from the Weitzes. To have another meal from that chef of theirs ... I remember wonderful evenings with Alan Pakula and his wife, Hannah. Yul Brynner was a regular. It was a New York life as a Virginia boy had always dreamed of it."

How then, one may ask, did the fruit of all this excellence and good breeding — Paul Weitz, 34, and his brother, Chris, 30, the co-directors and producers of "American Pie" — grow up to

make a hit movie whose central joke is ... masturbation?

"It is curious," Chris says with a smile. The brothers live in Los Angeles, but were back East just before Christmas to see their parents, who now spend most of their time in a big, comfortable house set down in the middle of a potato field near Bridgehampton, N.Y. Chris is reflective, with a dry sense of humor, while Paul is more extroverted and can size up the idiocy in a situation pretty quickly. Both have their parents' good looks and manners. "Our dad never wanted to be seen as a bourgeois parent, urging his children to pursue careers," Chris continues. "He and my mother were great in that sense. They held a creative life to be a cut above the rest."

"Of course," says Paul, "in the beginning, our dad had a slightly different idea about how our careers should proceed. He kept saying, 'Don't Merchant and Ivory need someone to write their screenplays?'"

Chris nods. "He kept saying, 'Write a letter to Merchant and Ivory ...'"

THE THING TO UNDERSTAND ABOUT THE Weitz brothers is that they — and, by extension, their movies (they wrote "Antz" and are currently directing a remake of "Heaven Can Wait," starring Chris Rock) — are really the product of two remarkable European families, the Weitzes and the Kohners. Robert Salomon Weitz, their paternal grandfather, was a successful German Jewish businessman who was part of the social set in Berlin described by Christopher Isherwood. He was an infantry hero in the First World War and was awarded the Iron Cross. "Which in Germany after the war," says Wolfe, who wrote the forward to Weitz's 1992 biography of Hitler's Foreign Minister, Joachim von Ribbentrop, "was like being a Confederate hero of the Civil War. It's hard for anyone to understand just how glamorous that sort of background was."

Bobby Weitz, as he was called, after the fashion for English nicknames, also had a fondness for bathroom humor. "Both my father and Susan's father were raucous men," says John, sounding pleased, when I see him and Susan a few days later. "That I can vouch for," Susan says placidly, as she sits curled up on the couch in their apartment.

Clockwise, from above: Paul and Chris, ages 8 and 4, sharing a bond that would lead to writing collaborations like "Antz"; John and Susan on their boat, in the 70's.

Lawrence Pressman, an actor who has known the Weitzes for years and who had a small role as a lacrosse coach in "American Pie," says, "Whatever fierceness that John had as a father was highly ameliorated by the fact that both boys knew he could descend to that level." He adds: "There's something reminiscent of the Old Country in John. I would go even further — the Old Testament. He's biblical. With John, there is right, and there is wrong, and no shilly-shallying between."

Susan's father came over from what is now the Czech Republic with William Wyler and went to work at Universal Studios, producing pictures. Paul Kohner later became a big agent, representing John Huston, among others, and a lot of Europeans, like Ingmar Bergman and Max von Sydow. Almost all of them passed through the Weitzes' living room when the boys were young. Bergman even took them to the circus.

That must have been interesting, I say.

"Well," replies Chris, "Ingmar Bergman at the circus to begin with ——"

"Is quite a concept," Paul says.

The brothers have a tendency to complete each other's sentences, as well as to yell "Cut!" at the same time. Which probably isn't surprising, given that, as children, they were often dressed identically in Lacoste shirts and blue blazers. That was done mainly to help Susan keep track of them in the park, but also, one suspects, to conform to their father's aesthetic ideal — what he called "the Anglophilism of an English upbringing, little boys in camel's hair coats and so on." It was all wrapped up in his own experience before the Second World War as a student at St. Paul's, the English boarding school, and, ultimately, in his tremendous success as a designer.

Wolfe says: "Only I, probably, only I would

'I remember Dad telling me that Fred Astaire wore a tie as a belt,' says Paul.

have noticed that when the Duke of Windsor's estate went to auction, there were about a half-dozen pairs of John Weitz socks from the 60's."

The brothers have a marvelously complicitous way of describing all this. It's almost as if they are looking at these two exquisite creatures … their parents. Pressman says that when they were kids, they even had a kind of private language. Anyway, you can see why they became writers and directors. Growing up Weitz gave them plenty of material.

"The thing that I think about," says Paul, "is the double standard that existed for the great figures in fashion history, and then us. I remember Dad telling me at one point that Fred Astaire wore a tie as a belt, that this was really

chic. But one night, when I was trying to sneak out to a disco and I was wearing a tie as a belt, my dad stopped me and would not let me leave."

Chris laughs and says: "Our dad thought he was protecting us from gross blunders. He used to talk about the image that people project and how it's relevant to how they're perceived. So when we were leaving the house looking to him like transients, as he often pointed out, he expected that we would be treated accordingly."

Paul, who for a while took to wearing a buzz cut with a single lock of hair down the middle of his face, observes of life Chez Weitz: "Everything was just so. I remember we had a cook for a lot of our childhood. We weren't the kind of kids to take that for granted. We always thought it was a bit of a freak show to have a cook living in the back of the house ——"

"And dressed," says Chris, "in a white jacket with a black bow tie."

They don't seem to have been much affected by the stream of film people, either. That was largely because of Susan, who, despite a couple of Golden Globes and an Academy Award nomination for her role in "Imitation of Life," gave up acting when she married John. Also, as Pressman points out, she herself grew up in a pretty glamorous atmosphere. Her pals were the children of people like Loretta Young and Ernst Lubitsch, who directed "Ninotchka." So fame wasn't a big deal to her. "She's an extremely modest person," Chris says. "She wore all that stuff very lightly."

Naturally, their father is proud of the fact that Paul and Chris finally got things together, after doing a little of this and that and living, for what he feared might be forever, on the parental dole. But Weitz, who also has a son, Robert, 47, and a daughter, Karen, 49, from a previous marriage, prefers to explain the boys' success by emphasizing the ordinary. "I know only one thing," he says, "and that is they got hugged and they got kissed and they got hugged. People say, 'Oh, you shouldn't do that.' Yes, you can. As long as they know you love them and that you trust them — well, that's it."

Touching, but not ultimately satisfying, from a man who has always stood his ground like a sequoia, who never shied away from a fight or an opinion and whose humor flowed straight back to sexy old Berlin. Chris and Paul tell the story of their 76-year-old father going to see "American Pie" at a theater in East Hampton. He loved it, of course. Roared his head off.

Now Paul says: "The next day he was at a dinner, and there was another old gentleman, who said to him, 'Well, I guess you're pretty proud of your sons for that movie.' My dad said he was, and the other guy said, 'Well, I thought it was pretty vulgar.' I'm sure my dad raised his voice, because he's really confrontational. He said, 'I'll tell you what I think is vulgar is people doing drugs and shooting each other.' Then he said to the fellow, 'Haven't you ever masturbated in your life?'"

Paul smiles. "So he defended ——"

"Our honor," says Chris. ∎

my experience of his film also freed me to fight for my own independence, not only from my mother but also from my society. In the end, I too became a filmmaker.

> …Hollywood…made questionable use of such fabulous talents as Lena Horne and Rex Ingram and Ethel Waters—talents that were never given the respect of a truly objective evaluation. Louise Beavers…Mantan Moreland…Juanita Moore…I had met them and found them three-dimensional human beings…They all were reduced by the requirements of a racist society and an industry that knew how to reflect the society racially in only that one way.
> —Sidney Poitier, *The Measure of a Man: A Spiritual Autobiography*

Sunday morning, February 20, 2000. Lazily, I was browsing through the decidedly whimsical "Fashions of the Times," a Sunday *New York Times* supplement. Susan Kohner's name catches my eye. Her name is in an article that promises to answer what is inherent in the paradox of "Growing Up Weitz." This article highlights Paul and Chris Weitz, Hollywood's hottest new filmmakers. Their credits include *Antz, American Pie*, and an upcoming remake of *Heaven Can Wait*, retitled *Down to Earth*, starring the "now" comic, Chris Rock. The author, Cathy Horyn, a *New York Times* fashion critic, states that "the thing to understand about the Weitz brothers is that they…are really the product of two remarkable European families."

Proudly, I immediately lay this nugget of information at the feet of my long-dead mother. "See," I silently yell out, "I told you so! Class, sex, and race are trump cards. Where is that brilliant actress Juanita Moore now in relation to Susan Kohner Weitz's sons?"

Paul and Chris Weitz: In addition to being white, male, rich, and loved, they are heirs to two dynasties—those of fashion and film. Then there's Chris Rock: high school dropout; hails from a middle-class Black family; genius and heir apparent to Richard Pryor; potential commercial success as a star in a time-proven vehicle, *Down to Earth*, a.k.a. *Heaven Can Wait*. As one of the film's producers, he hires the Weitz brothers to write and direct his star vehicle.

Mouthing "So what?" my mother shrugs her shoulders and turns her back on me, bored. I also retreat from our ongoing, now silent argument. But it's only because I do believe that today Chris Rock has more opportunities than Juanita Moore did. Or does he? Later that year, Juanita Moore suddenly reappears.

On Sunday, July 9, 2000, I opened the Calendar Section of the *Los Angeles Times*. The lead story, "A Hard Lesson from Hollywood's Past" by Eric Harrison, was an update on actress Juanita Moore. "After her Oscar nomination for *Imitation of Life*," the article states, "Juanita Moore was never again to find work of equal stature. At 77 and working again, she's no longer bitter." It seems that Ms. Moore had accompanied her grandson, a young aspiring actor, into an agent's office. He took one look at her and immediately hired her for a new Bruce Willis vehicle, Disney's *The Kid.* In this film, she is no longer a maid, she is now a grandmother. In the article, Ms. Moore goes on to praise Nick Stewart, a serious Black actor who cared about training other Black actors in the craft. Her mentor, Stewart gained fame acting on *Amos 'n' Andy,* the 1950s television program. He trained Juanita Moore in his Ebony Showcase Theater, along with other well-known actors such as Beah Richards, Isabel Sanford, and James Edwards. In Stewart's relatively unknown Los Angeles playhouse, these actors played serious roles in works such as James Baldwin's *Amen Corner* and Jean-Paul Sartre's *No Exit.* Ms. Moore, despite the fact that in July 2000 she is still unable to play a role that challenges her as a talented actress, is still working.

Susan Kohner Weitz reads my chapter for this book and also weighs in: "My sons have pretty much made their names for themselves on their own," she proudly reports, "and Chris Rock hired them, not the other way around." There is a pause in our conversation. "Is race the only factor for success these days?" she tentatively asks me, and I do wonder. Permanent wealth, access, and longevity are plums granted to Hollywood's family dynasties like the Weitzes, the Mankiewiczes, the Kohners, the Spielbergs, and the Lucases. Therefore, I'm skeptical, for this permanent quality of success somehow eludes most of this industry's successful influential Blacks, such as the Bill Cosbys, the Gordon Parks, the Alex Haleys, and the Spike Lees. Untimely deaths, financial losses, or controls to access somehow seem to "keep us in our place."

So, yes, I am curious as to the final outcome. And so I holler these questions at my mother's slowly retreating back: Where will Paul and Chris Weitz's children be then? And where will Chris Rock's children be in relation to the Weitz brothers' prodigies? And where will Juanita Moore's great-grandchildren be in relation to the great-grandchildren of her colleague Susan Kohner Weitz?

I wait for the rest of time's answer.

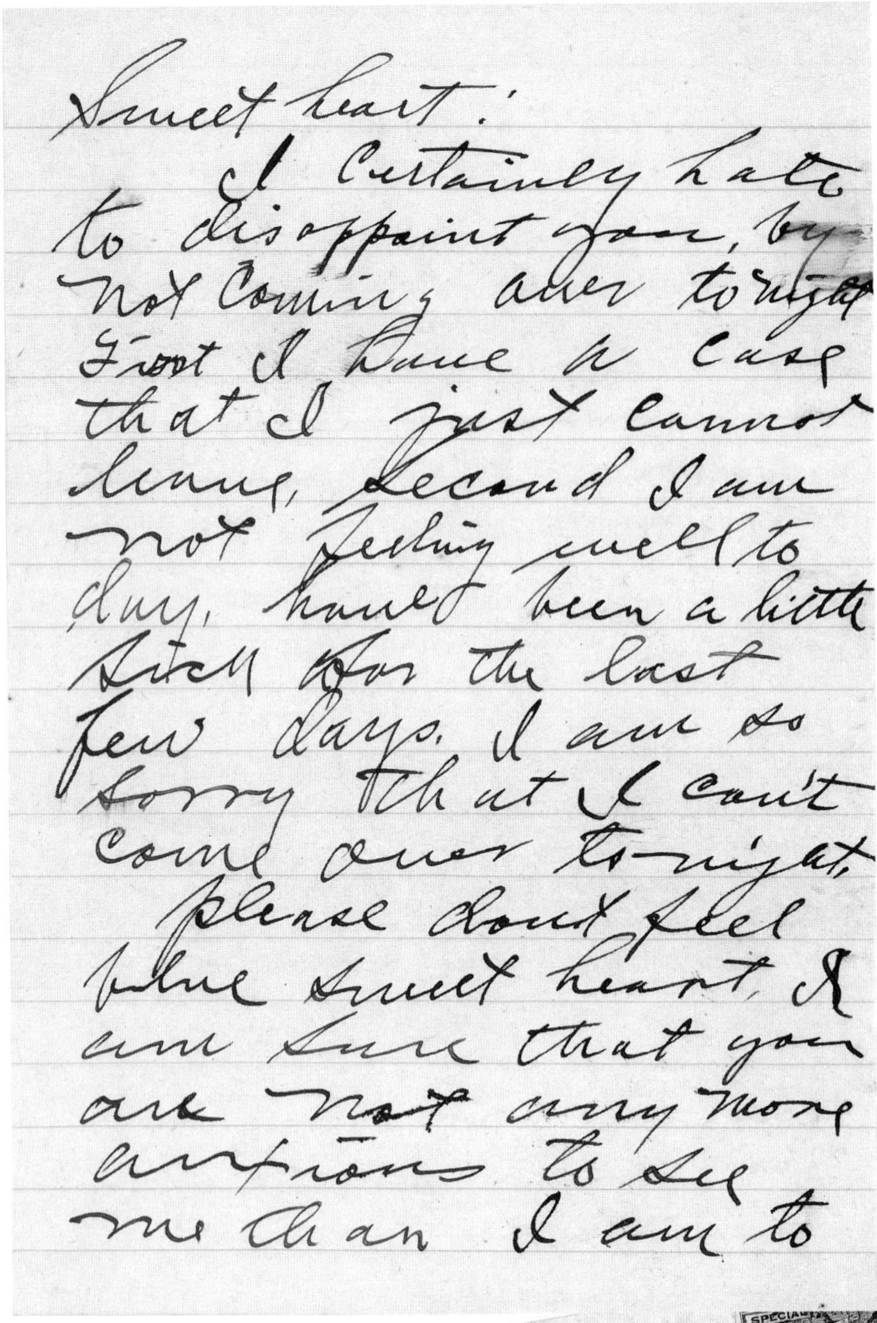

Sweet heart:

I certainly hate
to disappoint you, by
not coming over to night
First I have a case
that I just cannot
leave, Second I am
not feeling well to
day, have been a little
sick for the last
few days. I am so
sorry that I cant
come over to night.
Please dont feel
blue sweet heart, I
am sure that you
are not any more
anxious to see
me than I am to

September 23, 1933

Sweet heart:

I certainly hate to disappoint you, by not coming over tonight. First I have a case that I just cannot leave, second I am not feeling well to day, have been a little sick for the last few days. I am so sorry that I can't come over tonight.

Please don't feel blue sweet heart. I am sure that you are not any more anxious to see me than I am to see you.

Celeste darling you certainly can write some sweet letters. Oh! I just enjoy them so very much. I love them. I even look for them when they are not due— Sweet heart you can write such encouraging letter I feel so much better after I read your sweet and uplifting letters.

Honey I hope that it wasn't to late to pay the note. Sorry that I was a little late. Sweet heart I am sending you some thing to live on.

Things are getting better.

Celeste darling just as soon as I get better and this case is alright I am coming over. Celeste sweet heart I love you, and shall always love you—you are such a darling little "girl."

Trust that you are feeling well and getting along nicely.

Honey I am so anxious to get our little home fix up so that you can move in it. I know that you are not so happy there. You know Celeste that I know you. I dont want to be away just now because I may miss some that will be of some help to us, and too I just don't feel well enough to make the trip, and also have a case that I just can't leave.

How is our little son?

Tell him that Dad certainly want to see him.

Well Sweet heart be sweet until I can see you all

Much love to you all Celeste

From

Dad

He love you Celeste

161

ANNUAL REPORT
1968

SOUTH CENTRAL BRANCH

YOUNG MEN'S CHRISTIAN ASSOCIATION
OF THE GREATER HOUSTON AREA

"Developing Human Resources
for a Changing Society"

YMCA SERVICE AWARD

DR. FRED D. PARROTT

A long-time Y layman and campaigner, general chairman of the 1958 membership campaign; member of the Board of Managers since 1956; member, Health and Physical Education, World Service, and Christian Emphasis committees; and former chairman, adult program committee.

A distinguished member of the dental profession, Dr. Parrott's numerous affiliations and services include: Deacon, St. John's Baptist Church on Dowling; Chaplain, Business and Professional Men's Club; Treasurer, Charles A. George Dental Society; Gulf State Dental Association; Harris County Dental Association; Area Democratic Chairman.

The most admirable thing about the fantastic is
that the fantastic does not exist; everything is real.
—André Breton

Chapter VIII **When Louisiana Married Texas**

I am a workaholic. At the very least, I do work very hard to follow the rules, the social mores, and the work ethic of any group in which I find myself. It's automatic. I do it to fit in. Yet, I know I will never belong. Because there is that exception. Whenever I believe I am unjustly treated by anyone, I dig in my heels. Deep. They travel into a refusal buried inside the depths of my being. Once my bottom line is outwardly reached, my inner refusal to comply becomes unshakable.

My steeled resolve seems to have developed through my continuing relationship with my mother. I suspect my unwavering focus grew out of my desperate needs. The loss of my mother's love in my life left me empty, yet with a spirit full of a chronic, emotional pain. I don't remember my exact age, but I do remember I was in elementary school when I became aware that my mother didn't love me.

On this particular day, my mother and I were going to one of her meetings. She was always going to meetings. I wanted to wear one dress; she wanted me to wear another. I resisted. She won. I saw red.

As she drove us away from the house, I pouted. Simultaneously, I held my anger in check. Silently, I obeyed her every command, to the letter. Because she could not catch me in any specific technicalities of the kind that would allow her to just reach over and smack me hard, her frustration welled up and bubbled over. I was quiet, polite, measured. And sullen. She simply couldn't find a way to justify punishing me for being sullen.

What was also galling to her was that she had both won and lost at the same time. And we both knew that. The winning was obvious. I was wearing the dress. She lost because she would suffer a severe loss of face if she used physical blows to stem my heavy silence. So she decided to fight me back by attacking the invisible inside my heart.

By then, we had reached the meeting site. Resolved, she turned off the car's motor. I could hear the crickets start to signal the end of the day. Turning to face me, she looked directly into my eyes with a shameless and open disgust.

Up to that point, the day had been uneventful. But when I looked into the raw anger in my mother's eyes, I felt something odd. I felt my mother's anger at me in its most naked, primal force. From that moment on, the day took on unforgettable proportions.

Her words were precise, her tone was civilized, and her voice's tenor was remarkably well measured:

"You are absolutely despicable," she coolly observed, looking at me with an unwavering detachment. "If my blood did not run through your veins, I would not have anything else ever to do with you."

She was always good at delivering deliberately long and pregnant silences after dropping verbal bombshells. But on this day, in that silence, I watched the life in her eyes turn from anger to disgust to hatred. The shifts were slow and almost invisible, like the subtle change of color in the sky during a spectacular sunset.

Even worse, the hatred toward me in her eyes continued to evolve, finally turning into a cool detachment. It was as though I ceased to exist for her. I believe that it was around that time that she officially lost even her casual interest in me. But now and again, I sometimes wonder if she ever learned to care for what was human inside of me at all.

From what I've heard from her sisters and my cousins, I don't believe she ever bonded with me as an infant on any emotional level. Some have said that after my birth my father watched how my mother treated me as her baby. At that time, she was drowning in postpartum depression. Her distress seemed to him to interfere with her ability to mother me. Based on what he saw, he intervened, sending my mother away for several months. Her older sister, Alberta, or Birdie, as she was called, was paid to care for me while my mother was gone. Later, I heard these casual family jokes about how, upon her return, I failed to recognize her as my mother.

But there was yet another wrinkle. This temporary hiring of my aunt eventually led to my aunt becoming our maid for ten years. My aunt's new job as her sister's maid essentially relieved my mother of the role of parenting me. That is, until I began my final years of elementary school. Around that time, my aunt and my mother had this huge fight that no one ever dared to talk about.

My aunt always resented being her baby sister's maid. This meant my aunt also resented me. My mother was the only family member out of sixteen brothers and sisters with a college degree. Aunt Birdie had always been a maid; she was too poor and untrained to work as anything other than a maid. As a young adult, I read a Richard Wright story about another Black woman who was a maid in a white home. So I would imagine that my aunt would prefer to work for her sister rather than be exposed to the cruelty of working as what would be a slave for a white. Yet even that sense of freedom began to wear. I slightly remember my mother—while playing at the role of the lady of the manor—discussing with my father the pros and the cons of giving my aunt a raise. Things began to wear and fray between them. Essentially, my aunt's role as the family maid—caring for me as an child, being my surrogate mother, cleaning the dirt in every part of my mother's house, washing and ironing our clothes, shopping for and then cooking our meals, serving as my mother's confidante mostly about my father's chasing other women—exacerbated these class divisions between my mother and her sister. For years after their argument, they barely spoke to one another. That argument and the subsequent deep-seated tensions in their relationship were my first introduction to class as power in America.

As I write this, I realize that my mother probably left me alone too soon after my birth. Our lack of physical contact in my earliest months of life may have stunted any possibility for an emotional bond to exist between us. Over the years, my perceptions of her actions toward me led me to believe that my mother never loved me. She didn't appear to comprehend that the absence of her acceptance of me in my life hurt me badly. Her emotional withdrawal devastated me.

But on that day, I didn't quite grasp the effect of our silent confrontation as we sat in her car, staring back at each other. It really was quite a long silence that followed her horrific statement to me. I did not flinch. I managed to hold her stare by remaining poker-faced. I concentrated on forcing myself to dull my eyes to register no reaction.

I was able to do this by keeping my eyes facing outward while I was turning my feelings inward. I tamped my emotions down, stemming my impulse to flush my sorrow out as tears. On the way down inside, I also grabbed my crushed heart. Behind my eyes, and deep inside my darkness, I drove all that was left of myself into that river of resolve flowing at the bottom of my soul.

Pushing. Swallowing. Staring. That effort helped to hold my tears back. I concentrated by reading the subtle, shifting degrees of my mother's spite. That and my invisible hands gently holding my heart inside to heal its pulsing screams in the warmth of my own liquid currents of resistance kept me occupied.

I did, however, realize that something was very wrong. My mother's anger at me had flared into hatred because I didn't want to wear a dress that she liked more than I did. I didn't quite know why it was wrong. But it was then that I decided to focus my spirit solely on survival. To forget forever about love. I knew then that I had to hold on to my life long enough to be able to walk, physically whole and mentally intact, out of my parent's house. So I focused on that decision and on keeping alive my hidden dream that somewhere, somehow, out there, there had to be enough love left in the world that could find me. And hold me. And nurture me back to health.

Later, when I was an adult, I once asked my mother what she thought of me.

"About you?" she paused to think. "You." It finally hit her. "You always had too much pride," she retorted. I suppose that behind this "pride" that she experienced of me was my dogged refusal to comply with unjust demands made by anyone.

In May 1999, Peter Dress, a former student of mine who had taken every class I had taught during his tenure in the department, thanked me for being his teacher. Peter made top honors in his class, graduating summa cum laude. He publicly honored my contribution to his education at the graduation ceremonies. He named me as the teacher who had influenced him the most during his college career. I was stunned.

For his graduation gift to me, Peter took me to see the movie *Eve's Bayou*. He wanted me to see a film made by a Black woman with a young Black girl in the starring role. He told me that he had learned to appreciate the beauty of the Black experience through my teaching. *Eve's Bayou* exemplified this dignity for him.

What he didn't know was that he took me to a film that showed me a faint reflection of my very own life. My soul's river in this film is a bayou—Eve's bayou. But rather than being a river full of rushing rapids, traveling to a vast ocean, it is an inlet. Stagnating. Standing still. Festering.

Set in Louisiana in the 1950s, *Eve's Bayou* tells the coming-of-age story of Eve, a young girl from a professional-class Black family. Her father is a doctor. My father was a dentist. Her mother is an elegant lady. So was my mother. Their family has secrets that everyone agrees to hide. So did mine. Eve fights back. So did I. Her philandering father's death occurs under the shadow of his possible incest attempt on her older sister. Eve, the girl, starts the film by saying that she had killed her father.

Kasi Lemmons, the film's writer-director, has created a film that dares to speak publicly about family secrets—those of womanizing, incest, and murder in a Black, middle-class, educated family. Many Black people I've spoken to about the film dismiss it. When I ask if it is because of the incest, they say it is because Eve seems to feel no remorse over the death of her father. They feel that at the center of this film's heart is a morally corrupt value.

Morally corrupt? How can that be? It is a film that circumscribes the essence of my life. My own father used to masturbate in front of me. I was about eight or nine years old when I finally got up enough courage to tell him to stop. No one else would. That experience of my defiance, coupled with watching my mother's eyes grow cold with hatred at the very sight of me around the same time, was more than enough to make me question, for the rest of my life, the notion of the sanctity of the family.

Was the director wrong to leave room for her audience to decide that the child has no remorse? Like Eve, I have guilt for leaving, for exposing my family as a fraud. But I have no remorse for saving what I could of my sanity so that I could live. For me there was no other way out. I had to stay with these parents of mine, crazy or not, until I was old enough to leave. Then I had to leave, and now, to write and therefore unmask the lie.

I was able to stay for as long as I did by turning the core of my soul into an underground river. This river's waters were made out of the unshed tears of my resistance. I lived only because I dared to drink from my fight to survive. There were no brothers or sisters or relations or friends or community members available to help me.

I fed myself from myself.

Like Eve, would I have killed one of my parents if I could have? I am still too socialized to even dare to think of murder as an appropriate answer. I do, however, thank *Eve's Bayou* for allowing me the luxury of having the permission to imagine this frightening question. I did kill the lie of my family's official, public pose that we functioned well as a family. I do know that both my parents and Eve's parents were encased in the terrible racial, financial, and sexual oppression of everyone who lives in this country. What the film shows me is that Eve's parents were so preoccupied with their personal agony that their children were always a second thought. And that their children—like me—were in the way.

169

"I want a Sunday kind of love . . . a love that lasts past Saturday night. . . ."

The film's music actively expresses this heart-breaking longing for wholeness that remains from the experience of being trapped in the cruelty of what it means to be Black in America. Etta James. Bobby "Blue" Bland. Little Junior Parker. Ray Charles. Eryka Badu. All southern Black music holds at the back of its structure the blues and the gospel. Devil and Angel. Happiness and Sadness. Love and Hate. That melancholy tension poised by great artists enhances this film's story line by drawing the audience into reflections of themselves, which is why television commercials using the same music are so effective. The music laid under the message entices the viewer to buy. However, *Eve's Bayou* uses the mu-

A New Song of the South

LOS ANGELES TIMES THURSDAY, NOVEMBER 6, 1997

Cult actor Kasi Lemmons turns to writing; the result is her dream-like 'Eve's Bayou.'

BY EMORY HOLMES II
SPECIAL TO THE TIMES

"It's not that I didn't have luck as an actor," says writer-director Kasi Lemmons—a supporting star in several cult classic films, including "Silence of the Lambs," "Fear of a Black Hat," "Vampire's Kiss" and "Candyman"—"but it wasn't taking me where I needed to go."

Her highly personal debut film, "Eve's Bayou," which opens Friday at selected theaters, has taken her to the front ranks of emerging American filmmakers. It received a rare standing ovation when it premiered at the Telluride Film Festival in late August and has already generated a significant critical buzz.

"We say we want something different from our cinema," Lemmons, 34, says between sips of iced tea at a West Hollywood restaurant. "I'm not saying that 'Eve's Bayou' is the answer, you know, because some people will like it and some people won't. But I think that this is one of the answers."

Lemmons says she was trying to create a new style of storytelling.

"I wasn't certain at first if it was going to come out as a movie or a book. I have been very influenced by magical realism and the great novelists Toni Morrison and Gabriel García Márquez," she says. "I wanted to create a piece that was visual and lyrical with characters speaking in the rhythms that I remember from my childhood [in the South]. Since it was personal, and I didn't plan on showing it to anybody, I could be totally free with the questions I was asking myself. As a matter of fact, the questions could be more important than the answers. Like: What is reality? What is the nature of memory?"

Her questions, as well as the elusive waves of truth and ambiguity that her film explores, have their metaphorical twin in the dreamy, looking-glass pools and mists of the Louisiana bayou of the film's title, with its stunning, enclosed gardens of personalities and flowers, its secrets, its wild things and peccadilloes, its extravagant, roiling passions and skies.

"I was trying to create something I hadn't seen before," says Lemmons, "an African American Southern Gothic. The story is told from a child's point of view, and there is definitely something happening on a couple of levels. This is the kind of movie that I would want to see, and I think that is the truest way to create: You make a movie that you would really want to see."

"Eve's Bayou," which stars Samuel L. Jackson (who also served as one of the film's producers) and Lynn Whitfield, is set in 1962 in a languid storybook marshland just outside New Orleans. The film's hero clan, the Batistes, are articulate, funky, powerful and gorgeous. The story deals with deeply personal, human dilemmas, rather than racial, sociological or political baggage.

"The Batistes are so isolated and in their own world," Lemmons says. "There is a lot that they don't have to deal with because they are the ruling family in a very small town. On the other hand, they have the wherewithal and the money to get their clothes from France."

"Eve's Bayou" not only depicts the mysteries of the real world through the eyes of a child, it probes the imaginative dream world of its two seers, Mozelle Delacroix (a radiant Debbi Morgan) and Elzora (Diahann Carroll).

Lemmons allows her camera to tell its stories slowly, lingering over the subtleties and beauties of the faces and of the unhurried, rustic pace of the bayou.

"I had to fight very hard to keep the pacing in the movie. You get these people who feel you should pace it up, but to me, it means something to have this little girl walk out of the graveyard and across the bridge, moving through space."

Lemmons, who was born in St. Louis, considers herself a student of the foibles, superstitions and rhythms of the South because "both my parents are deeply Southern, and I spent a lot of time in my grandmother's house in Tuskegee, Ala." Her film is not autobiographical, although it draws on her childhood memories, some from her own family.

Although she dabbled at writing as a child and as a young actor writing short scenes for friends in drama school, she never considered herself a writer. She attended NYU, and UCLA and finally the film school at New York's New School of Social Research. But her writing career started, in her words, "by accident."

"I had gone to film school to be a documentary filmmaker. When I got out of film school, I made this little film that I was very proud of and I got an [acting] audition for the 'Cosby Show.' So I showed my film to Mr. Cosby. He watched it, and I can't even remember if he had much to say about it. But what he said is, 'What I really need is a writer.' And I said, 'I'm a writer. Now, I really wasn't, but he said, 'Write me a scene.'"

Lemmons (with two writing partners) wrote her first script and received her first story credit on "The Cosby Show" on the strength of that scene. Meanwhile, her acting career picked up. She landed supporting roles in several films that have become cult classics, including "Vampire's Kiss," (1988) opposite Nicolas Cage, and Jonathan Demme's "Silence of the Lambs" (1991), in which she played Jody Foster's roommate, but her writing career had stopped cold. After "Silence of the Lambs," Lemmons moved to Los Angeles and made several attempts to script a feature film, with no success. She decided she was not a writer after all. It was then that she turned to the private musings that eventually became "Eve's Bayou."

Lemmons' husband, actor Vondie Curtis-Hall (a notable writer-director), first read the script that emerged from her assemblage of impressions, questions and personal vignettes.

"He was lying across the bed and I was sitting at my desk. I was very nervous. I kept asking him 'What page are you on?' and he would say, 'Go 'way.' Finally, I came back in and he was finishing it, and he looked up and he had these tears in his eyes and he said, 'This is beautiful, this is beautiful.' Vondie was the one who convinced me to show it to more people. He is so supportive and so proud of me and has been totally behind it the whole way."

Lemmons' next task was to secure an agent, who sent "Eve's Bayou" out as a writing sample. It arrived on the desk of Caldecot "Cotty" Chubb, who had produced a number of quirky films, including "To Sleep With Anger," "The Crow" and "Good Morning Babylon."

Chubb was looking for writers to adapt a novel that he was developing. But when he got "Eve's Bayou," Chubb recalls, "two pages into it, I felt that I was hearing a new voice. I thought it was extraordinary writing, simply and beautifully written."

He and Lemmons formed a handshake partnership and began considering who they'd like to direct. "Cotty was bringing up all these wonderful directors, people who I really admired," says Lemmons. But Chubb also asked her to consider some well-known actors, who had no directorial experience, in hopes their high name recognition would add some cachet to Lemmons' artful, offbeat little melodrama.

Recalls Lemmons, "I woke up on my birthday and I thought, well, they've never done it before, but I went to film school and I wrote the script. So I called up Cotty and my agent and said, I've had an epiphany and I'm going to give myself a birthday present; I want to direct 'Eve's Bayou.'"

Chubb agreed on the condition that Lemmons first script and direct a short film. Lemmons responded by writing "Dr. Hugo," a 20-minute short, starring Curtis-Hall (he also has a small role in "Eve's Bayou"), that captures some of the beauty, simplicity, wit and sensuality of "Eve's Bayou."

Lemmons credits her director of photography, Amy Vincent (a recent graduate of the American Film institute), with the sumptuous visual appeal of both "Dr. Hugo" and "Eve's Bayou."

Since she scripted "Eve's Bayou," Lemmons' writing career has taken off. Her original script "Privacy," exploring the world of tabloid journalism, was commissioned by Michelle Pfeiffer after Pfeiffer read an early draft of "Eve's Bayou."

"Privacy" is in development. Lemmons has also written a script for Whitney Houston, "Eight Pieces for Josette," which is also in development. Moreover, she has completed scripts for a horror film and a musical, both of which have generated some interest. But her dream right now is to complete a script with her husband.

"We are writing a movie right now," she says. "My dream is that I will either find material or create material that I feel as deeply about as I did 'Eve's Bayou.' I have a lot of stories to tell. It happened accidentally, but I am a writer now, you know?"

sic to seduce its audience into thinking: about right and wrong. Incest. Murder. Adultery. Judgment. Forgiveness. Love.

Love. My mother came from Texas, my father, from Louisiana.

It wasn't until the late Marlon Riggs hired me as a field producer for his last film, *Black Is . . . Black Ain't,* that I began to understand. For the first time, I went as an adult into my memory of Louisiana. My father grew up in Mansfield, an upstate Louisiana hamlet. When I visited as a child, the town setup was fairly uncomplicated. Mansfield consisted of a white-only general store across the street from the Negro-only general store. White men owned both of the stores. Along the side of the two stores was a railroad track. This was all there was of Mansfield the official town. Houses and run-down shacks with yellowed newspapers shellacked down as wallpaper dotted the farmland surrounding the meager village. Every abode had an outhouse. Small churches lay hidden within tree groves with whispers of graves next to them. Black people's lives sang with fear. The energy of it covered the sky, the air between, and the earth.

After the death of Alex Edward Parrott, my grandfather, in 1906, Henrietta Parrott, my father's illiterate, strong-willed, and incredibly soft-spoken mother, raised their children by herself, living off the farm land that my grandfather had actually legally owned. Although this fact is a source of great pride in my father's family, how this possession happened, or how my poverty-stricken grandmother managed to keep her dead husband's land, is a mystery to me. And this land is still owned by my family.

As a young adult, my father permanently injured his leg working in a sawmill. Crippled with a limp and a sixth-grade education, he migrated to Houston from Louisiana. There he successfully restarted his education, and finally graduated with a high school diploma. After his graduation, he found work as a chauffeur. He drove rich white people all over the United States and Canada. He, a former professional driver, later taught me how to drive. He then became a Pullman porter. From both jobs, he saved enough money to start dental school at Meharry Medical College in Nashville, Tennessee. He enrolled in the very last class of doctors, dentists, and pharmacists who only possessed a high school diploma. The very next year Meharry required college diplomas of its entering classes. His life was spent "slipping under the wire," leaving him never feeling "good enough."

In the mornings, he would whisper to himself while dressing, acting out all parts of any troubling situations that might happen during that day. He would play himself and then answer his comments with the words of his upcoming nemesis. Snatching his clothes over his head, buttoning his shirts, he would whisper back and forth, his voice rising and falling, with the powerful one overtaking him, the weak one.

Sometimes, in a surprisingly gentle tone, my mother would take it upon herself to analyze my father's ways.

171

"He's not like me, you know," she would inevitably begin. "Really." She spoke forcefully to convince both herself and me. "He has an entirely different set of values . . ."

She would then drift off into a deep yet confused thought. Overhearing his daily prework ritual in her bedroom, my mother would shake her head in silent disgust. She would fiercely suck the insides of her teeth and then talk to herself, admonishing him for being so spineless and unsure of himself.

"If he'd only make us some money . . ." Some days she would wonder aloud about my father's aimless ways, ". . . that's what it takes to be a real man."

I grew up listening to my parents' dual yet solitary conversations. Early in the mornings, while I dressed for school, the echoes of their whispers would float from one room to the other.

One day, in one of my mother's soliloquies, she surprised me when she volunteered that she never loved my father. She had married, she said dryly, out of desperation. "He was the last thing on my horizon," she sighed. "Every other man was gone."

Every other man? She was hinting to me that I best not wait too long. But what struck me was how, to her, men seemed to be things. Chess pieces that one could move around to suit the day, the time, the place.

172

My mother's relatives in Texas were different. Her father was an ex-slave and a landowner who could read. He used his reading skills to translate Bible readings and thus become a Baptist minister. Rather than a spiritual calling, his choice of profession was the economically expedient thing to do. My mother seemed to feel that her father's ministry was a career move up to the edge of the Negro middle class, or whatever there was of a Black middle class in Texas in the early 1900s. My mother's family moved to Houston sometime around 1908. They settled in and helped to build Independence Heights, the first Black chartered town in Texas. There my grandmother, Polly Carroll, and her oldest daughter, Lena Carroll, joined with three other women to cofound the Greater New Hope Baptist Church, a church that still stands.

My grandmother had Native American, African, and white blood in her veins. She appeared to be a full-blooded Native American in her photograph. She wore her long black hair in two braids on either side of her face. As a child, I kept looking in her photograph for a headband and a feather to cap her head.

Like my maternal grandmother, my mother had high cheekbones; thin lips; a narrow, sharp nose; and long, straight hair. My mother was proud that she was not all Negro. She was the baby and the darkest-skinned member of her family. She caught hell for her color; she spent her adult life making up for being nicknamed "Blackie." And my mother's family members were all of a lighter color than my father's. There was talk in the Carroll family of a white man, of German or Irish ethnicity, who had perhaps fathered my grandmother. My mother insisted, to all our disbelief, that as a young child her mother would take her to visit her white relatives in Halletsville, Texas.

Because she was the baby of the Carroll family, there was enough money from her older brother to help send her to Tuskegee Institute. Still, it took time. She was thirty-seven years old when she finally graduated, with highest honors, from the Houston College for Negroes. She was the only Carroll with a college degree. Later, her graduate degree provided her with an even greater sense of self-importance. Being the only family member with a postgraduate degree instilled in her a right to an unspoken privilege in her family that my father also seemed to achieve in his. But to my mother, he was not as high up in respectability as she. As a family leader herself, she always approved of any leadership role I took among my classmates and playmates.

"You are to lead, not follow," she would often admonish.

But my parents' lifestyles were opposites. In many ways, their marriage was a forty-eight-year power play, a constant fight for his rule over hers and her rule over his.

What I learned while making *Black Is . . . Black Ain't* is that the core of self-esteem one develops in one's upbringing sometimes establishes itself rock solid until death; that my mother was told in Texas that she could achieve, and my father was told in Louisiana that he could not; and that the particular corner of Louisiana where my father grew up was full of a fear that my mother managed to escape in her family environment in Halletsville and Houston, Texas. The difference in their cores so divided them that it seemed to me that rather than support each other they turned against each other and, in doing so, hurt each other. My parents died over twenty years ago, my father in 1974 and my mother in 1976. I remain eternally attached to both of them. No matter. My heart is still empty. I still desire their love. I still love them.

". . . Don't let the sun catch you crying, crying at my front door. . ."

This film's lush, full cinematography captures the light of the South, the insides of Black homes, the gleam on the wood polished by hands taking pride in ownership, the people at the parties wearing a sweat from dancing that turns into passion, the bits of green in the yard as a way to catch a beauty denied by segregated parks and beaches, a moss that sways in the wind, the bayou that is still.

Cinematographer Amy Vincent's camera does more than paint with light. Those shadows both hide and expose the invisible: the unspoken fears, the ghosts who live in spite of death. The camera in the hands of a skilled practitioner stalks at the atmosphere in order to capture a story's essence. In *Eve's Bayou*, Vincent's camera becomes one of the story's characters. Yet how it becomes center stage is the question.

> In the hands of a free spirit the cinema is a magnificent and dangerous weapon. A film is like an involuntary imitation of a dream. The cinema seems to have been invented to express the life of the subconscious, the roots of which penetrate poetry so deeply.
> —Luis Buñuel, "Poetry and Cinema"

Surrealism, magic realism, mysticism, the dream. The films of Luis Buñuel make him one of my heroes. He uses the surreal and the dream in his work to mock our lies. But what happens when surrealism and dreams are used in film to tell the story of being Black in the world? Amaki Cantong, my friend from Ghana, believes that "the West leaves those artists of Third World countries and those artists that are powerless with nothing more than the dream to fashion the truth." "And," she continues, "as long as our artists resort to surrealism and the dream in art, these artists will sublimate what it takes to feed the audiences' spirit to revolt."

But there is also the dream. It is said that Africa's Bambara people believe that as we dream in our sleep, our souls leave our bodies to confer with the spirits of the dead. The messages we get through our otherworldly conversations with our ancestors help us to return to our bodies with the wisdom that will assist us in our lives when we awake from our nightly dreams. As an artist, I believe that both statements—the political and the spiritual—are true.

To enter a river is for the soul to enter the body...
The body leads a precarious existence; it seeps away
like water, and each soul possesses an individual body;
its temporary habitation, its river.

—Heraclitus

Part III **My Life**

GARMEL

Mary McLeod Bethune, *Founder*

International Debutante Ball
NATIONAL COUNCIL OF NEGRO WOMEN, INC.
Hotel Commodore — 42nd Street & Lexington Avenue
New York 17, New York

National President
Dorothy I. Height

August 1960

Honorary Chairman
Mrs. Franklin Delano Roosevelt

Honorary Co-Chairmen
Miss Marian Anderson
Mrs. Ralph Bunche
Mrs. Edward Dudley
Miss Lena Horne
Mrs. Sophia Yarnall Jacobs

Dear

It is an honor to submit to this distinguished organization an invitation for participation on behalf of the National Council of Negro Women.

The President of the United States has signed the Resolution passed by Congress authorizing the NCNW to erect on public land in the nations capitol the first Memorial to an American Negro.

As the opening of our Silver Anniversary and to launch our campaign we are holding as a benefit an International Debutante Ball at the Hotel Commodore, Friday, September 23, 1960.

Under the Honorary Chairmanship of Mrs. Franklin Delano Roosevelt, the ball will symbolize the highest qualities in womanhood, service and achievement for which the National Council of Negro Women was organized in 1935 by Mary McLeod Bethune and other distinguished women leaders.

It would mean a great deal to have your organization sponsor a debutante. You may consider sponsoring one of our debutantes from another country or from the United States who desires a Sponsor, or one of your own choosing. The Gala Dinner and Divertissement will be a real spectacular! The Sponsor assists the debutante with all or part of her contribution of one hundred dollars to the Educational Fund and helps assure her of her table in the dinner-dance.

This Century of Freedom Memorial Project is the biggest thing Negro women have undertaken with a unity of purpose. Your support in this effort will never be forgotten. Our 850,000 women will be deeply grateful.

Sincerely,

Dorothy I. Height
National President

Please reply to:
200 West 57th Street
New York, 17, New York
#1301

180

Chapter IX **September 23, 1960**

I remember the letter and that it was hot and muggy when it arrived. I heard the mail fall through the postal chute. Shortly afterward, my mother let out a shout of pure joy. "Carroll Ann! Come here!" I flew through the house. She was proudly reading out loud. "The President of the United States has given the National Council of Negro Women," she paused breathlessly before continuing, ". . . Incorporated, the authority to memorialize Mary McLeod Bethune!" My mother's eyes were dancing. She had that "Can you believe it?" look on her face. "This is the first time in our history that an American Negro will be so honored. And that Negro is a woman!"

I remembered Mrs. Bethune's fierce eyes and strong voice. The power of her conviction was unforgettable, even to me as a six-year-old in 1949, as I watched her speak to a Black women's gathering in Houston. That particular meeting was held at the Masonic Hall near the corner of Dowling and McGowen Streets. The building was near our church, St. John's Baptist Church on Dowling. With a sweat-drenched face, she implored the crowd with just her voice. I don't remember her words, but her fervor was absolutely compelling. After her talk, I remember shaking her hand as her fierce eyes peered directly into mine. I'm so grateful to this day that my mother introduced me to this now mythic figure.

I took the one-page letter that my mother waved in front of me and started reading it from the beginning:

FOR IMMEDIATE RELEASE

REPRESENTATIVES OF UNITED
NATIONS POLITICS AND THEATRE
SET FOR NCNW DEBUTANTES' BALL

The National Council of Negro Women's Silver Anniversary Debutante Ball will be held at the Commodore Hotel in its Grand Ballroom Friday night, September 23rd. It will be highlighted by some of the most outstanding personalities of stage, screen, radio and television. It will also be like a Social Summit Conference event with some of the top representatives of the United Nations, attending.

The Silver Anniversary Debutante Ball is being sponsored by the NCNW to inaugurate a two year drive to raise the necessary funds to establish an educational center and erect a monument to honor the late Mary McLeod Bethune in Washington, D. C. The center and the monument to the founder of the National Council will mark the first time that a Negro woman has been so honored in the Nation's Capitol.

In view of this historic event, the Silver Anniversary Debutante Ball will have among its guests outstanding patrons from all over the world.

Among those who have accepted invitations and purchased tables are Presidential nominee Senator John F. Kennedy, whose family contigent will be led by his sister, who will also attend if a speaking engagement will permit. Edward W. Brooke, who is running as the first Negro ever nominated for Secretary of the State of Massachusetts, Rodman Rockefeller, who will lead an entourage of Governor Rockefeller's friends, Sir Lawrence Oliver, the great English film star; Metropolitan Opera dancer, Carmen De Lavallade and television star, Lonnie Satin.

From the United Nations will come Ambassador and Mrs. Quaison-Sackey, Ghana; Ambassador and Mde. Adam Pachachi, Iraq; Sir Patrick and Lady Dean, United Kingdom; Ambassador and Mrs. C. S. Jha, India; Ambassador and Mde. Rafik Asha, United Arab Republic; and Sir Claude and Lady Correa, Ceylon. Also Ambassador and Mde. Berard, France; Ambassador Barnes and Counsel General David Thomas, Liberia; Ambassador Abdul Monum Rifa'i, Jordan; and Mr. C. G. Jury.

Also United States Ambassador and Mrs. James J. Wadsworth and Ambassador and Mde. Mehdi Vakil, Iran. These and other dignitaries from at home and abroad will make the Silver Anniversary Debutante Ball of the National Council of Negro Women a social Summit Conference.

It is the largest and most pretentious affair ever sponsored by the 850,000 member organization. It will be both a dinner and dance and highlight the progress of the group founded by the lady they are now honoring.

DIPLOMATIC COMMITTEE

HONORED GUESTS AND HOSTS

TRY	GUESTS	HOSTESS
OR	His Excellency Dr. Jose A. Correa)	
IA	Consul General David Thomas)	Mrs. W. C. Handy
	His Excellency Ambassador & Mrs. Quaison-Sackey	Dr. Jeanne Noble
	Consul General Kofi O. Darko	Mrs. Stanley Alexander
	His Excellency Ambassador & Madame Adam Pachachi	Mrs. Louis P. Morris
N	His Excellency Ambassador Sir Claude & Lady Corea)	
D ES	Attorney Edward W. Brooke Secretary of State of Massachusetts)	Miss Alexandra Barry
KA	H.E. Ambassador Nathan Barnes	Mrs. Lillian Alexander
	H.E. Ambassador & Madame Mehdi Vakil	Mr. & Mrs. Nathaniel Meade
	H.E. Ambassador & Madame Carlet R. Auguste	Mrs. Gilbert Brown
O ES	Dr. Zelma Watson George Alternate Delegate to the 15th General Assembly, United Nations	Miss Wilhelmina Drake
PIA	His Excellency & Madame Tesfaye G. Gesaye	Mrs. Wiliam Epps
LIC OONS	His Excellency Ambassador Charles Okala	Mrs. Carolyne H. Mitchel'
LIC ZAVILLE)	His Excellency Ambassador Stephane T. Chichelle	Mrs. -Carolyne H. Mito'

HONORED GUESTS TO BE HOSTED

. Permanent of France to the United Nations (2)

. His Excellency Ambassador & Mrs. James Wadsworth (WILL ARRIVE LATE)
United States ;Mission to the United Nations

. United Kingdom of Great Britain and Northern Ireland (2)
(Kwame)
. His Excellency Mr.(Nkrumnah)
President of Ghana

. His Excellency Monsieur & Madame Sekou Toure
Prime Minister of Guinea

. His Excellency Ambassador & Mrs. Aage Hessellund-Jensen
Permanent Mission of Denmark to the United Nations

- 2 -

HONORED GUESTS TO BE HOSTED (CONTINUED)

7. His Excellency Marshal Josip Broz (TITO)
President of the Federal Peoples' Republic of Yugoslavia
&
His Excellency Ambassador & Mrs. Dobrivoje Vidic
Permanent Mission of the Federal Peoples' Republic of Yugoslavia
to the United Nations

8. His Excellency Ambassador Andre Gustave Anguile
Republic of Gabon

9. Foreign Minister Justin Bomboko (Republic of Congo - Brazzaville)
Monsieur Josias Pele (·Republic of Congo - Brazzaville)
Monsieur Louis Ilufa (Republic of Congo - Brazzaville)
&
Miss Lillie Lobel (Interpreter)

10. H. E. Ambassador J. Toura Caba
Republic of Chad.

11. His Excellency Ambassador Issoufon Saidon Djermakoye
Republic of Niger

12. His Excellency Ambassador Francois Apolgan
Republic of Dahomey

13. His Excellency Ambassador Louis Rakotomalala
Republic of Malagasy

14. His Excellency Ambassador Sylvanus Olympio
Republic of Togo

15. His Excellency Ambassador Momadan Coulibaly
Republic of Ivory Coast

16. His Excellency Ambassador Zenon Rossides (Republic of Cyprus
&
Monsieur R. M. Malyal (Republic of Cyprus

17. His Excellency Ambassador Bakary Traore
Republic of Upper Volta

18. His Excellency Ambassador Hadji Farah Ali Omar
Republic of Soualia

Mr. L. Edward Nichols
23 Years old.
Studied abroad   Field of Medicine
Speaks 3 languages Fluently Including
French.

POSSIBLE HOSTESSES

1. Mrs. Henriene Ward Banks

GARMEL

The Committee invites you to the
International Debutante Ball
A Gala Dinner and Divertissements
Silver Anniversary Benefit for the N.C.N.W. Educational Fund
sponsored by the
National Council of Negro Women, Inc.
under the Honorary Chairmanship of
Mrs. Franklin Delano Roosevelt

Co-Chairmen

MISS MARIAN ANDERSON   MRS. RALPH BUNCHE
MRS. EDWARD DUDLEY   MISS LENA HORNE
MRS. SOPHIA YARNALL JACOBS

Hotel Commodore
Friday, September 23rd, Nineteen hundred Sixty   WHITE OR BLACK TIE

AT EIGHT O'CLOCK

It is an honor to submit to this distinguished organization an invitation for participation on behalf of the National Council of Negro Women.

In the end, my mother paid for me to be one of the two delegate debutantes from Houston. In fact, we were all honored that two of Houston's young ladies—Johnnye Ruth Davis and Carroll Ann Parrott—were going to represent our city. Quickly, she began to tally her finances. Because I was in college in Boston, the cost to travel to New York City would be minimal. She figured she'd find the money, somehow. We were under the impression that we had done something truly magnificent to be asked to participate in this incredible event. We viewed this as one of the highest honors for the cause of Negro womanhood. A Black woman's honor was always in question. To be a debutante? In New York City, at some famous hotel? In a ballroom peopled with famous Blacks and diplomats from around the world? This was a fantastic validation of our worth!

The ball was special. Even in today's terms, it was a boldly innovative concept. Most cotillions are closed according to class and race, but this one was different. It was an international debutante ball. The forty-nine young women in attendance came from all continents and races, including a large contingent of young women from African and Asian nations. Ralph Bunche's wife was one of the honorary co-chairs of the event, along with the legendary singers Marian Anderson and Lena Horne. Ralph Bunche, then the only Negro Nobel Prize winner, was one of the major architects of African and other Third World independence movements through his United Nations post. Unusually highly placed in both the United States and the United Nations, Bunche had finally convinced Western colonial powers that it was economically prudent to relinquish direct governing of Third World countries. African leaders like Ghana's Kwame Nkrumah, Guinea's Sekou Toure, and Kenya's Jomo Kenyatta were his respected colleagues. His highly sophisticated UN initiatives had helped to bring these leaders and their countries to independence. Eleanor Roosevelt was the ball's honorary chairperson. High-level representatives from many UN member nations were to be in attendance.

My mother and I never looked at this event as a fund-raiser. For us, this introduction to society was our way to buttress our still fragile dignity. But behind the scenes, the keen farsightedness of Dorothy Height, the National Council's president, was wisely at work. In staging this event, she accomplished at least two objectives. She acknowledged the emerging Asian and African independence movements. African, Indian, Caribbean, and Asian debutantes were among us. The notion of the United Nations was ever present, and its concept of a world government was not lost on me.

Simultaneously, in 1960, Miss Height obtained a congressional decree to establish this country's first memorial to any African American. It had taken over

August 15, 1960

Mrs. Leola Edwards
200 West 57th Street
New York 19, N.Y.

As Co-ordinators, it is our objective to aid the Committee Chairmen in bringing the International Debutante Ball to a successful conclusion:

From now until the evening of the 23rd of September, it will be of the utmost importance that we stay constantly in touch. To that end, we will send out weekly memos to help you keep in touch with what the other committees are accomplishing. We MUST know from you:

    (1) Exactly where you are at this point in the project.
    (2) What your immediate problems are.

PLEASE send in as complete a report as you possibly can from your committee immediately. The SUCCESS of the BALL depends on YOU ! ! ! ! ! ! !

MEMO NOTES:
    Meeting:-- August 11, 1960 - Attending:---Mr. Philippe, Miss Dorothy Height, Mrs. Prudence Black, Miss Garnette Henderson, Mr. M.A. Lockhart

There was a general discussion on all points of the Ball. Mr. Philippe was concerned that there was not enough publicity. He pledged his full support in assisting from his office. The invitations were a major concern to Miss Height, who wanted to make sure that they were in the hands of the proper people before she left for Chicago. Floor plans, table arrangements and the program were checked on. A general overall strategy was developed for insuring the success of the Ball.

INVITATIONS--These were delivered to Mrs. Anna C. Perry by Mr. Lockhart.

RESERVATION TICKETS--These were delivered to Mrs. Claramae Long by Mr. Lockhart.

PUBLICITY--Mr. Lockhart has been in touch with Mrs. Evelyn Cunningham on several occasions. A plan for publicity has been worked out that will garner full coverage for the affair. Please send any interest notes along to this office.

DEBUTANTES--To date, there are only nine debutantes committed to the Ball. Please submit any possibilities that you may know of.

ESCORTS--We have 54 escorts that have expressed the desire to participate.

RAFFLES--The books are now ready for distribution. Contact Mrs. Gadsen for your supply. Time is of the essence. We need all the sellers we can recruit.

Please be sure that your address and telephone number is correct, so that we will have no difficulty in contacting you. Send this along with your report.

Mrs. Ada Fisher Jones--Floor Plans and program were sent to Mrs. Fisher.
Mrs. Maude Gadsen-- Returning from California on Wednesday.
Mrs. Prudence Black--All Committee Chairmen will be hearing from Mrs. Black.
Mrs. Ophelia DeVore--Will be away for two weeks, but is appointing a replacement to handle contact for international debutantes.

one hundred years and Miss Height's persistent urging for the United States to officially honor Mary McLeod Bethune. It was the weight of the 850,000-strong membership of the National Council and this group's money that helped to create the Washington, D.C.–based monument and the Bethune Council House. The strength of a united group of Black women with political and purchasing power was yet another lesson not lost on me.

Even so, the ball's fund-raising efforts had been a hair-raising race to the finish line. Imagine my surprise when I uncovered the truth at the Mary McLeod Bethune Council House Archives in Washington, D.C. I discovered some meeting notes dated August 16, 1960. The minutes briefly noted that as of August 11, there were only *nine* paid debutantes! There were fifty-four male escorts volunteering, but then they didn't have to pay. These women were in a state of high panic. In haste, the main office dispatched a letter to all the chapters "giving them the honor of sending their young ladies as debutante representatives to the ball." In addition, the rumors were that Winthrop Rockefeller, one of the Rockefeller men—a young, eligible one!—would be at the ball. We got the letter at the end of August. August 1960 was the postmarked date. We both were too excited to notice that it was unusual that the letter had no exact date on it.

"It would mean a great deal to have your organization sponsor a debutante." The cool, high-minded tone in this letter hid any notion of the organization's financial desperation. We had no idea that, nationwide, 849,999 other Black women had been contacted. We were too busy being in absolute bliss that we had been asked to participate. Almost immediately my mother had me married to Winthrop Rockefeller. "Just think, Carroll Ann," she mused, with an uncharacteristic girlish delight, "we could be a princess like Grace Kelly, couldn't we?" Yes, I could imagine that "we" were Mrs. Winthrop-Rockefeller-Princess-Grace-Kelly-Rainier. She continued with her reverie, "We could be buying outfits from Neiman-Marcus and Sakowitz for the receptions before, during, and after the wedding." She was talking about us getting outfits from two of Houston's finest apparel stores—stores that had no prices in their windows. My cousin Mae Lois Hoffman had already pointed out that this absence meant these clothes were far too expensive for us. I liked it that my mother saw my upcoming marriage to a Rockefeller as "our" marriage to him. We spent the rest of the day gloating over the myriad possibilities that lay ahead for us, all flowing in with Winthrop's impending marriage proposal.

On September 23, 1960, forty-nine young women were introduced to proper society. The actual event was a blur in my memory. I flew into New York City after my first week as a Boston University freshman. I left Boston with a prepaid round-trip airline ticket and $25, which was a lot of money in 1960. It was to last me three days. As the plane landed, I watched the skyline of the city of my dreams with great anticipation. From the time I hit the ground in New York City it must have been crystal-clear and obvious to all that I was a country hick. The shameful truth of it hit me by the time I reached my hotel room. The bellboy dropped the luggage and put his hand out. I quickly realized that I had exactly two dollars left. Surprised, I looked at the money, his outstretched hand, and then at him. "Do you have any change?" I sounded timid even to myself. He didn't flinch as he fired back, "No, I don't!" To me, his response sounded more like a dare than an answer. He leaned forward, towering over me. He narrowed his eyes, clearly insulted. "Look, lady, you had two *very* heavy pieces of luggage here…" He was impatient. He seemed to be shouting at me. Then, to my surprise, this bellhop let out a real scary laugh—something like Richard Widmark's hideous laugh just before he pushed that old lady in a wheelchair down the stairs in the 1947 film noir *Kiss of Death*. Then this crazy guy pushed his hand out, closer to me. I hurried up and put one of the two crumpled dollar bills in his hand. Snatching his clenched fist back, he turned and walked away real quick like. "Thank you," I meekly called out to his back. His reply was a disdainful door slam.

After calling home collect for more money, I found the hotel's grand ballroom. When I walked into this huge room, I saw the walls lined with neatly dressed young ladies. Most of them seemed to carry themselves as if they were to the manner born. Our male escorts all looked safe, dull, and entirely predictable. They were the kind of young men that mothers would approve of their daughters marrying. Winthrop Rockefeller was nowhere to be found. I gave my name and was promptly introduced to my escort. To this day I don't remember a thing about him, other than that he was Black. In fact, the only face I can remember is that of my Houston colleague, Johnnye Ruth Davis—and the faces of the famous people that I saw that night.

Suddenly, some man with a pencil-thin mustache was barking short and very sharp commands at all of us as we rushed to make what he called straight lines, turning large turns, and going through some mysterious, yet tightly prescribed movements. This person had absolutely no patience with any of us. I felt like I was in a herd of bleating sheep being pushed from side to side by an angry sheepdog determined to keep us huddled together and moving forward. Then some really dressed-up women suddenly appeared. They all seemed to have heavily powdered faces, white gloves, and strong perfume smells. They took over. "You young Negro ladies are the cream of the crop," they sternly admonished us, "and you are to conduct yourselves as such." No one ever detailed exactly what this meant, but I do remember observing that all these women crossed their legs at the ankle and not at the knees.

At some point, the great and lovely dancer Carmen DeLavallade floated like an angel into the ballroom. Her job that evening was to swirl around us, Tinker-Bell-like, and hand out some little package of a "specially prepared" perfume made in

Paris only for us. It was called "Debutante International." I do remember that as I opened the bottle, the perfume smelled cheap and rancid. As the women were leaving, the man started barking at us again. This time we were commanded to curtsy with a very deep bow. To be honest, I was just learning how to wear heels. I could barely walk in a straight line with them on. And so to be ordered to "float like I was being led by a dainty feather" was not an easy concept for my oversized and clumsy high-heeled feet to conquer.

As I struggled to keep up, I remember that I was mostly ignored. And that I was lost in the mass of it all. There was food, flowing champagne fountains, and a lot of people who seemed to take this event very seriously. I remember the important girls kept getting pulled away from tables to take pictures with famous people. Class certainly played a part in it. In 1960, Houston, Texas, was a backwater, small southern town to most of these upper-class East Coast Blacks who vacationed in the very tony Martha's Vineyard. I was not in the "right" class, so I did not get to meet the Edward Brookes (he later became a U.S. Senator), the Ralph Bunches, the Sekou Toures, Lena Horne, Daisy Bates, or Kwame Nkrumrah, who, I was told, were among the evening's notables.

Color also played a major role. When I look at the photographs, I see a majority of light-skinned girls everywhere. I remember the queen of the ball was very fair. As the queen of the ball, she got to meet Winthrop Rockefeller. Or was it Rodman Rockefeller? Anyway, I still don't understand how she got chosen. As for me, my crowning glory came at the actual ball. Carmen DeLavallade floated toward me and handed me this packet of perfume tied up with a ribbon that had a balloon at the top. Somewhere out there was an *Ebony* magazine photographer who snapped his camera at that special moment when she reached toward me, with the result that I too ended up in the December 1960 *Ebony* magazine with Harry Belafonte on the cover and me at the top of page 48. Later, back in Boston, I got the attention of all the Negro coeds in the Boston and Cambridge area. The appearance of my photograph—the second largest in this *Ebony* article—was a major feat. Here I was, an unknown with no privilege-class or light-skinned-color credentials. Yet luck had smiled on me. My image was there beside all those proper young ladies and men who were the cream of the Negro race. And even though Winthrop (or Rodman) never called me, I got over it. Meanwhile, an important fact was not lost on me—and that was the power of press coverage. As it records events, mass media also freezes snapshots of our cultural history. And it's odd how the passage of time shifts the meanings of events. How different our perception of race is today when we think of African Americans in the military. Close to sixty years ago, *Life* magazine reported that Blacks were inexperienced in military fighting. In 2000, I watched a ceremony in honor of Black soldiers who courageously fought to save Italy in World War II. The same is true regarding women's sexuality. As I

DEBUTANTE BALL QUEEN GREETED

Winthrop Rockefeller shakes hands with Elenor Epps, right, queen of debutante ball, at Commodore hotel in New York Sept. 23. Women in center, from left, are Helen Maxwell, actress Lena Horne and Deborah Wolf. U.N. delegates attended the ball, unique because non-white girls outnumbered white debs thirty-two to eight. Event was sponsored by National Council of Negro Women to raise funds for an educational center in Washington as a memorial to famed Negro educator Mary McLeod Bethune.

NEW YORK, N.Y.
WORLD-TELEGRAM & SUN
W. 453.331 SAT. 174,917
SEP 26 1960

Society Today

U.S. Art Expert Biddle Expects A Masterpiece

JOSEPH X. DEVER.

ALMANACH DE GOTHAM: The Jimmy Biddles will soon be three! He's the American art expert at the Met Museum. She's the former Louise Copeland of the Du Pont dynasty. . . . Post-deb Cheray Zauderer of the racing and realty clans seems to have shifted from broker Geist Ely to banker Earl Mack. . . . Dyed-in-the-wool Republican Dick Cowell is devoting all his time to coralling Elephantophiles for the $100-a-plate Nixon-Lodge dinner at the Astor on Thursday. That is when Dick isn't heeding the call of the hearty Faith Dane, who introduced herself to us as "I'm the bugle-blowing stripper from 'Gypsy.'" . . . Tree-shaded Belmont opens its 24-day autumn meeting today and all of turf-minded society who would trade their kingdoms for a horse will be on hand—trading.

Cheray Zauderer

* * *

We attended the Silver Anniversary Debutante Ball on Friday night at the Commodore, timed for the 25th anniversary of the National Council of Negro Women, founded in 1935 by the late Mary McLeod Bethune. Proceeds of this gala will be used to build a monument in Washington to that great educator—a child of onetime slaves—who became herself a monument of democracy. Forty debutantes representing 14 countries were presented to more than 1000 members of the N.C.N.W. and their friends. The silver canopy overhead, candlelit tables with red covers and trellised arbor on stage furnished a setting as attractive as any deb affair we can think of, as the young ladies curtsied low and descended the stairs as their names were read. The debs themselves were chosen by the 850,000 members of N.C.N.W. as "symbolizing the highest qualities in womenhood, service and achievement," a criterion that strikes us as exemplary for debs everywhere. Emcee Hy Gardner informed us that Honorary Chairman Mrs. Franklin D. Roosevelt, a great friend of Mrs. Bethune, was away in Cleveland. But most of the others were too busy admiring Lena Horne who headed the receiving line to notice. Many U.N. dignitaries present including Iranian Ambassador Mehdi Vakil and the French Congo's Foreign Minister Justin Bamboko, not to forget a tall, serious young man not so much interested in deb parties as worthy causes — Gov. Rockefeller's son, Rodman.

* * *

thumbed through the archives of this event at the Bethune archives, I ran across a *World Telegram and Sun* society column, dated September 26, 1960. Although this article highlights the cotillion, the lead story announces the arrival of a Biddle baby. Forty years later, another Biddle family member is now infamously known as "The Mayflower Madam."

But alas, my fate was not to become a socialite. It was to turn in yet another direction. In August, I had just turned seventeen. Feeling my oats, I had gone to a Boston University freshman mixer. There I loudly started expressing my opinion about some recent Hollywood film. "It was boring," I declared.

Instinctively, I sensed melodrama was too predictable a solution for my demanding tastes. I had seen one too many Rock Hudson and Doris Day films. Even the "serious films" like *A Town without Pity* seemed to be too clichéd. Overhearing my sophomoric complaints, an upperclassman suggested I go to see a certain film. "I don't think you'll find this one very predictable," she said. I did go that very weekend to a movie art house on Massachusetts Avenue, four blocks away from the dorm.

That's where I inhaled *Hiroshima, mon amour*.

From that film's very first frame, I fell under the sway of a magic that I had never before experienced in viewing a film. The unfolding of a woman's life drove this story. Our heroine is a free spirit who appoints her heart as her authority. But wait. In addition to showcasing an independent woman's love, the film is also a strong commentary on war, race, power, female socialization, and a beautiful woman breaking society's rules. The acting was flawless, the directing sensitive, the cinematography beautiful, the editing pristine. *Hiroshima, mon amour* was the first film that gave me the experience of having all of my aesthetic sensibilities fed.

I was very fortunate, as a future filmmaker, to be in Boston from 1960 to 1965. European film was flourishing, and Boston was one of this country's ports of entry for this golden age of a new cinema. And in Boston, these films found highly receptive audiences. I began to study the films of François Truffaut, Jean-Luc Godard, Luis Buñuel, Louis Malle, Luchino Visconti, Vittorio De Sica, Federico Fellini, Ingmar Bergman, Michaelangelo Antonioni, Satyajit Ray, Tony Richardson, and Alan Resnais, among others.

I also remember seeing *Shadows*, a film with inferior sound recording, grainy images, and an erratic plot structure. Still, for an American film, there was something almost too precious about it. What held my attention throughout was that it treated Blacks as equals. *Shadows* introduced me to the work of John Cassavetes, a filmmaker whose works I followed until his death. While I was a UCLA Film School student, I had the pleasure of being an extra in a crowd scene in his film *Opening Night*. I relished the opportunity to watch him direct. I also saw the late Shirley Clarke's *The Connection* and later her groundbreaking film on a group of

Harlem's Black teenagers, *The Cool World*. When I knew her at UCLA's Film School, she was preoccupied with making a film on Ornette Coleman, the jazz musician. She was a committee member for my thesis film, *Varnette's World: A Study of a Young Artist.*

The only Hollywood films that did impress me in the early 1960s were those that dealt with race. Thus, *A Raisin in the Sun, Paris Blues,* and *Nothing but a Man* stand out as my American cinematic guideposts. As I gained knowledge of world cinema, my cinematic tastes gradually became more refined, and I began to be much more selective. I first noticed how much I had changed when my mother and I watched our last film together in the summer of 1967. Delicate strains of Simon and Garfunkel's "Scarborough Fair" floated over radio airwaves. Finally, *The Graduate,* Mike Nichols's acclaimed film, had come to Houston.

On the same occasion, I also became aware of how much Houston had changed. Everything my mother had worked for had come true in her lifetime. She had even been a part of the Texas Southern University students' protests, sit-ins, marches, and arrests that led to Houston's integration. Transportation, schools, movie houses, theaters, and restaurants were now open to all races, creeds, and colors. Why, whites and Blacks even lived together in some Houston neighborhoods. We went to the Majestic, Houston's famous formerly white-only movie house. In the pre-mall days, the Majestic was located downtown on Main Street, next to Foley's, the city's main department store. Without incident, we bought two tickets. This time I took my mother to the movies. Based on my budding film knowledge, I suggested we watch this film, proud that she was going to sample some of my cinematic tastes.

My mother was unusually quiet during this film. I was absorbed as well. I was into the cinematography. The camera's point of view was so fresh in some scenes. Then there was the music and the editing. And how the actors were performing. That Dustin Hoffman and Kathleen Ross were closing the door on the angry crowd of adults now trapped inside frankly exhilarated me. I cheered as the couple escaped to freedom, not disregarding that they did it from the back of the bus, a place so long ago delegated to Negroes. When the house lights went up, I realized my mother was sitting there frozen with anger.

"That old hussy knew better than to entrap that boy." My mother's words were like ice-cold water thrown on the warmth of my enthusiasm. "Whatever was she talking about?" I pondered, "Clearly this film was an important work to be hailed." I was quiet. We moved with the crowds through the air-conditioned lobby. Her grumbling continued as we walked out onto the street. "And just how did those young people plan to make a living? That boy had no job . . ." I finally got it that she was talking more to what she thought my ideas of love were than to the issues raised in the actual movie. As we were walking to the car, she continued to won-

194

der. I was driving, so I let her in the car. She turned to look at me directly, "I hope and pray to God that you have something better than that planned for your life . . ." I paid at the parking booth and started the long drive home. I wasn't saying much of anything because I realized that she didn't get it at all.

Movies were her way of teaching moral lessons. The morals in this particular film went deeply against the grain of all she believed to be righteous and true. By now I had lived with films like *Belle de Jour, Viridiana, Rocco and His Brothers,* and *The Virgin Spring.* These films got at the heart of morals in ways that advocated radical change, a change that was far from my mother's wildest dreams. It was 1967, and the smell of revolution was in the air all around us. Smoke from marijuana joints, along with burning bras and American flags, filled this country's air. The free speech movement was on, the civil rights movement had birthed Black Power, and even Martin Luther King Jr. was on the antiwar bandwagon. Crowds of protesters of every kind were filling the streets.

By then I was so committed to fighting back on these larger issues that I no longer needed to challenge my mother's core beliefs. I was united with all of those who hadn't reached thirty yet. Together we were all going to change the world. I was cheerfully absorbing the messages in this film's energy, delighting so much in my emerging political consciousness that I had forgotten about her. Instead of fighting her, I was beginning to learn how to fight the society that had helped to shape us. When I returned home from my first semester in Boston, I knew I was not cut out for the life that my parents had envisioned for me.

That 1960 Christmas season my mother had a round of parties celebrating my coming out as a debutante. I own two photographs that encapsulate me during that time. In one, my sixty-year-old mother and I are framed by her two older relatives, Emma Carroll Jones, her sister, and Lillie Bell Porter, her cousin. They were among the ones who made fun of her by calling her "Blackie" while growing up.

She was the only one in her entire family to go to college, marry a professional man, and get a master's degree. Now here she was, the president of the colored YWCA board, dressed in black and proudly hosting my reception in the Y's building. I am standing by her side, dressed entirely in white, her trophy daughter.

In the other photograph, I had just finished arguing with my mother in the Sylvan Beach Auditorium bathroom. My defiant determination shows up in how I hold my mouth. On the other hand, my father, caught in the middle of our fight, has "a deer in the headlights" look in his eyes.

At the time, I was the only family member ever officially introduced to high society. And what an introduction! My photograph had been taken in New York City at the International Debutante Ball, and I had even been in *Ebony* magazine. How accomplished my mother must have felt at the time.

I, on the other hand, had tasted something new, yet entirely familiar in Boston. Now I was driven by Gwendolyn Brooks's *The Bean Eaters*, James Baldwin's *Nobody Knows My Name*, Langston Hughes and Roy DeCarava's *Sweet Flypaper of Life*, Miles Davis's *Kind of Blue*, Thelonious Monk's *'Round Midnight*, and Lorraine Hansberry's *A Raisin in the Sun*. Although I didn't understand it at the time, I had left the world my parents had dreamed for me. I was desperately in search of some way, any way to join the ranks of those who were creating the art that expressed who I was. My parents also left me a rich legacy of being the "race people" that Mary McLeod Bethune articulated so well in her final will and testament, published in *Ebony* magazine in 1955. Now, as heir to a legacy of a mighty vision, I was hungry to become an artist. I had no idea where my aspirations would take me. All I knew was that I had to name myself.

Suddenly my mother fell silent in the car. Too quiet for me. Her silence broke my reverie. Taking my eyes off the road, I turned in the car to see fury clearly planted on her face. "I care about her," I remember thinking, as I watched my mother's underlying fear of the future being mashed down by her seething anger.

She liked my cooking. After we arrived home, I sat her down in the kitchen, and I set about fixing dinner. She sat pensively at the kitchen table, still ranting on about *The Graduate*. "I really liked the symbolism of the cross over the church door," I tentatively ventured my opinion while chopping onions, ". . . using it to block the door was brilliant, given all that the church has done to oppress people."

Dinner was ready. I put the food on the table and sat down. Honoring her routine before eating, I bowed my head with hers in a silent prayer. Then as I dipped into the salad bowl while she cut the chicken, she queried me, "But, baby, the people in the church were right." Really? I was thinking. "Maybe," I said aloud. But to my mind, in that film my generation was clearly winning. We had barred the church doors with a cross. Her generation was locked inside, screaming silently through the windows, looking on helplessly at Dustin Hoffman and Katharine Ross as they escaped, happy and free. Looking directly into her eyes, I realized I too had won. I was no longer joined at the hip of my mother's belief system. I was free. I had finally come into my own. I was going about the business of becoming an artist. I looked over at my mother, an elderly, bewildered woman who looked askance at these confusing times. I wanted to comfort her: "Ma," I said as I reached out to touch her with assurance, "it's only a movie . . ."

Looking into my eyes, she mirrored my smile. I watched her worries fade as her smile turned into our mirth. And we sat there, at the same table where so many years before she had told me, a child too young to hear, her terrible dream. Now we sat facing each other and we laughed. We were never, in our lifetime together, able to reconcile our differences. Still, we both cherished the value of shared laughter.

My Last Will and Testament*
By Mary McLeod Bethune

Sometimes as I sit communing in my study I feel that death is not far off. I am aware that it will overtake me before the greatest of my dreams — full equality for the Negro in our time — is realized. Yet, I face that reality without fear or regrets. I am resigned to death as all humans must be at the proper time. Death neither alarms nor frightens one who has had a long career of fruitful toil. The knowledge that my work has been helpful to many fills me with joy and great satisfaction.

Since my retirement from an active role in educational work and from the affairs of the National Council of Negro Women, I have been living quietly and working at my desk at my home here in Florida. The years have directed a change of pace for me. I am now 78 years old and my activities are no longer so strenuous as they once were. I feel that I must conserve my strength to finish the work at hand.

Already I have begun working on my autobiography which will record my life-journey in detail, together with the innumerable side trips which have carried me abroad, into every corner of our country, into homes both lowly and luxurious, and even into the White House to confer with Presidents. I have also deeded my home and its contents to the Mary McLeod Bethune Foundation, organized in March, 1953, for research, interracial activity and the sponsorship of wider educational opportunities.

Sometimes I ask myself if I have any other legacy to leave. Truly, my worldly possessions are few. Yet, my experiences have been rich. From them, I have distilled principles and policies in which I believe firmly, for they represent the meaning of my life's work. They are the products of much sweat and sorrow. Perhaps in them there is something of value. So, as my life draws to a close, I will pass them on to Negroes everywhere in the hope that an old woman's philosophy may give them inspiration. Here, then is my legacy.

I LEAVE YOU LOVE. Love builds. It is positive and helpful. It is more beneficial than hate. Injuries quickly forgotten quickly pass away. Personally and racially, our enemies must be forgiven. Our aim must be to create a world of fellowship and justice where no man's skin, color or religion, is held against him. "Love thy neighbor" is a precept which could transform the world if it were universally practiced. It connotes brotherhood and, to me, brotherhood of man is the noblest concept in all human relations. Loving your neighbor means being interracial, interreligious and international.

I LEAVE YOU HOPE. The Negro's growth will be great in the years to come. Yesterday, our ancestors endured the degradation of slavery, yet they retained their dignity. Today, we direct our economic and political strength toward winning a more abundant and secure life. Tomorrow, a new Negro, unhindered by race taboos and shackles, will benefit from more than 330 years of ceaseless striving and struggle. Theirs will be a better world. This I believe with all my heart.

I LEAVE YOU THE CHALLENGE OF DEVELOPING CONFIDENCE IN ONE ANOTHER. As long as Negroes are hemmed into racial blocs by prejudice and pressure, it will be necessary for them to band together for economic betterment. Negro banks, insurance companies and other businesses are examples of successful, racial economic enterprises. These institutions were made possible by vision and mutual aid. Confidence was vital in getting them started and keeping them going. Negroes have got to demonstrate still more confidence in each other in business. This kind of confidence will aid the economic rise of the race by bringing together the pennies and dollars of our people and ploughing them into useful channels. Economic separatism cannot be tolerated in this enlightened age, and it is not practicable. We must spread out as far and as fast as we can, but we must also help each other as we go.

I LEAVE YOU A THIRST FOR EDUCATION. Knowledge is the prime need of the hour. More and more, Negroes are taking full advantage of hard-won opportunities for learning, and the educational level of the Negro population is at its highest point in history. We are making greater use of the privileges inherent in living in a democracy. If we continue in this trend, we will be able to rear increasing numbers of strong, purposeful men and women, equipped with vision, mental clarity, health and education.

I LEAVE YOU RESPECT FOR THE USES OF POWER. We live in a world which respects power above all things. Power, intelligently directed, can lead to more freedom. Unwisely directed, it can be a dreadful, destructive force. During my lifetime I have seen the power of the Negro grow enormously. It has always been my first concern that this power should be placed on the side of human justice.

Now that the barriers are crumbling everywhere, the Negro in America must be ever vigilant lest his forces be marshalled behind wrong causes and undemocratic movements. He must not lend his support to any group that seeks to subvert democracy. That is why we must select leaders who are wise, courageous, and of great moral stature and ability. We have great leaders among us today: Ralph Bunche, Channing Tobias, Mordecai Johnson, Walter White, and Mary Church Terrell. [The latter now deceased]. We have had other great men and women in the past: Frederick Douglass, Booker T. Washington, Harriet Tubman, and Sojourner Truth. We must produce more qualified people like them, who will work not for themselves, but for others.

I LEAVE YOU FAITH. Faith is the first factor in a life devoted to service. Without faith, nothing is possible. With it, nothing is impossible. Faith in God is the greatest power, but great, too, is faith in oneself. In 50 years the faith of the American Negro in himself has grown immensely and is still increasing. The measure of our progress as a race is in precise relation to the depth of the faith in our people held by our leaders. Frederick Douglass, genius though he was, was spurred by a deep conviction that his people would heed his counsel and follow him to freedom. Our greatest Negro figures have been imbued with faith. Our forefathers struggled for liberty in conditions far more onerous than those we now face, but they never lost the faith. Their perseverance paid rich dividends. We must never forget their sufferings and their sacrifices, for they were the foundations of the progress of our people.

I LEAVE YOU RACIAL DIGNITY. I want Negroes to maintain their human dignity at all costs. We, as Negroes, must recognize that we are the custodians as well as the heirs of a great civilization. We have given something to the world as a race and for this we are proud and fully conscious of our place in the total picture of mankind's development. We must learn also to share and mix with all men. We must make and effort to be less race conscious and more conscious of individual and human values. I have never been sensitive about my complexion. My color has never destroyed my self-respect nor has it ever caused me to conduct myself in such a manner as to merit the disrespect of any person. I have not let my color handicap me. Despite many crushing burdens and handicaps, I have risen from the cotton fields of South Carolina to found a college, administer it during its years of growth, become a public servant in the government of our country and a leader of women. I would not exchange my color for all the wealth in the world, for had I been born white I might not have been able to do all that I have done or yet hope to do.

I LEAVE YOU A DESIRE TO LIVE HARMONIOUSLY WITH YOUR FELLOW MEN. The problem of color is worldwide. It is found in Africa and Asia, Europe and South America. I appeal to American Negroes — North, South, East and West -- to recognize their common problems and unite to solve them.

I pray that we will learn to live harmoniously with the white race. So often, our difficulties have made us hyper-sensitive and truculent. I want to see my people conduct themselves naturally in all relationships — fully conscious of their manly responsibilities and deeply aware of their heritage. I want them to learn to understand whites and influence them for good, for it is advisable and sensible for us to do so. We are a minority of 15 million living side by side with a white majority. We must learn to deal with these people positively and on an individual basis.

I LEAVE YOU FINALLY A RESPONSIBILITY TO OUR YOUNG PEOPLE. The world around us really belongs to youth for youth will take over its future management. Our children must never lose their zeal for building a better world. They must not be discouraged from aspiring toward greatness, for they are to be the leaders of tomorrow. Nor must they forget that the masses of our people are still underprivileged, ill-housed, impoverished and victimized by discrimination. We have a powerful potential in our youth, and we must have the courage to change old ideas and practices so that we may direct their power toward good ends.

Faith, courage, brotherhood, dignity, ambition, responsibility -- these are needed today as never before. We must cultivate them and use them as tools for our task of completing the establishment of equality for the Negro. We must sharpen these tools in the struggle that faces us and find new ways of using them. The Freedom Gates are half-ajar. We must pry them fully open.

If I have a legacy to leave my people, it is my philosophy of living and serving. As I face tomorrow, I am content, for I think I have spent my life well. I pray now that my philosophy may be helpful to those who share my vision of a world of Peace, Progress, Brotherhood, and Love.

*Originally published in **EBONY** (August 1955).

Interlude #3 **May 1975**

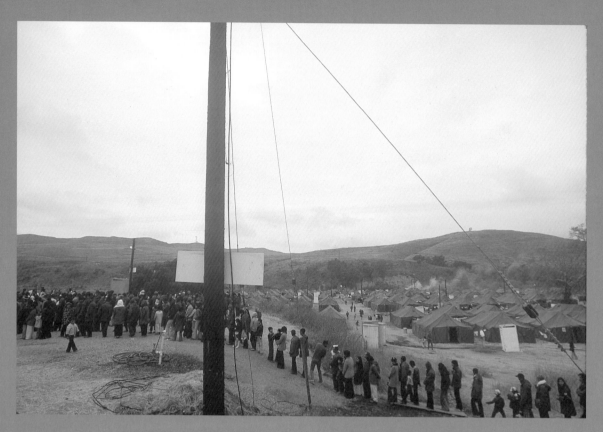

202

203

Da Nang, South Vietnam
Camp Pendleton, California
May 1975

Part I

"The Nam . . ."

I still remember the feel of the bitter
sting from his slap across my face
turning sharply into his voice:
"You haven't earned the right to say that . . ."
His voice was like ice: smooth,
hard, cold inside an angry truth

He had been there,
he had fought there,
risking his life to return
to an ungrateful wall
covered by Marvin Gaye's
"What's Going On."

He had been there; I hadn't.

May 28, 1975

Hi Baby, I received your thought waves daily — Do you get mine — I send thought waves as soon as my eyes fly open and before they close at night and all through the day. In fact I think of you almost constantly. Though distance separates us we are always together in my mind.

How is life going with you? How is the photography? My class is over — I learned very, very little. Too many professionals in the class. They pitched over my head.

I am now at the food stamp center. I work in the center every Wednesday as a volunteer.

Mrs. Carroll Ann Blue
939 Burns Court
San Diego, Calif 92113

May 28, 1975

Hi Baby, I received your thought waves daily—Do you get mine—I send thought waves as soon as my eyes fly open and before they close at night and all through the day. In fact I think of you almost constantly. Though distance separates us we are always together in my mind.

How is life going with you? How is the photography? My class is over—I learned very, very little. Too many professionals in the class. They pitched over my head.

I am now at the food stamp center. I work in the center every Wednesday as a volunteer. I shall be coming to L.A. sometime in June. I hope I can come to see you then, as I told you before I would like to spend a week in San Diego. Hope you have located a place for me to stay, if this is not too much trouble. If it gives you too much concern I can find a place by phone when I arrive in L.A.

All is going well with me. My two girls are lovely to me. They make it so family like especially when Jane cooks an African dinner.

Much love to you and your friends

Mother

Did you receive my last letter?

I shall be coming to L.A.
sometimes in June. I hope I
can come to see you then, as
I told you before I would like
to spend a week in San Diego.
Hope you have located a place
for me to stay, if this is not
too much trouble. If it gives
you too much concern I can
find a place by phone when
I arrive in L.A.
All is going well with me
My two girls are lovely to me.
They make it so family like
especially when Jane Cooks an
African dinner.
Much love to you and
your friends
Mother
Did you receive my last letter?

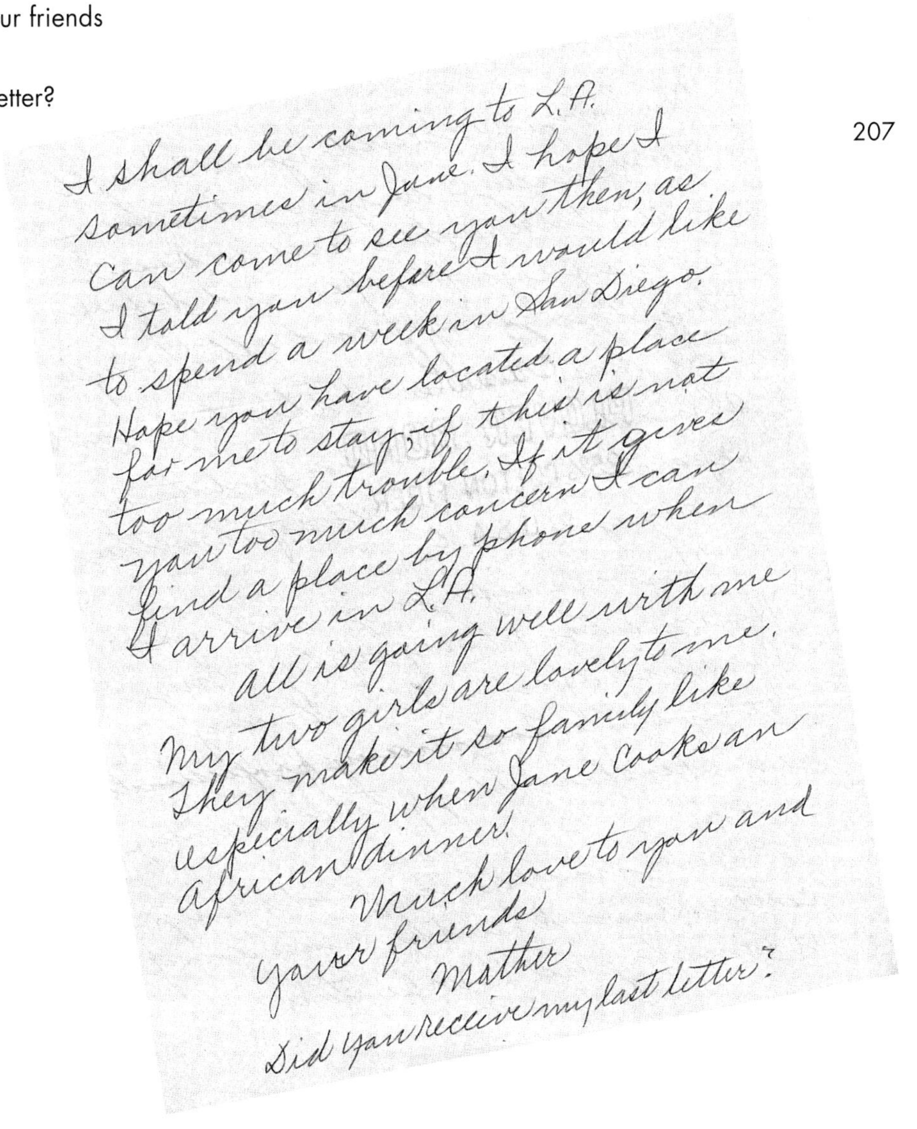

Part II

"The Nam."

Seeking like a child to imitate him,
I mouthed it only to be close to him.
I'd sensed his emptiness after hearing
him and his war buddies caress the
sound of those words with loving
distance in their eyes

Warm utterances that were full
Of shared-in-common secrets
Memories flooded with there.
Vietnam, the place where
I wasn't.

June 3

Dear Mother –

I've recieved both your letters and I was particularly touched by your last letter.

Things are moving busily for me. I was able to photograph the Vietnam Refugees at Camp Pendleton for a local newspaper and I've finished a Student Health Handbook for San Diego State that will be printed for the Fall 1975 semester.

So I'm pushing foward in many respects. In spite of the lack of proper lab facilities (working at Cal Tech really spoiled me) I'm able to experiment more and more. My personal work is beginning to get more and more abstract as I am beginning to open myself more and more to the invisible worlds, such as imagination, fantasy and dreams.

The fortunate thing is that more work and results of research work are being released to the public and therefore more information is available for me to study and compile and eventually construct into a coherent whole.

So I've read some really exciting material this year. There is one book that comes to my mind that you really would enjoy reading. And it comes in paperback: Carl Jung's Memories, Reflections, Dreams. This is the autobiography of a man who spent his lifetime approaching and attempting to understand the unconscious sector of mankind. I feel you would particularly enjoy his descriptions of his travels around the world. He edited another beautiful book called Man and His Symbols. A lot of his work has been inspirational to me and helpful in an encouraging way for me to continue my search for ways to express my feelings about the world.

So, overall, I must say photography has taught and is continuing to teach me a lot about life and in this result, it has been extremely enriching.

June 3, 1975

Dear Mother,

I've received both your letters and I was particularly touched by your last letter.

Things are moving busily for me. I was able to photograph the Vietnam Refugees at Camp Pendleton for a local newspaper and I've finished a <u>Student Health Handbook</u> for San Diego State that will be printed for the Fall 1975 semester.

So I'm pushing forward in many respects. In spite of the lack of proper lab facilities (working at Cal Tech really spoiled me) I'm able to experiment more and more. My personal work is beginning to get more and more abstract as I am beginning to open myself more and more to the invisible worlds, such as imagination, fantasy and dreams.

The fortunate thing is that more work and results of research work are being released to the public and therefore more information is available for me to study and compile and eventually construct into a coherent whole.

So I've read some really exciting material this year. There is one book that comes to my mind that you really would enjoy reading. And it comes in paperback: Carl Jung's <u>Memories, Reflections, Dreams.</u> This is the autobiography of a man who spent his lifetime approaching and attempting to understand the unconscious sector of mankind. I feel you would particularly enjoy his descriptions of his travels around the world. He edited another beautiful book called <u>Man and His Symbols.</u> A lot of his work has been inspirational to me and helpful in an encouraging way for me to continue my search for ways to express my feelings about

939 Burns Court
San Diego, California 92113

Mrs. Fred Parrott
3520 Delano Street
Houston Texas 77004

the world.

So, overall, I must say photography has taught and is continuing to teach me a lot about life and in this result, it has been extremely enriching. I can understand your first experience with a photography class. It can put you off, hearing so many unfamiliar terms. But If you can persist, going at your own pace, it would be very soon that you could see improvement on your own. Practice makes perfect, you know well I'm sure!

I have not made arrangements for a room because hotels want to know a specific date. So when you find out exactly when you are coming, please let me know and I can place a reservation. What kinds of things would you be interested in doing here in San Diego? Is there anything special you would like to do?

Well, again, it was good to hear from you and to know that you are thinking good thoughts each day for everyone and your health is good.

God bless you,
Carroll

212

I can understand your first experience with a photography class. It can put you off, hearing so many unfamiliar terms. But If you can persist, going at your own pace, it would be very soon that you could see improvement on your own. Practice makes perfect, you know well I'm sure!

I have not made arrangements for a room because hotels want to know a specific date. So when you find out exactly when you are coming, please let me know and I can place a reservation. What kinds of things would you be interested in doing here in San Diego? Is there anything special you would like to do?

Well, again, it was good to hear from you and to know that you are thinking good thoughts each day for everyone and your health is good.

God bless you,
Carroll

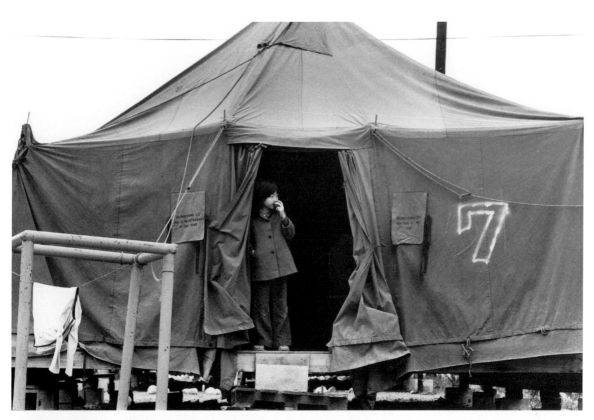

Part III

"End the War!"

Vietnam? No.
I wasn't there.
I was in the streets,
part of the public scream
spreading from my country
to the world—Toronto,
Mexico City, London, Paris,
and yes, even Saigon

Where sitting in the hot sun
Buddhist monks poured gasoline
on themselves to burn to death . . .

Ashes for their beloved Vietnamese soil

Part IV

"I will not seek re-election."

Together. It was our fighting,
protesting, losing, dying, our
rebelling that broke the
President who could no
longer lead us.

For Lyndon Baines Johnson's voice
no longer had spine as our boys
retreated back to our shores
to hide from the war we lost.

9/30 Dear Mother:

I would have written sooner, but things have proven so hectic.

I am still researching and learning about slide presentations for the tennis tournament. Also, I did a interview on Dizzie Gillispie, a jazz musician.

Currently, I'm studying color film and so I have to take pictures from the sunrise to the sunset to see how the sunlight effects the film from different angles. Basically, I am learning how to control the light based upon the light sensitivity of the film. Color film is far more fragile than black & white and so very tedious precautions must be taken to get a technically correct exposure. Also, each hour of the day conveys a certain mood — so the subject matter must match the mood. For example, why don't you take a walk in the morning as the sun rises and observe what's happening around you. Try to focus on images that capture the mood of the morning. Take into consideration the people you see, what they are doing and how the light from the sun is hitting them. Also, observe the trees, the flowers, the houses and the streets. Perhaps you can see how hard it is to capture the flavor of the moment. Also, remember that the film cannot see the way you see: it has a much weaker eyesight than you do. So you must remember at all times the film's limitations and make your mind act like a sieve and cancel out the many images that flood your mind that the film is unable to capture.

9/30/75

Dear Mother,

    I would have written sooner, but things have proven so hectic.

    I am still researching and learning about slide presentations for the tennis tournament. Also, I did a interview on Dizzie Gillespie, a jazz musician.

    Currently, I'm studying color film and so I have to take pictures from the sunrise to the sunset to see how the sunlight effects the film from different angles. Basically, I am learning how to control the light based upon the light sensitivity of the film. Color film is far more fragile than black & white and so very tedious precautions must be taken to get a technically correct exposure. Also, each hour of the day conveys a certain mood—so the subject matter must match the mood. For example, why don't you take a walk in the morning as the sun rises and observe what's happening around you. Try to focus on images that capture the mood of the morning. Take into consideration the people you see, what they are doing and how the light from the sun is hitting them. Also, observe the trees, the flowers, the houses and the streets. Perhaps you can see how hard it is to capture the flavor of the moment. Also remember that the film cannot see the way you see: it has a much weaker eyesight than you do. So you must remember at all times the film's limitations and make your mind act like a sieve and cancel out the many images that flood your mind that the film is unable to capture.

219

939 BURNS COURT
SAN DIEGO, CALIFORNIA 92113

Mrs. Mollie Parrott
3520 Delano Street
Houston, Texas 77004

So you learn to see with your eyes and also to see with your mind as it acts to translate the language of the film.

Also, I had to return to Camp Pendleton to interview and research more on the Vietnam Refugees. Security has gotten tighter up there and I'm sure that if I were just starting to photograph now that I would be unable to get in unless I had more press credentials.

Also, I've learned one basic rule in photography: SAVE EVERYTHING. So I find myself literally hidden in negatives, and piles of prints. This means I need some kind of proper filing system.

Other than that, we are all well here, trying to do the best we can. I hope all is good by you also. What do you think about all these crazy white women trying to kill the president? They say the last one was a spy for the FBI. She's here in San Diego. I sure would like to photograph her and interview her. They say she grew up in the same town with Charles Manson, the leader of the cult that the other girl who tried to kill Ford was a member of. At any rate, the whole scene is bizarre. Ronald Reagan doesn't want any other Republican in California but himself (smile).

Well, write and let me know how you are doing. I enjoy hearing from you although I don't write as often as you do.

Love, Carroll

So you learn to see with your eyes and also to see with your mind as it acts to translate the language of the film.

Also, I had to return to Camp Pendleton to interview and research more on the Vietnam Refugees. Security has gotten tighter up there and I'm sure that if I were just starting to photograph now that I would be unable to get in unless I had more press credentials.

Also, I've learned one basic rule in photography: SAVE EVERYTHING. So I find myself literally hidden in negatives, and piles of prints. This means I need some kind of proper filing system.

Other than that, we are all well here, trying to do the best we can. I hope all is good by you also. What do you think about all these crazy white women trying to kill the president? They say the last one was a spy for the FBI. She's here in San Diego. I sure would like to photograph her and interview her. They say she grew up in the same town with Charles Manson, the leader of the cult that the other girl who tried to kill Ford was a member of. At any rate, the whole scene is bizarre. Ronald Reagan doesn't want any other Republican in California but himself (smile).

Well, write and let me know how you are doing. I enjoy hearing from you although I don't write as often as you do.

love, Carroll

Part V

The Nam. The slap. What's Going On.
End the War! I will not seek re-election.

The wind strewing ashes
from Da Nang, South Vietnam.
to Camp Pendleton, California.

May 1975.

The first wave of Vietnamese,
Cambodian, and Hmong refugees
arrived here on the heels of our retreat.

I was there to meet them.
Walking among them,
I remembered everything.

That we ended the war.
That my camera was my
eye, ear, voice, my heart.
And that I became an artist the day
that Vietnam came home to me.

And the peace of God, which passeth all understanding,
shall keep your hearts and minds through Christ Jesus.
—Philippians 4:7

Chapter X **Peace beyond Understanding**

Creatively, Roberto Legato was the closest male counterpart I had. In my honest opinion, our only difference was that he was more talented than I. And he was born with even fewer financial and emotional resources than I was.

Lucinda, his ex-wife, described his condition in unsentimental terms: "Carroll," she would tell me with her matter-of-fact dryness, "his parents first met in a sleazy, disreputable bar. His father was Filipino and his mother Irish. Now everyone knows that Roberto is what you call a cheap combination." Then Lucinda would stop and sigh. "Anyway," she continued sadly, "neither parent ever really wanted Roberto." She would then hesitate, thinking, "He spent his entire life fighting against that lack of love."

We were kindred spirits. Roberto and I both lived under that dark cloud of feeling unwanted from birth; we both sought refuge in photography.

Visually, Roberto had an even more natural affinity for the photographic image than I did. He was also a former East Los Angeles gang banger with a fierce, broad streak of mean anger, and he could barely read or write. His broken nose and deep-down hungry eyes made his past history public in spite of his efforts to hide who he was. The only thing that prevented him from going straight from juvenile hall to prison was his love of the beauty in a well-made photograph and his almost insane drive to capture that essence. It was through manipulating the highlights and shadows of the photographic image that Roberto found a way to express the essence of the sweet and bitter contradictions layered inside himself.

He was truly a wild man, a completely out-of-control maverick bravely painting with light to capture precisely the stillness inside a moment when it was pregnant with a golden shimmer.

September 1971. Los Angeles Trade-Technical College. The grounds were teeming with a different kind of student: combat soldiers returning from Vietnam; women bus drivers who loved books; incredible artists who, out of practicality, chose to study dress design; LVNs who dreamed of a better life; and former high school students who just wanted a leg up in society—all sought deliverance in training for the blue-collar yet reputable trades that would pay more: Auto Repair, Metal Shop, Culinary Arts, Library Assistants, Appliance Repair, Fashion Design, and Commercial Photography.

Roberto and I met right after our first photography class let out. He was quicker than I. I was planning to go to lunch. He was like a groundhog moving toward cover. Immediately, he scoped out where every resource was hidden. From the first hour, he ascertained just how he was going to use every bit of this facility to expand his art. I spotted him out of the corner of my eye, using the dry-mount press over in the corner to put his photographs on poster board. I spied his photographs spilling out of the red-orange Agfa photographic paper box.

His work was stunning. It was brilliant. His fresh images pulled me over to him and made me ask to see his work. As he reluctantly pulled out his 11x14 color prints, I marveled at how his images jumped off the page, literally singing energy. Roberto was shy and self-effacing. Having barely gotten a G.E.D., he didn't understand that his pictures had a magnetic strength. He felt insecure about his work and himself. He worked as a printer in a custom-color laboratory off Sunset Boulevard. Though the job never paid a decent wage, it did allow him free time and supplies to print his own work. I felt akin to him. I was working full-time at night at Central Juvenile Hall as an attendant so that I could go to school. I felt I was too old and, besides, I was one of only a few women in the class. There were three Black women. The other two, Nalita and Ann, were years younger than I. Roberto and I were taking a serious chance on ourselves, and we were in the absolute wrong place to do so.

Years later he told me that he knew right away, on that first day, that we were going to be friends. He'd even made up his mind that Lucinda, his wife, and I were going to be friends as well. Because he was a womanizer, he decided to tell me early on not to tell Lucinda where he was most of the time. He was most likely somewhere trying to get into some pretty woman's panties. Almost immediately, he treated me like a sister. The really coincidental thing was that the couple lived within blocks of me on the edge of Echo Park, that part of town now immortalized in Alison Anders's film *Mi Vida Loca*. Lucinda and her mother used to shop at the Ranch Market on

Sunset and Echo Park. They taught me to make Chiles Rellenos and Spanish Rice. And in time, both of them and their families grew very dear to me.

What bound Roberto and me together so quickly was our mutual love of and respect for the art of photography. We both were inspired by the work of the same photographers—Henri Cartier-Bresson, Jerry Uelsmann, Duane Michals, and Marc Riboud. We were also seeing Riboud's radical left-wing documentaries on China at neighborhood meetings in Chinatown.

What also brought us together was that we were locked out of any access to this rarefied art world. At least three strikes ousted us from the real game: we weren't in it for the money, we both possessed a fierce motivation to create images that could sustain our aesthetic growth, and we didn't know how to love ourselves. In this indifferent, if not hostile, society, our vulnerability beat us down so deep into the ground that we almost disappeared. For we were pushing ourselves out of a ground that filled our eyes, noses, ears, and mouths to the point of almost smothering us to death. Roberto and I were both fighting like hell to stay alive.

We were truly desperate. And so we grabbed on to that tenuous thread of satisfaction that came from shaping a personal expression that was reflected in a well-executed still photograph. Almost simultaneously we had reached a plateau of frustration over our lack of technical skills. Our desire to improve drove us to search for the training that could improve our technique. And that's how we ended up, at the same time, in a very low-cost training program. We were both full of hopes of learning how to master film processing, lighting, all camera formats, and of gaining greater shooting experience. All would combine, we hoped, to bring us closer to being the skilled artists we so admired.

Instinctively, Roberto was always trying something different—in the darkroom, in the camera, in the shooting style. Innovation was simply part of his nature. He took to the surreal like a duck to water. I would watch him and learn from his joy. Roberto taught me to embrace the experimental, to play with it. I learned from him that the abstract is the heart, the underpinning, for the realistic.

Ultimately, his natural inclination toward the avant-garde opened me up to the work of Luis Buñuel. Although I had seen Buñuel's work while in college, in 1970 I saw a remarkable double bill of *The Battle of Algiers* and *Belle de Jour* at a now defunct art movie house on Wilshire Boulevard, close to MacArthur Park. The program was a magnificent cinematic juxtaposition that brought the political and the surreal together in such a way that it freed me to experience opposites as two different sides of the same coin. Buñuel opened me up to surrealism. It is as though the time span for consciousness is twenty-four hours. It extends from the waking hours of acute consciousness into the twilight subconscious awareness of the dream world. Reality is seeing inside the day, and the dream is the experience inside the sleep of night. Together, night and day construct an expanded view of

reality. For Roberto, and later for me, the abstract was a living part of reality, not some esoteric theory far removed from the practical.

Roberto taught me to use mirrors, double printing, color painted onto the print. His brilliant mind could have invented Photoshop. He taught me the pride needed to search for the underpinnings beyond what life served up as real. His journey into capturing the photographic essence encouraged me also to explore. Because of Roberto's total acceptance of the experimental, I continued to look at the force of the avant-garde in cinema: Dziga Vertov, Walther Ruttman, Jean Vigo, Joris

Ivens, Luis Buñuel. I also began to look at the experimental in photography: Man Ray, John Hartsfield, László Moholy-Nagy.

Years later while in film school, I met one of our former Trade-Tech classmates who had come from a family with money. Richard Arrindell had escaped from Trade-Tech to Pasadena's Art Center College of Design. After finishing his artistic training, he worked for advertising agencies and gained a certain level of commercial success.

"You guys should have gone on to the Art Center like I did," he admonished me as he and I walked through his well-appointed studio. "You two were so talented…" Shaking his head in despair, he talked about me to me as if I were not there. "What a waste," he continued wearily. He could, I thought, afford to blame us, the victims. He was, after all, white, with parents who both subsidized and eagerly supported his growth. I couldn't find a suitable answer to his glib, yet entirely logical assessment. Anyway, by then Richard was successful, Roberto was too long dead, and I was, at such a late age, so ashamed to be poor and still struggling in film school.

January 1976 was the beginning of America's national bicentennial celebration. Three deaths happened that month that had a tremendous impact on me. My mother died mysteriously in a fire in my brother's home. On the way back from her burial, my brother requested that the limousine driver turn on the radio. The men in the front seat of the limousine breathed a sigh of relief. The funeral was over. The Super Bowl football game was in full play. At some point during this game, it was announced that Paul Robeson had just died.

It was reported that Paul Robeson became increasingly withdrawn and depressed before his death. For years he was under house arrest in this, his native land. He was systematically denied access to work by this country's anti-Communist policies. His controlled isolation and inability to work are said to have broken his spirit. He was one of my heroes. At the time of the radio announcement, I remember I held my breath in fear because I'd always been told that death came in threes. The Super Bowl game continued.

Nalita Cassell met me a few days later at the Los Angeles airport. Nalita, Roberto, and I had been Trade-Tech classmates. Surprised, I was curious as to why she was there. And how she knew that I was coming in. Roberto was supposed to meet me; I was to stay at his place before going back to San Diego. I looked at her. Her face was tense and drawn. She looked back at me, straight into my eyes. Ignoring her hangdog look, I asked, "Where's Roberto?"

"Carroll, Roberto's dead," her calm words were like a strange, cool, hard slap on my face. When I had called Roberto three days before, he'd made it a point to tell me good-bye a second time. I didn't think it odd until Nalita told me he was dead. Then I realized he had meant good-bye forever.

230

The day he killed himself had been quite an ordinary Los Angeles kind of day. The rush-hour traffic on the Hollywood Freeway was thinning out. The sun was setting in the usual rush-hour smog. Roberto was walking on the sidewalk of a freeway overpass. People on the street near him say he was ranting and raving like a mad man. Lucinda told me later that he'd started smoking angel dust again and had become increasingly violent and depressed.

He stopped, looking over the bridge. He was observed watching the approach of a gas tanker. He quickly climbed up to the top of the short, sturdy metal bridge railing and aligned himself to the tanker's lane. He jumped quickly. The driver says he never saw anything until the impact of Roberto's body rocked the cab.

January 1976: First my mother, then Paul Robeson, and now Roberto.

My mother's death was entirely unexpected. She was in robust health and in full possession of all her faculties. An electrical fire broke out in the kitchen of my brother's home. My mother was trapped inside. She died from smoke inhalation. Her body was found with her mouth drawn open and her neck muscles strained as she had gasped for air during the fire. In my brother's home, the black smoke covered the walls, and its overpowering smell permeated her possessions for weeks after the funeral.

I have one letter from her, written months before her death. In it, she apologized to me and asked me to forgive her. At the time, I was in pain from her past cruelty and could not hear the plea behind her words. It has taken me twenty-five years to finally read beyond her words and feel a deep measure of sorrow for her. I am grateful that finally I can feel awe and compassion for her.

When I compare her letter to my brother written days before my birth with the one she wrote to me months before she died, I sense the maturing of a woman fighting against the brutality inflicted on her by a society that never knew she existed.

In that letter to my brother, she admonishes him for incorrectly spelling words. "You must learn to be better because you are a Negro," she sternly tells him. He was living in Chicago in 1943. "You are going to high school up North so that you can observe the white children. Take this opportunity to learn. You must compete with them for the rest of your life."

"Forgive me," she wrote, pleading with me in October 1975, three months before her death. "Only now do I know that words can hurt and damage. I did not know the power of words before. Now that I do, I am telling you that I am sincerely sorry for using my harsh and bitter words to destroy you."

In another one of her last letters, she encouraged me: "You say that you want to go to film school and that you don't have the money. I was the same way. . . ."

As I read, I remembered her telling me about her fiftieth class reunion at Alabama's Tuskegee Institute. How funny everyone looked. I recalled the warmth

231

in her smile when she told me that the class president who had run off with all the class graduation money had the nerve to return to the class reunion. Now no one even cared anymore, she told me. Everyone was just happy to be there to see who else was still alive. Time, she told me, had erased the bite in the memory. Her laughter echoed through my memories. I returned to her letter.

"But unlike you, Carroll Ann," she continued to write, "I had faith. You need to learn to have the same quality of faith. You must believe that God will guide you toward your goal. Believe with all your heart and you too shall succeed." She wrote me that she prayed every day for my well-being. Her prayers and her teachings have been effective. Today, I am a filmmaker and a college professor.

Sharon Grant-Henry visits me. Over thirty years ago, we met as young women engaged in making the world better. I was a photographer. She was a Black Muslim. We spend some of the time now reminiscing about the 1970s and how we are still working for peace and justice some twenty years later. I have just gotten out of storage some of the photographs I took during that time. Deborah Willis uses some of these photographs in her important book *Reflections in Black: A History of Black Photographers 1840 to the Present.* I show Sharon photographs from a rally oddly coproduced by Reverend Jim Jones and Waleed Muhammad. These pictures were taken in Los Angeles just months before the infamous Jonestown deaths. I ask her the name of one of the Nation of Islam men in the photograph.

After we put the photographs down, Sharon tells me that she's on to something. She'll be meeting soon with a psychologist who is documenting the emotional damage that slavery has done to African Americans. Sharon feels that this research will help to answer many questions about African Americans, including why we can be so cruel to each other. "Anytime a people are subjected to a sustained trauma, they are affected. Especially with multiple crosses to bear, such as slavery, prolonged poverty, racism, and lack of access to full citizenship. And when combined with the injustice that their slave labor has made the society that now locks them out, then they as a group suffer from the disease of traumatic stress syndrome." I ponder her words. Sharon believes that as a group our actions toward each other reflect this mass affliction.

When I think about my relationship to my family, I have to agree with her. Something went very wrong that killed the natural spirit of familial love between us. That something was both within and outside of our influence. So yes, certainly my family is responsible for their part, and I for mine. But how could any of us be better or do better when the poverty of spirit that caused us to damage each other also comes from our social, economic, and political condition? Our conversation reminds me of that old saying: "It's hard to be loving, kind, and generous when there's an elephant sitting on your face."

REFLECTIONS IN BLACK

A HISTORY OF
BLACK
PHOTOGRAPHERS
1840 TO THE PRESENT

Deborah Willis

W · W · Norton & Company · New York · London

Carroll Parrott Blue (b. 1943)
413. Kathleen Cleaver (b. 1945), civil rights activist, in San Francisco
C-print, ca. 1968
Courtesy of the photographer, San Diego, California

Carroll Parrott Blue (b. 1943)
414. Fannie Lou Hamer (1917–1977), civil
rights activist, in Berkeley
C-print, ca. 1967
Courtesy of the photographer, San Diego,
California

Carroll Parrott Blue (b. 1943)
415. Free Huey! Los Angeles Black Panther headquarters after shootout in December
C-print, 1969
Courtesy of the photographer, San Diego, California

In the 1970s, Sharon was in some kind of leadership role in the Nation of Islam and I was doing street photography. She helped arrange for me to videotape Louis Farrakhan's San Diego speech. I was just starting to learn about the moving image, and I had gotten the Farrakhan assignment through San Diego's public access channel. The photographs I took and the videos I made over thirty years ago are now historical documents. My photographs of Angela Davis, Kathleen Cleaver, and Fannie Lou Hamer are in Deborah Willis's book.

Most Black women's creative works are still invisible. One of the last things Aunt Henrietta Houston gave me before her death was a quilt made by my great-grandmother. She was a slave. Her quilt is over 150 years old. My father's grandmother, his mother, and his sisters all made quilts. Aunt Henrietta told me that "your great-grandmother was the best of all. She was a master quilt maker. She was known for miles around and made quilts for both the colored *and* the white people." My aunt always emphasized "and the white" because she believed colored people's actions had importance only when white people showed an interest.

I believe my great-grandmother's quilt is magical. I know that when I hurt inside, when I feel as though I cannot continue to endure, I lie under my great-grandmother's quilt and I cry. Oftentimes I fall asleep wrapped inside. In the morning when I awake, I always discover I have the strength and resolve to move on.

In one of many conversations we had as he lay dying, Marlon Riggs once told me that he envisioned his last film, *Black Is . . . Black Ain't,* as a quilt. "It is in this work that all kinds of Black people are brought together, sewn together by the experience of Blackness in America. When I leave, I'll provide the woven tapestry of all of us together. This is my gift to us." After his death, at his memorial service, I saw Faith Ringgold's quilt that she made for Marlon. When I experience the healing power of my great-grandmother's quilt on me, it all comes together somehow. The African American women's quilts are a way of marshaling together what we all bring to the table as Black people, whether we understand each contribution or not. It is the culmination of what the Bible calls "the peace that passeth all understanding."

Faith Ringgold has memorialized Black women's contribution to quilt making and storytelling through her art. She uses her quilts to tell her, and therefore our, stories. I asked Ms. Ringgold if I could use her work in this memoir. "Take it," she said, "I'll do what I can to help you." I'm honored that she understands that the "you" she describes is collective. That my mother's and my story are part of a very large quilt. The self that I express combines with all the other voices, and, blended, our voices become one sound. Quilt making is like gospel singing, which doesn't require that all the voices be classically trained or even audibly good. It is the sound of the many voices together that blended give witness to the richness of the story.

237

1 Being here with you Marlena, my darling daughter, is a true Moroccan holiday. I have just completed these paintings of four great men in our history. A gift to you, my love, to celebrate our women's courage. Had I been born a man I would have been just like them. It is their courage that will not allow me to be a victim, Marlena. Never be a victim, Marlena. Never never, Marlena.

2 When your father died I knew it would be too hard to keep you and Pierrot in Paris and pursue my art. Given a chance, I could secure a good life for all of us. The world doesn't need another black mother alone with her children. Still it was a great sacrifice to send you and Pierrot to live with Aunt Melissa in the States. "So are you saying, Mama, what you did with your life you did for me and Pierrot?"

3 Yes, Marlena. A mother can never forget her duty. It doesn't matter where you are, or who you are with, your heart is always with your children. "Mama, please do not go over the mother-daughter-Aunt Melissa argument again. I have heard it all my life and there is no resolution to it." But, Marlena, since you have never understood how I feel as a mother, how can I help but explain it to you again and again?

4 "Mama, like the men, you put your art first. None of them have anything on you. Frederick Douglass, Marcus Garvey, Malcolm X, Martin Luther King Jr., these are men who devoted their lives to our freedom. It is as if we are their children. You have done the same as an artist. I am your daughter, an artist, the beneficiary of your success. And so how can I blame you for not being there as a mother too?"

5 Marlena, do you know what the world would be like if women could do exactly as they please the way men do? "Mama, is there something you wanted to do with your life that you did not do?" Yes, my darling Marlena, I would have had children, become a celebrated artist but never married. "Yet you were married for only a few years before Papa died." Yes, but still I had such a sense of duty.

6 "It's as if you were never married, Mama. Papa died and Aunt Melissa raised us. Where was your duty?" Admit it, Marlena, you blame me for not being a bitter old woman who never got her chance. "Aunt Melissa is not a bitter old woman. On the contrary she is a powerful woman who took care of us and had her own catering business too and we have never had a problem with this." Yes, but that is only because Aunt Melissa is your aunt and I am your mother.

7 "You are a mother because you carried Pierrot and I in your belly for nine months? Was that your duty Mama? Is there a way for you to live in this world without guilt?" Yes, Marlena, I could have sacrificed my art for motherhood and had anger instead of guilt. But who wants to be an angry old woman?

Moroccan Holiday
(The French Collection Part II: #12)
Faith Ringgold

8 Marlena I want you to know there is a heavy price to pay for being a black woman. For one thing no one ever expects you to know anything, to have anything, or to be anything. So you must focus on your dreams and never, never let go. On the other hand there are white people whose feet never touch the ground. Do you sometime wonder what it is like to have their good fortune, freedom, success, happiness and a send of duty too?

9 "No Mama. I find it difficult to fathom the lives of white people, especially those whose feet don't touch the ground. I only know I really want to be an artist, but if I marry and have children I will try hard also to be a wife and mother. And if I do it wrong, I'll face up to it. No matter what I do, I hope I won't feel guilty and spend my life in denial."

10 What's a mother to do, Marlena? "Face the facts and move on, Mama." A mother is forever, Marlena, so there is no place for me to go. "What's a daughter to do, Mama?" You are the future, Marlena, *you move on* and try not to repeat the past. "None of us wants to be like our mother, Mama, yet many of us probably will be."

11 The world wants daughter to surpass mother, but why must we compete, Marlena? Why must we make a winner of daughter and a loser of mother? Can't we have a team, a sisterhood maybe? Motherhood should be a noble cause not a thankless duty. But we know if it is done right, it is wrong, and if it is done wrong that is wrong too. Motherhood is too often a trap, an excuse women have for giving up their lives to others.

12 Fatherhood is a noble cause because men are leaders and therefore can father the world, not just their brood. We need to rewrite the book of life to make men the mothers and women the fathers. That alone would end our mother-daughter debate. We would be too busy solving problems of war, world hunger, disease and ignorance to continue this futile women's war.

13 "You not only feel guilt but anger too, Mama. You are guilty because you gave up motherhood for art, and you are angry because despite the fact that you have lived your life exactly as you pleased, you still can't have the power of men. You want it all, Mama, and what's more you deserve it. Pierrot and I are proud of you, Mama. We love you and we know you love us."

14 "In your way you have nurtured and protected us and given us the best kind of life. And you have not only shown me how to be a woman but an artist as well. It is wonderful to be with you for my first Moroccan holiday. However it is not just Douglass, Garvey, Malcolm and Martin who should be here with us, but Aunt Melissa also. She is our courage too, Mama. She is right up there with you and these men."

Traumatized and energized by the 1960s, I became a writer, documentary filmmaker, and still photographer. I wanted to tell personal stories that were about everyone.

The 1984 article "Lights, Camera…Affirmative Action" in *The Independent* magazine describes the kind of education I received at UCLA's Film School from 1976 to 1980. This independent, feminist, avant-garde, and Third World cinema training was unusual in its day. It came about in 1968 as the result of UCLA students using effective grassroots agitation to bring about a change in that university's policies. Through the combined efforts of its Asian, African, Latino, and Native American students and scattered faculty, UCLA's Ethno-Communications program came into being. In 1976, I came in on the tail end of this program. It seemed to be over before I left in 1980. Fortunately, Robert Nakamura, one of the original student founders and now a UCLA professor, is continuing the Ethno-Communications tradition in UCLA's Asian American studies program. Bob was my teacher in photography and film. Still reinventing himself, he is also my mentor.

So is Mandy Richardson, my paternal great-grandmother, whom I never met. She was a master quilt maker who took cast-off patches of cloth and created beautiful covers that also warmed her children's bodies on cold Louisiana nights. I slept under one of her magical quilts, one she made in the late nineteenth century. I knew her through her quilt, my only family heirloom for a short time.

On March 25, 2002 my great grandmother's quilt was stolen due to the United Parcel Service's procedural mishandling of it during shipping. UPS representatives later informed me that her quilt never left San Diego's airport. Tragically and ironically it, according to them, ended up in an unknown San Diego landfill. This was an irreplaceable cultural loss, for so few handmade nineteenth-century quilts by African American slaves have survived. As a metaphor, the loss reflects how our country treats the powerless.

And my mother? My mother was a different kind of quilt maker. She quilted people together to fight for civil rights for all Americans. Her successful community activism helped to create the Houston, Texas, we know today.

I too have inherited the African American woman's treasured ability to make something out of nothing. I quilt together images and words to teach, make films, photographs, books, and digital media.

For our story is one of many African American women's stories tucked inside the twentieth century. I compare our journey—that of our women—to the history of America's Black soldiers, who are so devalued in the face of their courage. Their persistence, in spite of this country's remarkable hostility to their willingness to die for it, is legendary. They have placed their lives on the line to free a country that denies them and protect a people who scorn them.

In 1770, our country's patriots revolted against British corporate authority. The subsequent Boston Massacre sparked this nation's beginning. Crispus Attucks, a runaway slave, led the patriot's charge. He was the first American killed for this country's freedom. Midway through the Revolutionary War, one-third of our Continental Army was Black. Since the Revolution, African Americans have fought in every American war except the 1846–1848 Mexican War. Our soldiers' valor, ever-present during our simultaneous negotiation through a master-slave-parent-child relationship, is at the heart of what we, as the United States of America, will become. Ours is a complex journey. We, who created this country to end corporate abuse, have become the world's greatest corporate abusers.

There is more to this story. Today in the twenty-first century, all races from around the world people the United States of America. What fruit will our combined interpretations of the American dream bring to bear?

Lights, Camera...
Affirmative Action

It is ironic that Hollywood has of late become enamored with the portrayal of 60's rebels now grown up—as if to prove the industry mill can swallow any social convulsion and spit it out pasteurized. But the media itself was not shielded from the times, as Third World and progressive peoples demanded—and won—not only a presence within it but a redefinition of its form and content.

The Ethno-Communications program, which began in 1968 at the University of California at Los Angeles (UCLA), was one catalyst to that movement. As an affirmative action program Ethno-Communications opened the door to Asian American, Black, Chicano and Native American students in significant numbers for the first time. As a film training program it went far beyond the traditions of form-conscious but conscience-less preparation for the industry.

"The Ethno-Communications students were trying to find leaders in their community—like political leaders, or Chicano artists—and make films about them," explained Sylvia Morales, who is currently the executive director of the Latino Program Consortium and the producer of *Los Lobos: A Time to Dance*. In her first year at UCLA prior to the Ethno Program, Morales was the only Chicana in the entire film department and, she recalls, "The non-color students were involved with films concerning relationships, personal films. But for us there was a sense of urgency, so we set aside our desire to make personal films in order to make ones which reflected our communities."

These students were not alone in their challenge to the status quo. The independent film movement was beginning to take shape at the time, and many Ethno alumni went on to join its ranks. The films produced since, with a strong commitment to the visual articulation of their people's history, have their moorings in the spirit which infused the Ethno program.

Prominent among the Ethno graduates are Asian American and Chicano independent producers who have remained in the Los Angeles area, home to both the nation's largest Asian and Chicano communities and the movie industry. The way in which the Ethno-Communications program changed the color of independent filmmaking, the success of its graduates and their ongoing work within their own communities are all an antidote to present-day attacks on affirmative action programs.

BEFORE ETHNO

1968 at the UCLA film department: Francis Ford Coppola had just completed his MFA. There were two Chicanos in the graduate and undergraduate programs combined with a handful of other minority students. If the media industry was a bastion of the status quo, then film schools trained its palace guard. In 1968, film studies at UCLA was as it had always been.

Elsewhere on campus and across the country, minority students were organizing with demands for affirmative action and ethnic studies and agitating against the Vietnam war. At UCLA, Campbell Hall was transformed into the left-American equivalent of the Harvard Center for International Affairs, housing Afro-American, Asian American, Chicano and Indian studies. And in that same year the new political realities hit the film school full gale.

Moctezuma Esparza is the executive producer of *The Ballad of Gregorio Cortez*, a three-hour indie feature about a legendary Mexican hero. In 1968 Esparza was a history student and organizer active in the founding of UCLA's Moviemento Estudiantil Chicano de Aztlan (MECHA). He was asked by Elyseo Taylor, the only Black (and only minority) professor on the faculty of the film department, to join the newly-formed Media Urban Crisis Committee (MUCC). With a dozen other minority students as well as sympathetic faculty such as white profesor John Young, the MUCC group, dubbed the "Mother Muccers," was organized.

The original 13 Muccers staged sit-ins and protests to successfully agitate for affirmative action in the film department, resulting in the formation of the pilot program for Ethno-Communications which established the program's basic structure. According to Esparza, the curriculum was modeled after the department's existing course of instruction. Each student produced a short S-8 and 16mm film, followed by a thesis film. Some additional workshops or seminars were established in Third World aesthetics and community-related issues. But the singularity of Ethno's curriculum lay in the types of films produced which, in turn, reflected the program's philosophy.

"Ethno-Communications gave them [Black students] a sense of purpose because the film department lacked structure," explained Black filmmaker Charles Burnett (*My Brother's Wedding, Killer of Sheep*) who was a teaching assistant in the progam. "Ethno-Communications had a definite purpose—to demystify filmmaking and get it out to the Black community, to get stories about Black people on film."

The essentially political orientation of the Ethno program was evident in the film *Requiem 29*, a major production of the pilot group (along with teaching assistant David Garcia). The 31-minute film documents the anti-war Chicano Moratorium of August 29, 1970 in East Los Angeles, and the subsequent inquest which implicated Los Angeles police in the shooting of reporter Ruben Salazar.

MOTHER MUCCERS GO FORTH AND MULTIPLY

As Native American filmmaker Sandy Osawa recalls the heady times, "You could really feel the presence of minorities on campus; I became aware of minority and media issues." Osawa quit her job to join the Ethno program. She now runs Upstream Productions, an independent video and graphic arts company with her husband Yasu, another Ethno graduate.

The original 13 students made films together and agitated together. One of their key victories was pushing an admissions quota policy through the student-faculty senate. According to Esparza, who was appointed to the body, the new policy mandated that 25% of all entrants to the undergraduate and graduate film programs should be from minority groups. Said Burnett of the affirmative action policy, "I thought it was absolutely necessary to set up a quota system because no one [at UCLA] took the responsibility of getting minorities into the program. To be quite honest, no one gave a damn." Burnett had been one of four Black Americans in the film program for the two years prior to Ethno-Communications. The "Mother Muccers" became active in recruiting succeeding classes, beginning with the 1970 entrants who constituted the first full Ethno program.

THE MOVEMENT IS THE MESSAGE

Ethno students were recruited from within UCLA and other area colleges, as well as from local communities. The recruitment and involvement of Asian American students is a history in itself. Asian Americans in the original 13 group—such as Betty Chen, Danny Kwan and Brian Maeda, all of whom continued in filmmaking—cooperated with the UCLA Asian American Studies Center to find candidates from within the Asian American community. Recruitees were found in interconnected movement organizations such as the anti-war community newspaper *Gidra*, the Asian American Student Alliance, and the "community college" which had been established during the summer of 1969 by future Ethno student Robert Nakamura, now a professor in the film department, and several other community professionals. Classmates Duane Kubo, Steven Tatsukawa and Eddie Wong would later join Nakamura to form the nucleus of Visual Communications, an Asian American production cooperative.

The Ethno program became the training ground for extending the movement work and

social concerns of its students. Tatsukawa remembers a special production class which was put together to "hit the road for a few weeks in California" to study location work. The Black Panthers in San Francisco, agricultural workers in the central California Loc region, Chicano Studies at Berkeley, and the Bay Area Native American Center were subjects of the workshop projects. Tatsukawa

Larry Clark's *Passing Through*, an early Ethno-Communications film, was acclaimed in Moscow.

says, "These visits stimulated films. The Loc footage became a Visual Communications film on Asian American farmworkers in the Delta entitled *Pieces of a Dream*."

Like *Requiem 29*, which won a Bronze Medal at the Atlanta International Film Festival, several early and significant Third World films came out of the program. Black filmmaker Larry Clark's *Passing Through* won the Grand Prize at the Moscow International Film Festival. Nakamura's *Manzanar* and Wong's *Wong Sinsaang* were widely distributed as Visual Communications' initial film repertoire. Nakamura recalls, "One of the most memorable things is Project 1, your first complete film on Super-8. After we completed it we put together a show, 'View from the Third World,' with about 50 short films. The Chicanos did things on the riots in the 60's, the Asian Americans did the [internment] camps—it's one of the best programs I've ever attended of Third World films. They were rough but they had a lot of guts."

Ethno films generated a mixed reception from white faculty and students. "Luis Ruiz did a real nice film that angered the whole faculty," Nakamura remembers. "It started out in English but after the two kids went into the house the rest of it was in Spanish."

Because of their close working bonds the Ethno students often had little contact with either white students or affluent foreign-born Third World students. "I think the [American-born] Third World students in Ethno hung out together, and for the most part were not included in the overall film program," explained Kubo. "During screenings at the end of the quarter I remember pitched battles between Third World and white students over content,

impact of the film, the way it was shot—almost everything. There were even a few fist fights in the middle of screenings."

But according to Morales, "It was those times. Everyone took a hard line—people were intolerant. All of the films were always attacked." Morales encountered contradictions within Ethno itself. "I found sexism in my own group," she recalls. Years later, when she returned to UCLA as a graduate student, she produced *Chicana*, a widely distributed and unprecedented film about the history of Mexican American women.

THE END OF ETHNO

Despite the fire of its first years, by 1973 Ethno began to fade. "It became a bad environment," according to Burnett. "No one in the University really wanted it. With Elyseo Taylor it was just like the Jesse Jackson thing in Syria: everyone hoped it would fail." The thread of disapproval remained throughout the program's lifetime, and it never received the concrete support necessary to make it last.

Nakamura remembers that there was a lot of criticism, the beginning of the anti-affirmative action backlash which eventually hit many such programs. "There was a certain amount of resentment on the part of other elements in the film department because some academic waivers were permitted [to Ethno students] and the unversity-wide Graduate Advancement program provided financial aid to minorities."

Unlike some other affirmative action projects, UCLA offered Ethno-Communications no special resources, with the exception of the commitment of faculty time and additional equipment access. Nakamura remembers more significant support as coming from Third World study centers in Campbell Hall. "We'd be able to get work study or graduate research assistantships through the centers to pay for school. Otherwise UCLA didn't put any money out; the program was just a big recruiting effort."

But Ethno-Communications was something more than that. It was a direct challenge to the status quo and traditions of the industry's concept of film training. According to Kubo, "David Garcia and other advisors to Ethno were constantly under fire from the rest of the faculty to produce competent filmmakers, as opposed to political activists."

Along with the lack of university support, internal problems and the increasingly conservative political climate were cited as contributing factors in Ethno's demise. John Rier (*Black Images from the Screen, There's a Mural I Know*), a Black filmmaker who entered the film department on the last leg of the program, echoes the sentiment of Ethno alumni that the students, too, had changed. "We had people who came in as individuals—students who came there to make it in Hollywood, unaware that there had been a struggle and a battle to even have Third World students [in the UCLA film program]."

As the Ethno program dissipated, a Third

World Film Students Organization was formed to lobby for maintaining Third World admissions and programs. A Chicano Cinema Coalition was also established, involving UCLA film students with Chicanos in the industry. But, according to Ruiz, that formation eventually petered out because post-Ethno students "didn't have to struggle like Ethno-Communications students did. So they didn't appreciate the struggle of Ethno-Communications."

THE ENTHO IMPACT

Since Ethno, the presence of Third World students in the film department has never been as extensive. But whereas Ethno students emerged in a relative vacuum, aspiring filmmakers since then enjoy the existence of a prolific, working Third World film community. Ethno alumni have been central to building that movement and forging that community.

Ethno alumni pioneered a minority presence in independent filmmaking and public television programming. Both Chicano and Asian American Ethno graduates have been active in founding and organizing the Latino Consortium and the National Asian American Telecommunication Association.

In 1975 Sandy Osawa wrote and produced television's first Native American series, consisting of ten 30-minute segments for KNBC-TV, Los Angeles. After leaving UCLA Luis Garza got a job at KABC-TV in Los Angeles as the producer of "Unidos," which became "Reflexiones," and hired a number of Ethno alumni. According to Ruiz, "the 'Reflexiones' group started television's magazine format. We didn't know video so we talked them into giving us film, so we'd go out into the [Chicano] community and do 30-minute pieces." Ruiz, Morales, Esparza and Francisco Martinez are among the Chicano alumni who have remained active in the production of documentaries about their communities.

What happened to the Black Ethno students? Ethiopian filmmaker Haile Gerima (*Bush Mama, Harvest 3,000 Years*), who was a UCLA film student at the time, says, "Asian Americans were more organized. The Blacks tried to organize like that but were not as successful, although people like Larry Clark did have direct links to the Black community. The Blacks seemed more interested in going into the industry, and that's where a number of them that I knew are now." Unlike the Black Ethno students, most of the Asian Americans went on to become independents.

Visual Communications, the oldest and most prolific of Asian American production entities, also has its roots in the Ethno program. Ten years after entering the program a number of Ethno alumni were key personnel on its landmark production *Hito Hata: Raise the Banner*, the first Asian American feature ever produced. Former Ethno students included executive producer Tatsukawa and co-directors Nakamura and Kubo. Working cooperatively in Visual Communications, they and other Ethno students had already produced over a dozen films and tapes about Asian Americans. "Ethno-Communications is what Visual Communications had become," explained Kubo. "It's what we thought we in the Asian American community could do with media."

Thus the true measure of Ethno-Communications' impact goes beyond the number of filmmakers it trained, the hours of programming produced or awards won. Ethno challenged the basic premise of industry training, and many of its alumni have never lost that spirit. Whereas the media, in its racism and neglect, has traditionally been anathema to Third World people, here, for once, Third World people had the skills and a voice. ∎

Wed night 4-9-75

My dear Daughter,

I am so glad to have your address so I can write you when I get the urge. This letter comes to try to reassure you that I love you and want you with all of my heart. I have asked God to bring us together; but God requires that we must want to come together. You need not feel alone in this world for your mother longs to see you, to be closely related and to be all a mother can be, but both of us must want to. I wish you could believe me and accept me. Forget the pass and come back to me

Life is so short, days, months and years pass so rapidly — The game will soon be over for me — I hate to think that this life will end without you. I will do anything, I will give anything just to have you. I have missed you so much during these years since you have been away. Please come back and let's have a good mother daughter relationship

Here's hoping and praying that that you can bring yourself to believe and accept me.

Love,
Mother

I wrote this after I had called many times Mary Lee had told me that you had said you felt so alone. She gave me your number and I started calling to try to reassure you that you were not alone

Wed. night 4-9-75

My dear Daughter,

   I am so glad to have your address so I can write you when I get the urge. This letter comes to try to reassure you that I love you and want you with all of my heart.
   I have asked God to bring us together, but God requires that we must want to come together. You need not feel alone in this world for your mother longs to see you, to be closely related and to be all a mother can be, but both of us must want to. I wish you could believe me and accept me. Forget the pass and come back to me. Life is so short, days, months and years pass so rapidly—the game will soon be over for me—I hate to think that this life will end without you. I will do any-thing, I will give anything just to have you. I have missed you so much during these years since you have been away. Please come back and let's have a good mother daughter relationship. Here's hoping and praying that that you can bring yourself to believe and accept me.

247

   Love,
   Mother

   I wrote this after I had called many times. Mary Lee had told me that you had said you felt so alone. She gave me your number and I started calling to try to reassure you that you were not alone.

Mrs. Mollie Carroll Parrott

Chapter XI **Mrs. Mollie Carroll Parrott**

I open my eyes and turn around. All of a sudden I discover I'm in a room of golden yellow walls. I'm mystified, but there's something incredibly familiar here. I sit up to find that I'm in my childhood bedroom. Had I been sleeping? Why am I here?

Outside I hear a gentle breeze. The tree leaves are rustling. The shadows from these waving branches holding fluttering leaves fall at an angle on the window screens. Then I remember. I'm home because she's dead. Have I overslept and missed my mother's funeral? I am frowning so hard it hurts. I sit up in a daze, struggling to sort things out.

Suddenly, the phone rings. I move toward the sound only to discover that there's no phone in this room. I keep searching because the sound is so very close. It's hard to believe it's not nearby.

I turn again toward the ringing. But now I'm lying down again. And everything that was before me is all gone. Quick, just like that. I find myself in San Diego, California. Yes, it is still morning. But the light outside my window is different. More white and washed out. And my phone really is ringing. I sit on the edge of my bed. Was I just dreaming? It was all so vivid and real. Too Real.

The ringing persists. I answer the phone. My brother tells me that my mother is dead. I am not at all surprised. I quickly realize and accept that when my phone rang, I had just come back from her funeral.

Both of my parents revealed themselves to me as they were dying. My sightings of them were strangely impersonal. There were no actual farewells, so to speak. No personal messages, no final words of wisdom. Just their distinct presence during a passing moment when they were traveling past me on their way to somewhere else. In my father's case, it was in the jolting sound of his "Hello," a greeting that quickly faded, decaying like a distant echo. With my mother, had it actually happened or was it when I was experiencing my dream of her funeral? And my dream just happened to come to pass on the morning of her death.

When I heard about my mother's death, I had mixed feelings. I sensed myself fluctuating between an intellectual sense of loss and a more odd and secret sense of relief. The relief was pretty concretely justified. There had been quite a few curious moments in the life of our relationship. The distance exhibited by my mother during a few telling moments finally led me to conclude that my mother never loved or even liked me. And that realization led to my ever increasing coldness toward her.

True, these moments served as wake-up calls. Ultimately, my coldness and her distance were instructive. I learned early on that I was on my own. Her stern yet consistent responses of "You figure it out" to many of my queries helped to teach me that I was never to expect support or help from her or anyone. But then there was the one time that she went too far.

My marriage was breaking up. I was in the midst of healing from a miscarriage when I asked my doctor why my body rejected the fetus. He told me to ask my mother if there was a history of "female problems" in my family. Fresh out of the hospital, I called her to inquire. I explained my situation and then asked her about our family medical history. Some of my relatives had told me that she had been pregnant after me and that she had not dealt with this pregnancy. So I called her to ask.

Even before the question, she sounded tense. She always seemed to cover her defensiveness with a steely tone of voice, haughty with pride. But after the question, she was downright frozen. She told me that she, unlike me, had a healthy body and that if something was wrong with me, it had absolutely nothing to do with her or the state of her body. Here again was another version of her standard "You figure it out."

Okay. This time I had information that allowed me to deflect her blame. Aware of family rumors, I asked if she had been pregnant after my birth. I wanted to know what happened to that child.

Her voice grew tighter, strident and snippy. "Yes," she snapped, she had gotten an abortion. "And that," she added, "was none of your business." Her attitude pained me. It was as if she disregarded that I was grieving the loss of my own child. And yet I persisted. I was determined to push down my sense of utter alienation. I let my curiosity take over. Why, I wondered out loud and directly to her, would she, a married woman, have an abortion? Her answer to my question was clear and unforgettable: "I killed that baby because I didn't want any more evil people like you being born into this world."

Time stopped. I absorbed the meaning of her statement. The words hit home. Dead straight aim: bull's-eye. It was her tone that stabbed me. Despair rammed itself deep into the most vulnerable part of my soul.

I paused. I remembered that when she was like this her words could hurt me so. She didn't hesitate; she was on a roll. She continued her angry accusations. I do remember that finally I stopped listening to her as she went on about how much trouble I'd given her, how she resented having a baby so late in life, and how good her life would have been if I hadn't been born. I was busy realizing how undeniable it was that my mother didn't love me. This thought kept crystallizing as a reality inside me.

I had lived inside her body as I transformed from an egg into a human being. But did she experience my growth inside her body as an event that could have created an emotional bond between us? Memories flooded in. I recalled my father telling me that after my birth she was so depressed that he had sent her away. And remembered that Aunt Birdie had laughingly said that my mother had been gone too long. That when she returned, I, as a baby, failed to recognize her as my mother. But her words marked the first time that I really began to believe that there was no hope. Something inside me died.

I was too numb to get mad or even cry. I remember being polite, patient, and even courteous. For once, I didn't challenge her mean-spiritedness. I was too overwhelmed with despair. I do remember that as we ended the telephone call, I quietly told her good-bye.

And I meant it. I planned never to see her again. And then I found out how remarkably easy it was to leave my family. I simply left town. And no one in my family tried to write to me or to find me. I was not at all surprised. For years I thought that I had been born unwanted. I just had never pushed hard enough to find out how true this was—until now. And so I disappeared.

In October 1975, I returned to Houston to see my mother. My primary goal was to look for some semblance of a peace between us. I brought my camera. In the mornings, I walked around my old neighborhood. I soon realized that everything in my childhood world was within walking distance of my parents' home, and that somehow everything in my line of vision then had blazed its imprint on what I was and what I would become.

Later, on a winter morning, I photographed it all: the morning sun hit me at an angle, drawing my shadow, as I recorded on film the places central to my youth. There was the railroad track that ran through my neighborhood. The steps of the

A SERVICE OF CHRISTIAN WORSHIP

IN MEMORY

OF

MOLLIE CARROLL PARROTT

Sunday, January 18, 1976 — 1:30 P. M.

St. John Missionary Baptist Church
2702 Dowling
Houston, Texas

The Reverend M. M. Malone, Pastor

LIFE CREED

To love someone more dearly every day.
To help a wandering child find his way.
To ponder o'er a noble thought and pray,
And smile when evening falls,
This is my task.
I've done my work.

LIFE EPITOME

Birthplace:	Halletsville, Texas
Parents:	The Reverend Andrew & Polly Carroll
Education:	Public schools of Halletsville, Texas; Old Colored High School, Houston, Texas, Tuskegee Institute, Wayne University, Prairie View College, Texas Southern University, University of Houston.
Marriage:	Dr. Fred D. Parrott, Sr. — December, 1924
Church Membership:	New Hope Baptist Church — St. John Baptist Church.
Occupation:	An invalued & committed volunteer & servant of mankind; a retired teacher - Halletsville Elementary School, Douglas Elementary, Eighth Ave. Elementary, Blackshear Elementary - HISD.
Affiliations:	Downtown YWCA - Bd. of Administration, Life Member; Blue Triangle YWCA - Bd. of Administration, Garden Club; Past Bd. Member VIPS - HISD; Women in Action; Church Women United; 1906 Art & Literary Club; City Association Federated Club; Charles A. George Dental Auxiliary; Retired Teachers; Harris County Democrats, Jack & Jills of Houston.
Life Departure:	Wednesday Morning, January 14, 1976 — Los Angeles, Calif.
Survivors:	Son, Dr. Fred D. Parrott, Jr., Los Angeles, California; daughter, Carroll Ann Parrott Blue, San Diego, California; many nieces, nephews, sisters-in-law, brothers-in-law, numerous friends.

young women's christian association of houston

metropolitan offices • 3515 allen parkway, 77019 • 523-6881

blue triangle branch
3005 mc gowen avenue 77004
224-0613

downtown branch
3515 allen parkway 77019
523-6881

cara root peden branch
11209 clematis lane 77035
723-4752

m. d. anderson – magnolia park branch
7305 navigation blvd. 77011
926-2601

spring branch – memorial
1102 campbell road 77055
468-1727

February 6, 1976

Mrs. Carroll Parrott Blue
c/o Dr. Fred Parrott
575 East Hardy Street
Englewood, CA 90301

Dear Mrs. Blue:

We continue to receive calls and condolences as more people hear
of your mother's death. We all miss her.

We thought you might like a copy of the comments of our president,
Mrs. Vickers, as well as to let you know we have received contributions
to the YWCA in Mrs. Parrott's name from the following persons -

Mr. and Mrs. Ben Blum
4306 Firestone, Houston, Texas 77035
Mr. Jack Cambron
P. O. Box 66883, Houston, Texas 77006
Dr. and Mrs. Benjamin D. Thompson
5655 Briar Drive, Houston, Texas 77056
Mrs. Julia Skarda
906 Bay Oaks Road, Houston, Texas 77008
Mrs. Edna T. Anderson
2404 Kipling, Houston, Texas 77098
Miss Thelma Mills
222 S. W. Harrison, Apt. 22-E, Portland, Oregon 97201
Mrs. Meda Levine
160 Birdsall, #49, Houston, Texas 77007
Mr. and Mrs. W. W. Terry
2534 Yorktown, #115, Houston, Texas 77027
Mr. and Mrs. F. G. Kitchen
3614 Brock, Houston, Texas 77023

Many contributions were specifically for YWCA memberships or camp schol-
for girls who are unable to afford them otherwise.

Anytime you are in Houston, we would love to have you drop by.

Sincerely,

Meda B. Levine
Executive Director

MBL:k

MEMBER YWCA OF U.S.A.

Mollie Parrott epitomized the YWCA.

"The Young Women's Christian Association of the United States
of America, a movement rooted in the Christian faith as known
in Jesus and nourished by the resources of that faith, seeks
to respond to the barrier-breaking love of God in this day.

The Association draws together into responsible membership
women and girls of diverse experiences and faiths, that
their lives may be open to new understanding and deeper
relationships and that together they may join in the struggle
for peace and justice, freedom and dignity for all people."

As President, on behalf of the Houston YWCA, I would like to express our
sense of loss at the death of Mollie Parrott.

A member of the Blue Triangle Branch Committee of Administration, the Downtown Branch Committee of Administration, the Metropolitan Board of Directors,
numerous internal committees which furnish research and information to the
staff and board, and as our representative to regional and National
meetings, her contribution to the Houston YWCA was immeasurable. She always
accepted responsibility for the task assigned to her; never waivered in the
courage of her convictions, yet was always open to another point of view.

As concerned as Mollie was with the service the Y brought to women and girls
in this community -- it didn't end there. She traveled all over the world,
studying the service the Y brought to women and girls in other cultures and
was very sensitive to the position of women and their needs in the global
sense. Her reports to us brought an insight and a broadened sense of our
YWCA purpose which we might not otherwise have had.

The Houston YWCA was indeed fortunate to have the benefit of her wise leadership over a span of so many years.

To assure that Mollie's influence will live on in the YWCA in a tangible and
visible way, and in response to the concern of many of her friends, the
Mollie Parrott Memorial Fund has been established in her memory.

Mollie's friendship, her beauty, both spiritual and physical, her kindness
and consideration, her warmth, her sense of humor, her intelligence were an
inspiration and a joy to us all.

How many lives this great woman must have touched! How many individuals
this great woman inspired by her work in the community of Houston (I didn't
say "black" community, for she worked in all segments of the larger
community.)

She believed in people. She believed in you and me, and I, like many
others, tried hard to justify her faith. She believed in the YWCA
perhaps because her life touched our organizational life, we can continue to
struggle for peace and justice, freedom and dignity for all people.

We will all miss her terribly.

Inga Vickers, President
Young Women's Christian Association of Houston, Texas
January 18, 1976

Houston Negro Hospital that led to the room where I was born. The church, the high school, and, finally, my parents' home. Inside this house sat my mother, with her family's portraits beside her. My photographic self-portrait ends here. In between are the streets, capturing the future in the form of the neighborhood children. Some of these young people were enthusiastically giving me Black Power salutes. This was a common practice among Black youth in the 1970s. No one sports that sign anymore.

On August 23, 1917, my mother watched how the Camp Logan mutiny froze Houston, Texas, into an entirely separate Black and white city for over fifty years. But change did occur. When I was born in 1943, it seemed to all of us that this arrangement was permanent. But by 1976, this country's bicentennial anniversary, Houston was finally moving toward integrated public spaces. All my mother's accomplishments as a community activist, knitted together with the history of all the others who participated in the struggle against injustice, helped to make this evolution happen. Mrs. Mollie Carroll Parrott spent a lifetime working with others to change an entire city. Houston, Texas, is now this nation's fourth largest city. It is a better place for everyone because of people like my mother.

How deep and pervasive are the unhealed wounds fostered by racism in this world? I don't know. But I can tell you that the insanity of it all in some way created a terrible loss in my own family. And it was this sense of loss abetted by racism that my mother's death brought home to me.

I continue to question the wisdom of our society's underlying values concerning race, sex, and class—especially when these values hold people down, people like a Mollie Carroll Parrott who are our invisible heroes, with so much to offer even when denied.

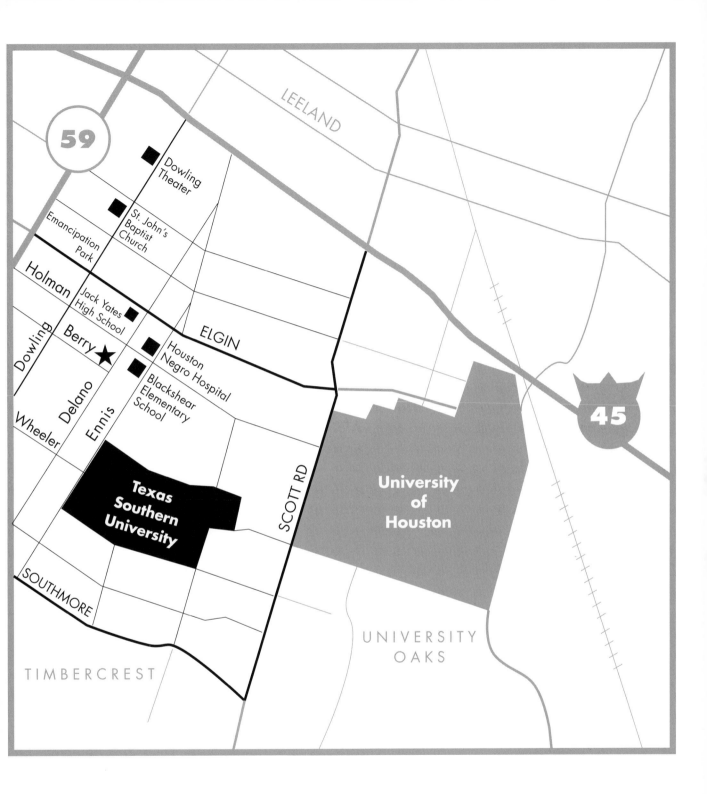

CHRIST THE HEAD
PROGRESSIVE NEW HOPE
BAPTIST CHURCH
REBUILT IN 1946 BY REV.
N.S. BROWN, A.B, BTH, D.D.
TRUSTEES
G. NORMAN   L. JONES
W.J. EDWARDS   P. ALLEN
W. ALIX   L.L. FOSTER
L. EVANS   M. SANFORD
C. THOMPSON   C.W. BELL
J.D. CLEVELAND
DEACONS
L. COOPER O.L. REYNOLDS
C. GORDON   M.C. CLAY
C. WHEAT   R. THOMAS
A. MOYE   A. CALLOWAY
REV. N.S. BROWN, PASTOR
SIS. L.M. RANDLE, CLERK
C.W. BELL, FIN. SEC'Y.
W.J. EDWARDS, TREAS.
CORNER STONE DONATED
BY J.E. BUCKLEY

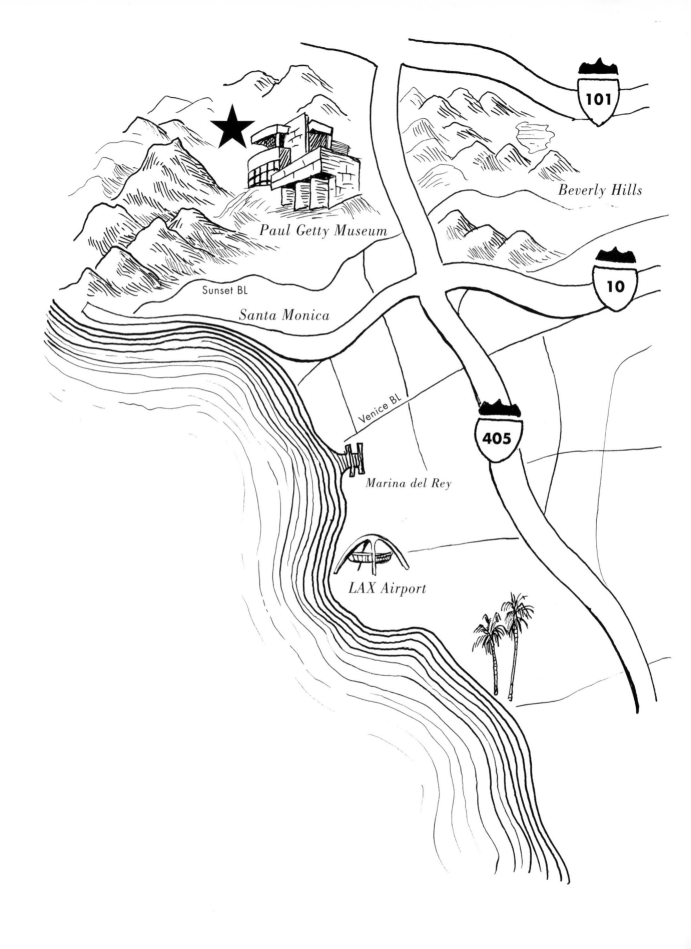

This vital connection between media and the economy's industrial core is a dominant feature of late-twentieth-century capitalism. TV provides the most spectacular means for transforming the audience into consumers. To obtain that audience is the holy grail of TV producers. When Dan Rather, the anchor of CBS News, along with other national anchors, was pulled out of Havana, where he was covering the Pope's visit, the reason was a juicier story—the president's latest sexual episode. Rather was quoted as saying, "I just didn't think it was practical to say no." *New York Times* TV columnist Walter Goodman put it this way: "The three masters of the media were not permitted by *their* masters to follow their better angels; our men in Havana had to follow that woman." 'It's about circulation and ratings,' Mr. Rather lamented. 'It's about competitive pressures.'"

—Herbert I. Schiller, on January 21, 1998, in *Living in the Number One Country: Reflections from a Critic of American Empire*

Chapter XII **blue@thegetty.january21.1998**

The natural beauty of the Los Angeles Basin comes through cleanest on a crisp, cold day after a winter rain storm. Soft yet steady, the rain washes the Southern California smog away. The air smells clean. The haze disappears. A veil of industrial waste is lifted. And the bright, clear rays of the dawning sun paint a cloudless sky pristine blue. This sky becomes an azure expanse that reigns over a shallow, wide valley bounded by a line of snow-capped mountains on the east and a glistening carpet of white, foam-capped ocean on the west.

On such mornings following gray days and black nights of heavy rains, I feel especially privileged, for I can behold the promise of a city that I have always loved. Los Angeles, the city of the angels. Suddenly, after the rain, every beautiful detail of this land's vastness reveals itself.

Wednesday, January 21, 1998. It is on such a day—coincidentally, my mother's birthday—that I drive up from San Diego to finally see the brand-new Getty Museum.

Although I have lived in San Diego for fourteen years and therefore call it home, I have never ever stopped longing for my version of Los Angeles. It is the only city in the world where I love to drive. As I wind my car through its streets and freeways, here and there cry echoes of my youth. Here, at Western and Adams, as stoplights blink at intersections, I am coming home from all-night parties. There, rushing past downtown on the Harbor Freeway, I'm on my way to punch that time clock at Juvie—Central Juvenile Hall—in East Los. Over there, on a lazy Sunday afternoon, I am following Sunset Boulevard from Olivera Street, this city's birthplace, "Bumping on Sunset" with Wes Montgomery's blaring guitar swinging on my car radio. Lazily, I slice across L.A.'s belly, continuing to follow Sunset to its end at the intersection of Pacific Palisades, at Sunset and Highway 101. There I gaze upon the grandeur of the Pacific Ocean. And years later, it's 6:00 P.M. and I'm cutting across Century City's rush-hour traffic to the lure of an all-night editing session at UCLA's Film School. As I drive, my memories of Los Angeles in the 1960s and 1970s stay fresh in the glimpses these streets provide me.

Wednesday, January 21, 1998. Today, I am on the same freeway as was O.J. Simpson's white Ford Bronco. I follow the path of his famous chase. My car radio is tuned to KPFK-FM. I'm listening to William Lee Brent, a former Black Panther, then an airplane hijacker, and now a fugitive living in Cuba. Considering himself a Cuban citizen now, he hasn't seen the United States in thirty years. Yet he speaks about our present condition with absolute clarity.

Immediately upon hearing the strength in his confident voice, I am filled with an unmistakable hunger for this kind of culture allowed in Los Angeles. It feeds me deep in my soul. I miss the music, the plays, the movies, the exhibitions, the ideas, and the energy so absent in my San Diego life. "San Diego is not a city," a friend reminded me once, "it is a military base." I keep forgetting the Gulf War was fought from here. Right now, because San Diego's culture doesn't honor the diversity in African American arts, I regret that I live there.

Getty Ctr. Dr. It's after ten in the morning. Soon after the Sunset Boulevard turnoff, I find this sign, the Getty Center Drive turnoff. I turn right and immediately I am in a massive line of waiting cars as hordes of people are being politely guided by men—primarily Black men in official guard uniforms—as they cross the streets. And there are the tour buses. Old people, young people, Japanese speaking Japanese, and Europeans speaking French and German. All these crowds are being escorted past my car, in long lines that surge forward in one direction through gates to trams that travel upward to the sky.

As I find my way from the seventh floor of an underground parking lot, I encounter eager, expectant tourists. Then there are those in uniforms: the Getty employees. What strikes me first is how proud these employees are. They exude pride in being a part of something special. What's more, most that I encounter this day will tell anyone who will listen that where they work is special. Before I board the tram that transports me to the top of this mountain, I have learned that the Getty cost one billion dollars to build, that there are 1,200 employees, that they are still hiring, that only a handful of Blacks work in any major positions, that the stone in all the buildings comes from Italy, that the crowds have appeared every single day since the Getty opened, and, finally, that this is *not* a museum, it is a campus.

As I leave the tram, I turn to look behind me. To my surprise, I have a view of the city I love. It is a panorama I have never seen before. Buildings and landmarks are situated differently than I have experienced them on the ground. When I travel east on Wilshire from Rodeo Drive in Beverly Hills, I get to downtown. Here, downtown is behind Beverly Hills, not next to it, as I have experienced driving down Wilshire. Perhaps Wilshire curves into a horseshoe shape?

I ask a guard for the employee entrance. I tell him that I know someone working here. He offers to take me there. On the way, I learn from him that employees get a discount on lunch food—10 percent. He opens the door of a building that has a long, wide corridor. I thank him and bid him good-bye. Inside, I pass a long wall on my right full of handprints cast in cement. I must appear puzzled. At least two passing employees volunteer that these handprints are from all the staff members present at the Getty's opening. As I walk past this huge mural I also see jewelry, photographs, sunglasses, and handwritten notes strangely sticking up out of this frozen concrete. I look up at the ceiling's enormous, exposed silver pipes. I realize I am inside a massive underside of what I can only describe as a city on top of a mountain. Later I find out that the Getty is a city built inside a mountain. But that's getting a bit ahead.

I am lunching with Rhodessa Jones, a very "en vogue" performance artist. We are Black women sitting in a sea of people and food. Rather than be distracted by the prevailing aura of being "in" with the "in-crowd," we have formed a secret pact to focus only on ourselves. To that end, we are having a funny, and at the same time, serious conversation about grandchildren and menopause: her grandchildren and our menopause. When we laugh much too loudly for the rarefied Getty atmosphere, heads turn politely at our hollering. Our "Black street" patois ("you go girl!"; "it ain't all that now…"; "what it is") slips in and out of our conversation on hot flashes, herbal remedies, and the seductive love of her grandbabies who call her "bab-boo," "Big Momma," and "Nana." Our laughter, intertwined with our slang, envelopes us like music. Its energy softly drapes around us. Relieved, we return from the pleasant courtyard to the interior of the temperature-controlled buildings. The sun shines in a way that highlights our weathered brown skins, for we are both becoming old women. Our words, our laughter, the tone of our voices, and the softness age renders on our bodies are weighed with memories that are at least a half-century old. For the time being, in this sea of civilized isolation, I feel my presence is justified.

Later, after lunch, I am alone. I walk through this city on a hill, this campus they call the Getty. I visit the galleries. Western art is at its finest and on exquisite display. The only glimmer that I am represented at all in this Getty worldview is through the work of the African-American woman photographer Carrie Mae Weems.

I photograph everything in my line of vision—the walls, the floors, the gardens, the crowds of people, the sky, the sun.

Monday, August 23, 1943. I can't really remember my birth, but I've heard the story so many times, of being slapped by the doctor who also cut my umbilical cord, that I clearly imagine I am seeing my first image. It is a bright ceiling light shining through a hazy foglike veil. What I do know is that on one of my later birthdays I awoke in anticipation of gifts, cake, ice cream, and celebration. Around the middle of the afternoon, it seemed certain no such activities were forthcoming. I remember asking my mother if there was going to be a proper birthday party for me that day.

"Why should there be a birthday party for you?" she asked me. Well, to my mind, this *was* my birthday. So, at first, her response took me aback. But then the rational calm in her tone of voice reassured me. "After all," she concluded, "it was I who suffered bringing you into this world. So you should give me a gift. In appreciation. For me giving you life, not the other way round." The clarity of logic in her argument must have blotted out any lingering doubt I might have been harboring. For many years after this conversation, I gave her gifts for my birthday.

Today, it is January 21, 1998. Near the end of the day, U.S. President Clinton will make his first appearance to counter his connection to Monica Lewinsky, to deny "a relationship with that woman." The Getty staff clusters around the one office television tuned to CNN. As I watch Clinton on the monitor, I reminisce. I realized that this is my mother's birthday. She would have turned ninety-eight years old today. What would my mother think of this man? It is twenty-two years after her death.

At the Getty, I experienced the luxury of viewing a Los Angeles never before available to me. I imagine access to this kind of leisure and atmosphere is available only to the very rich all of the time. There, surrounding me, is a circular view of the Pacific Ocean, Brentwood, Mount St. Mary's College, Westwood, Beverly Hills, downtown, South Los Angeles, East Los Angeles, the mountains, the sun, the crystal-clear blue sky. I am vaguely disturbed. There is a gnawing irritation inside me. I do not understand why.

I leave as the sun begins to set, casting a golden glow on all the buildings. A young man, another employee, waits next to me for the tram to arrive. And he talks to me with this irritating reverence in his voice. All these Getty employees transmit this enthusiasm and love of being in a unique place. He's reeling off even more new facts: "Right now we are standing on 2.5 million gallons of water underneath us. Literally, we're floating." He emphasizes this point by turning one finger down, toward the earth. He pauses for dramatic effect. When I ask why, he talks about earthquakes, hinting that some grandiose architectural design by the Getty will provide adequate prevention. For all that precious art I've just seen up there?

As for me, I'm thinking ahead. About my car parked seven stories underground. That I might be getting into my car when the San Andreas fault decides to stretch and have a tiny yawn. If that happens while I am opening my car door, then simultaneously I will be both flooded by an underground human-made lake and crushed by some intricately poured concrete. Besides, who would know? I'd forgotten to tell anyone where I was going. Just the thought of it all immediately throws me into deep contemplation.

My thoughts grow so loud they overtake my zealous guide's voice. But this young man doesn't hear my thoughts. Or see the fear growing in my eyes. Right now, he's busy pointing out Magic Johnson's hillside home across from us. As the tourists looking at us turn to see this former basketball player's domestic monument, I think about the billion dollars used to transform this mountain into a fortress with a floating moat for fine art, and I'm chilled.

Coming down on the tram, I see the five o'clock traffic crowd the freeway. The traffic gridlock brings me back to the present. With pride, I take advantage of my inside knowledge of Los Angeles streets. Turning down Sunset to Hilgard, I wind down over to Century City and then to La Cienega and Cadillac.

Now, on my way back to San Diego, I have to see Alden Kimbrough, who lives near L.A.'s tony Black development Fox Hills. Thirty-two years ago, he and I worked at Juvie as fellow probation officers. But that's not why I'm seeing him. In 1969, I was in the Bay area, occasionally photographing for the Black Panther Party newspaper. Alden, at the time, was collecting these papers. He's turned his collection into an archive. He has every copy of the papers. I am going to see them to find the papers that have my photographs.

The 1960s. I photographed every Panther rally, every rock concert, every protest march, every anti–Vietnam War demonstration, every People's Park event that I could. What brings me to Alden is Lee Lew Lee's documentary *All Power to the People*. Lee, a former Black Panther, has made a film on the rise and fall of the Panthers. When I first watched Lee's film, I discovered a rally with the late Fannie Lou Hamer speaking in the UC Berkeley quad. Déjà vu. I was there. I photographed that rally. I remember her blue dress and some of the faces in the crowd. I even have some of those photos. I wondered aloud to Lee about the ones I'd given to the Panther newspaper. Lee mentioned Alden Kimbrough as a historical resource. Immediately I remembered him because of his unique name.

So now I'm on my way to visit him. When we finally meet face-to-face, we speak of old acquaintances, people whose names are melted down somewhere in my reminiscences—forgotten old lovers, party buddies, supervisors, colleagues, and even some of the more remarkable, legendary juvenile prisoners.

During our conversation, the morning radio interview with Brent stays on my mind. I ask Alden about William Lee Brent. He goes through his box of old Pan-

265

DEATH OF A PAPER GOD

by Landon Williams

Since the beginning of time, man has been awed by the many so-called unexplainable and uncontrollable forces that make up the world we live in. The mysteries of life, death, fire, water, the stars and other natural phenomenon constantly challenges our reasoning from birth to the grave. In their endless search to find a meaning for life, some men turned away from the objective material world, rejected all their senses and began to seek the answers in the world of fantasy and spirits. The deceptive philosophy of idealism was born and the worship and belief in gods began. Since then everything conceivable has been worshipped as a god including evil. The early caveman felt that the fire that cooked his food, warmed his body and protected his cave from the beasts that roamed at night, was a god, and worshipped it as such. The ancient Greeks worshipped the sun god, Apollo, who they thought rode across the sky in a flaming chariot. During the course of human development the idea of a god has constantly changed with the values and morals of the society. Along with the development of these different gods, many different types of worship and religious practices came into being. To show reverence to their gods and to gain their good wishes and graces some people resorted to sacrifices and everything from corn and wine to human beings have been sacrificed by crazed idealists, in the names of so-called all powerful and all knowing gods. This useless waste of human lives is one of the tragedies of ancient human history, but with the ending of the dark ages and the coming of "civilization" this senseless slaughter, in the name of the gods, has become even more monsterous and barbaric. For worldly power and wealth, supposedly pious men have time and time again brought the world to the brink of destruction and all the while claimed to be following the wishes of some mystical, unseen, spiritual god.

UNDER THE SIGN OF THE CROSS

Around the 11th and 12th centuries, stories of the fabulous riches and beauty of the Moslem kingdoms of North Africa and the near east began to filter across Europe, which was just beginning to crawl out of the dark ages. There were tales of gold, silk, and diamonds beyond compare, cities of marble and streets of jewel. Up until that time the cities of the holy lands and Jerusalem were nothing but vague names in the Bible that no one in Europe had thought of as being real places for centuries. Soon, however, after the news of this wealth and untold riches reached Europe, the Pope of Rome got a divine vision and together with the greedy monarchs of Europe launched a "holy war" to save the holy lands. At the Pope's calling and in the name of God, tens of thousands of Christian knights rallied around the cross and rode off on the crusades. Those soldiers of God murdered, raped and plundered everything in their path. For the riches of this world those madmen who ruled Europe launched eight such crusades of holy wars that lasted 300 years and cost thousands upon thousands of lives including 50,000 children lost during the "children crusade" in 1212 A.D.

Cortez, the butcher, left from Spain in the 15th century and came to the new world, bringing with him all the advantages of European Christian society. He landed in Central America, planted the cross, knelt to pray, and then went about destroying and plundering a civilization that dated back hundreds and hundreds of years. The Aztec empire was sacked, the Inca Indians murdered, and their gold was blessed by the ever present priest who traveled with Cortez and sent back to fill the purses of the archaic rulers of Europe. As during the crusades, all this was done in the name of God. At one time the plunderers of the new world got so greedy until they threatened to plunge the monarchies of Spain and Portugal into war with each other over the booty. The situation was cooled however by the Pope when he, with God's graces, divided the world between these two powers. The church had its hand in many a filthy plot. During the Spanish Inquisition, the King of Spain with the help of religious fanatics in the church had thousands of persons sentenced to death and disposed of for not believing in the "true religion," the Catholic Church. In checking this shit out closely though, you begin to see it for what it really was -- another money making scheme of the rulers of Spain. It was simply a concentration of wealth, an elimination of competition. In the dungeons of Spain, the head of the family would be tortured until he "confessed" that he did not believe in the Catholic faith. Acts paralleled in their cruelty if not in their magnitude took place in America during the Puritan and Protestant directed Salem Witch Hunts. After the pseudotrial he would be branded atheist, guilty of heresy and his entire family would be sent to the executioner to be liquidated. Then all the property and wealth the family had would be turned over to the church and the state to be administered as the servants of God saw fit. The rulers of Spain lived high on the hog and ruled with an iron hand. The word of the monarchs and the church was law and they valued gold above human lives.

In 1492, Columbus sailed the blue looking for a trading route to the riches of India. Being a poor navigator he got lost and was lucky enough to stumble upon the Americas and thus saved himself and his crew from dying of thirst and starvation. Less than 130 years later in 1619, the first slaves were kidnapped from Africa and brought to America to begin to build the wealth that this country is based on. According to the crazed idealist preachers who justified it, the Africans had been damned by God and condemned to be forever slaves. What the good Christian slaveholding and the bourgeoisie classes of America did to the African slaves, while serving their God, is without a doubt history's most barbaric example of man's inhumanity to man. Over 50 million Africans were murdered in the course of the slave trade. In 1776, the bourgeoisie of America declared their independence from the monarch of England, King George and thus began the blood soaked 193 year old history of the most false God of them all, the American dollar.

BIRTH OF THE DO LLAR

Over the next 100 years of the American bourgeoisie under the guise of diving guidance, pushed their economic rule and exploitation all the way from the Atlantic Ocean on the east to the Pacific Ocean on the west. From the Canadian border to Mexico. Numerous treaties with the Indians were broken and the ruthless bourgeoisie murdered nearly all the original inhabitants of this land. From time to time, different areas of land were set aside as reservations for the Indians to live on and this lying, deceitful government made promises to leave those lands alone. As soon, however, as a way could be seen to make a profit off those lands, all the promises would be scrapped and the real meaning of this country's national motto, "In God We Trust," became crystal clear. More and more Indian land was stolen and plundered. The discovery of large deposits of gold in the hills spelled out the doom of not only the Indian domains, but also the doom of the Mexican possessions in North America. Built on a foundation made up of the blood, sweat and mangled bodies of black, red, brown, and white people the dream of the aspiring bourgeoisie class was realized. The American dollar soon had its place in the sun and its gold backing could be denied by no one. The dollar was stamped with the idealist phrase, "In God We Trust" and the American bourgeoisie worshipped and served the dollar like the early Greeks worshipped the sun god.

To further ensure the backing for the dollar and its economic growth, the U.S. went beyond its borders and the bourgeoisie forced the Monroe Doctrine on Latin America at the point of a gun. In books it is taught that the Monroe Doctrine was designed to protect South America from becoming European colonies. This is only a half truth, a deceptive bourgeoisie smoke screen that disappears when viewed objectively. It is true that the U.S. wanted to protect South America, but the protection was for the interest of the expanding U.S. bourgeoisie and not for the benefit of the workers and peasants who lived there.

Continued on page 21

"IT'S ONLY PAPER, AND IT'LL BURN"

E. CLEAVER MIN. OF INFO. B.P.P.

IN GOD WE TRUST

PEOPLE OF THE WORLD UNITE

LRW

LIBERATION
MEANS FREEDOM

What are revolutionaries? "Revolutionaries are changers." This response comes from the eager lips of the youngsters participating in the first liberation school sponsored by the Black Panther Party. The liberation school is the realization of point five of the ten point platform and program, that is, "We want education for our people that exposes the true nature of this decadent American society. We want education that teaches our true history and our role in the present-day society."

We recognize that education is only relevant when it teaches the art of survival. Our role in this society is to prepare ourselves and the masses for change. The change we want is within this decadent society. It's the implementation of the 10 point platform of the Vanguard Party. It's the destruction of the ruling class that oppresses and exploits the poor. It's the destruction of the avaricious businessman (the youth in the liberation school call him the "big, fat, businessman"). It's the destruction of the lying deceiving politicians, and most important of all, the destruction of the racist pigs that are running rampant in our communities.

Liberation schools will replace for the summer the Free Breakfast for School Children that was initiated in the beginning of this

youth, to guide them in their search for revolutionary truths and principles. Brunch and a well-balanced lunch is served daily. Three days of the week are spent in class. Thursday is Film day and Friday is set aside for field trips throughout the community. The 30th of June marked the opening of two additional schools in East Oakland, and Hunters Point in San Francisco, California. Additional programs are scheduled to begin in the very near future throughout the Bay Area and across the country.

The youth understand the struggle that's being waged in this society. It's evident by their eagerness to participate in the program. They understand that we're not fighting a race struggle, but in fact, a class struggle. They recognize the need for all oppressed people to unite against the forces that are making our lives unbearable. They're understanding manifests itself in their definitions, i.e. Revolution means Change; Revolutionaries are Changers; Liberation means Freedom and by their collective view of themselves as being part of a BIG FAMILY working, playing, and living together in the struggle. The beauty of socialism is seen through their daily practice while involving themselves in the program.

We call upon the people within the community

year and has since spread in chapters and branches of the party throughout the country. Liberation School is the second of the many socialistic and educational programs that will be implemented by the Black Panther Party to meet the needs of the people. The first program began Wednesday, June 25 at 9th and Hearst Streets in Berkeley, California. The program is a success with the maximum participation coming from the youth and volunteers throughout the community. The curriculum is designed to meet the needs of the

to join the Vanguard Party in putting forth the correct examples for our youth through their active participation in our liberation schools across this country.

Community Political Education classes will also be starting in the evening for adults. The education of the masses is primary to the Vanguard Party. People, take part in this revolutionary program to continue the struggle for freedom in this country."

ALL POWER TO THE PEOPLE!
ALL POWER TO THE YOUTH!

Panthers Valerie and Charlotte teach Children from Panther Paper.

Sister Valerie Pays Attention to Those Who Need It.

Fred tells the children about Huey P. Newton.

Children Have Opportunity for Self-Expression in Drawing Section.

Physical Education is Also Part of Liberation School.

Self - Expression and Collective Learning

Little "changers" listen up.

Marsha Has Always Been A Favorite With The Children.

Fred directs Outside Activities.

Panthers Have No Problem Getting Children To Concentrate.

ther papers and finds his photograph. I remember that brother! He was always behind Bobby Seale at rallies. Tall, thin, older brother with a mean look on his face. Yes, I recall his presence.

Then it's my turn to look. While I'm dipping into the box, I find one of the papers with my own photographs. It was my first photo essay, taken at one of the breakfast programs. I remember the school. I know the faces of these children. Those strong and serious Panther women. I remember Shirley Neeley and Erica Huggins, and all the other women I knew who worked hard, behind the scenes, for the party. Who loved the men. Who fixed the breakfasts. Who taught the children how to read. I smell the bacon cooking and hear them all singing "Black Is Beautiful, Free Huey!" with mouths full of food. Very poor children whose families didn't have enough food for them to eat in the morning. Chewing and singing. The black, white, and brown children. Then, I find the faces of the Panther men I'd seen and sometimes spoken to at the rallies. I discover the face of one brother I had photographed for this issue. It was the only photograph the Panthers had of him. I was the only one who had photographed him at this rally days before his death. This paper is dated August 23, 1969. It was printed on my twenty-sixth birthday.

It is very dark as I pass the Long Beach turnoff on the San Diego freeway. I am on my way back to San Diego. My home. Loud salsa music weaves through my car; it's my last chance to hear good music before the radio waves are lost in static somewhere in the Irvine hills. Every beat helps rush me back to the present. What do I make of today? Is it the Los Angeles of the 1960s that I always return to as I drive through this city? The memories of my youth? The idea that each day was a new discovery?

A week later, my developed film from that day arrives. The snapshots document the Getty against the backdrop of a clear aquamarine-colored sky, a sky that gets bluer as the day grows. I play with these pictures. I move them around, put them close to each other. Turn them, place them on top of one another. Finally, I spread four of them out. Paste them together. As I play with them, all I see are angles and lines: trees that are planted in rectangular beds filled with imported soil, gardens transposed in concrete beds floating on a tank of water.

In one photograph, I appear as a shadow. It is my style to photograph myself as a shadow. In the next, a corner of a wall faces an open sky. Rhodessa poses for me in a white room with a blond floor in the third photograph. One side of a large building hides a blue-green sky while dominating the last photograph's frame. Together, the four photographs tell the strange story of my day at the Getty.

Suddenly, on the pavement of the first photograph, I see a line. I place a ruler across the composite print, I follow its trail. This line crosses over into all four photographs. Individual photographs that were taken at different locations, at different times of the day, and at different angles. No matter. The single line persists in all the photographs. Through these images, the city reveals itself to be an inorganic overlay of angles, rectangles, triangles, blocks, corners, intersections. The gardens that house well-planted trees are built in shallow beds of soil. Nothing, not even the plant life, touches the core of the mountain's center of earth.

The photographs cluster, revealing an odd symmetry in the buildings, the walls, the flooring, the pavement. Odd because simultaneously this symmetry holds together two opposing qualities: it is both mathematically correct and it is organically inert. In short, Mike Davis is right. Los Angeles is dead.

The Getty architecture is a strange metaphor, somehow, of this death. I begin to understand why I am feeling unsettled. I realized that embedded in the city and the museum is an attitude of grandeur and denial. Both refuse to recognize that its human efforts are in an unequal partnership with the unknown power of nature. It's not about art or commerce. It's all about life, about honoring and supporting all that lives. What would happen if the billion dollars spent on the Getty could be spent to provide the highest quality of education to all the children in Los Angeles? Somehow the Getty vision, in its attempt to bend the natural impulse to its human bidding, forgets. Its very presence denies that it is the force of nature that bends the human incentive.

A week later, I have created yet another photographic collage that further clarifies my experience of that day. I am closer to understanding the role that creativity plays for me in my life.

My mother. Our relationship is so very complicated. Even death does not deter our continuing saga as mother and daughter. Yet, at last, she is becoming what she had demanded of me. On this day, my mother brings me a really precious gift. Her gift is wisdom—wisdom that is my awareness that our relationship appears within a string of seemingly unrelated events. What I bring to her gift is my creative process. With both our contributions, my heightened experience of this day bequeaths to me a richer perception of my world. January 21, 1998. Her gift confirms that she acknowledges my birth on her birthday.

271

To Africa in search of a heritage

By CAROL SPENCER
Post Reporter

She went to Africa, to see if she could find her roots. She also had another reason, too —her interest in the YWCA and its work throughout the world.

Mrs Fred D. Parrott (Mollie to her friends), who has just returned from seven African countries, will speak at 10 AM Tuesday at the downtown YWCA. A membership coffee will also be held.

MRS PARROTT, who speaks with a natural grace, traces her trip to many reasons.

"Over the years I've been interested in the Y program . . . not just here but all over the world and in the developing countries of Africa. My own roots were there. My parents' parents' parents came as African slaves. I wanted to see the place they came from . . . who knows, I might wander upon my tribe. Those were my main reasons."

Mrs Parrott, who left October 7, is in just the mood to talk — when fresh from a country, experiences are new and still very close inside. Even as a newly-returned traveler, she has much of it in perspective.

You see she has been preparing for a while for this trip her son gave her.

"IN 1967, I took a course in African anthropology at Rice University preparing for this trip."

She went alone. ("No, I wasn't afraid . . . not even in Senegal in the middle of the woods at night with a strange cab driver driving me in from the airport.") She traveled to Senegal, Sierra Leone, Liberia, Ghana, Kenya, the Congo, and Ethiopia, visiting a YWCA project in each country.

In Freetown, Sierra Leone "I observed a Y project operating a school for young women out of school . . . they started with 50 girls and now they have 500. They give vocational training in typing and cooking and laundry and house management — this is very very important in a developing country—knowing how to operate a home."

IN LIBERIA "I felt very much at home." (In fact, listening to Mrs Parrott she was at home wherever she went.)

In Nairobi, Kenya, "my, this is a going wide awake Y."

Then in Ethiopia she collected several of the special items that a traveler brings back. In her talk Tuesday she will show some crosses she brought.

"You know Ethiopia is the oldest Christian country in the world. For a long time they had trouble with the Moslems," and each Christian wore his own cross. She doesn't have any idea how old the crosses are. "I wish I did know."

FOR A LONG time she has worked with the Y as an all inclusive organization — "with no religious or racial discrimination. I feel a tremendous power in women working together for the good . . . with women of different ethnic and racial groups working for the development of the community . . . the Y is in 77 countries . . . and it is a way of working toward acceptance of all human beings."

There are other things — very poignant that she speaks of, talking wisely and gently about her background. One is slave beads she collected—that were said to be used "in exchange for slaves."

She believes probably her ancestors came from the Gold Coast in Ghana. "This is where American Negroes were brought from.

"It does seem unbelievable that my father and mother were slaves. My father was brought with his mother from Virginia to New Orleans. His mother was auctioned off and he was just left a little child. Somebody bought him and brought him to Texas."

And the story is closely the same about her mother.

MRS PARROTT was born in Halletsville where she lived "my first 10 years." And then she came to Houston as a young girl. In 1920, she went off to school to Tuskegee Institute, in Alabama.

There her interest in the Y formed. "Tuskegee had just a little chapter and the lady who was head of it was from Texas. She took me under her wings to the YWCA."

After school, "I was busy getting a husband," she said with a mighty special twinkle in her eyes. And she did — a dentist. "We were childhood sweethearts."

She later finished at Texas Southern, then received her master's degree from Wayne University in Detroit. She also taught for a while.

THEIR TWO children now are both on the West Coast — a daughter who is an art editor at Harcourt, Brace and World. And a son, a gynecologist in Los Angeles, who since 1964 has sent her on a trip each year.

Her husband leaves the traveling to her . . . and from her roaming this year she says she found out possibly what she really is.

"In Ghana, they told me they thought I was from the Ga tribe. So I said, all right, I'm a Ga now. Then in the Y cafeteria a man came up and said there wasn't a Ga tribe then. That there was the Twe tribe. So I ended up a Twe," she said, with a grand smile.

To grow up metabolizing hatred like daily bread means that eventually every human interaction becomes tainted with the negative passion and intensity of its by-products—anger and cruelty.

—Audre Lorde, *Eye to Eye: Black Women, Hatred, and Anger*

Chapter XIII **Legacies**

By way of Andrew Carroll, or "Pa," my mother's father and my grandfather, I am two generations removed from slavery. My mother remembered Pa as being so mean and angry that the whole family feared him. He physically beat everyone in his family. The worst beatings would happen when one of his children dared to sing. "Pa," she told me, "said that only slaves sang, and then it was only to ease the suffering." He told them all that none of his children would ever be slaves. With that pronouncement, he started beating the child who had dared to sing. His fierce, ironic cruelty to save his prodigy rendered all of his children tone deaf. Not one of my aunts or uncles could carry a tune. He beat the song out of every single one of them. He died very proud that he had raised no slaves.

One Sunday after church, I boldly approached my mother. I was tired of having her stand up, Sunday after Sunday, proudly rearing her head back to bellow out this foghorn-sounding, off-key voice that she called singing. Her hoarse, broken voice would rise above everyone else's, blare out the words so incoherently that the other children would giggle and point her out to their parents. And all those around us would share in the silent laughter. I was so embarrassed by the ugliness in her voice. Didn't she realize she didn't fit? I was puzzled by her pride. At the time, I remember being determined to shut her up. So I told her—point blank— that her singing was terrible. I recall that this time, my mother was not at all mad at me. She sat down and told me the story about her father's beatings. Perhaps she thought that by telling me this story, by telling me that slavery had soured her voice, I would understand her pride. The mere act of singing with a proud voice one generation removed from slavery meant a lot to her. Who else in the congregation was old enough to lay claim to the history she carried in her voice? Of course, at the time, I didn't understand either. I was too young then.

Years later, I learned that the Negro spiritual was created for people like her by slaves who understood exactly why they were fashioning a new song. Gospel absorbs all voices. It submerges all pitches into a united sound of a great faith, into the energy of a combined will to overcome. It is this united sound welling up from the energy of the group's essence that makes gospel's restorative power surge into the hearts of all who hear its song. Gospel's power does not lie in the individual singing voices. Its strength resides in the mingled sound of faith. My mother's

276

Crisis in North Ireland

1. Northern Ireland is a British province that covers about $\frac{1}{6}$ of the island. The other $\frac{5}{6}$ of the island is occupied by the Independent Republic of Ireland

Of the 1.5 million people 1 million are protestants .5 million (500,000) are Catholics Northern Ireland is mostly industrial.

In the 17 century Queen Elizabeth I settled English & Scottish families on land taken from the native Irish. Hoping that a protestant community would weaken the Irish Catholics' opposition to English rule. In 1920 England granted Ireland its independence but retained Northern Ireland as a province of England Since the creation of Northern Ireland there has been almost continual conflict pride came from her knowing that she didn't have to know how to sing to be able to contribute to this grand and fabulous sound. She knew it didn't matter that history had conspired to hinder her ability to "sing pretty." She was well aware that her experience of living left her with a sour hoarseness derived from the effects of slavery. That anguish blended with the sweetness in the group's harmony. She was delighted that her voice's particular quality added a much-needed weight to gospel's melody.

It was a cool, winter-lit Sunday, and I was still in elementary school when she told me this unforgettable story. What I heard in her story that day helped me to understand gospel's meaning later in life. And there's more...I understand that gospel is at the core of all African American music.

The force of the gentle, patient words that imparted her story somehow burrowed deep into my own life's motivation. As a result, I have become the magazines that my mother would read, I make the movies that do not mock us, I write the books that celebrate who we are, I teach the ideas that empower us to better generate our evolution.

One day, Uncle Alex, my paternal uncle, reminisced about his father to me. He told me that my paternal grandfather was so mean that while he lay dying, he got mad as he heard my uncle starting to cry. Angered by his child's noise, he got up out of his death bed to hit my uncle so hard that he never forgot his father's blows. "Everyone in the family tells me I had to be too young to remember," he paused slightly, "but, yes ma'am, I do remember that beating. Still, to this day..." Even so, as my uncle continued to tell me, he thought his father was a truly remarkable man. It was almost impossible for a Black man to own land in Louisiana in the late 1890s. Yet my paternal grandfather left his children the only inherited land that I own from either my maternal or paternal family.

My grandfathers. Both these men beat all of their children and wives unmercifully. Perhaps it was the horror in the struggle of it all that turned both my grandfathers so mean.

I was more my mother's pupil than I was her daughter. Her parents left her with little more than their memory of slavery. Their grim legacy swallowed her up with a motivation to change the world. What was left of her had to choose between a child and a people. Teaching rather than nurturing, she passed on to me what she left unfinished.

For as far back as I can remember, my mother read and wrote in her study almost every morning before dawn. After her funeral, I went through her personal effects. I found the books she was reading and her written notes to herself. She worked at this ritual almost to the day of her death. I discovered, neatly folded inside a tiny notebook, a *Los Angeles Times* article dated Wednesday, January 7, 1976. It is titled "Crisis in North Ireland—A History of Catholic-Protestant Conflict." There is no byline credit listed, so perhaps this story was pulled off the Associated Press wire services.

At any rate, this article had caught my mother's attention. In her notebook, I found my mother's handwritten notes on this article, dated seven days before her death. As I turned her notebook pages, I discovered single words written down with precise definitions scribbled next to them. She really did use dictionaries to teach herself spelling and the meaning of words.

I realized that my mother was reading this article to continue learning about the world. She began her days reading and writing because she was dedicated to self-improvement. She taught herself how to be—which is a pretty remarkable achievement for a Negro woman born in 1900 in a Texas country town named Halletsville. Her father had been a slave and her mother, an illiterate woman whose blood contained more Native American and Caucasian lineage than Negro.

Thus, it was not at all surprising for me to discover that, a week before her death, my mother was studying Northern Ireland. I believe she was really about the business of adding her voice to the sound of millions of other singing voices from around the world. These voices had fashioned songs from Ireland, Vietnam, East Timor, China, Tibet, South Africa, Rwanda, Palestine, Israel, Chernobyl, Kosovo, Cuba, Argentina, Mexico, the United States of America, Texas, and Houston. . . .

My mother knew her voice belonged to the world's song. On the day she told me her singing story, she taught me that human voices united emit a sound so deafening that it is inaudible to human ears. Sometimes it's so faint that it's unheard. Yet, its energy is not lost. Its vibrations pass into our subconsciousness. There, its unseen power is so persuasive that it melts away differences; its irresistible force sweeps us along. We answer its call when we commit to action.

Those who have gone before us live inside us. Their energy is part of this universal sound. They are this invincible music, lingering in our collective memory. Their song grows inside the core of our actions. Our ancestors' life essence remains their legacy to us.

The terrible conflict between my mother and me remains unresolved. We were so close that she was probably the worst enemy I'll ever know. I'm left with the strange knowledge that though her body gave me life, it also housed her spirit, which was so angry with me for being alive. She was my mother. She was my teacher. She was terrible. She was wonderful.

She was so desperately alone. And she hid it well, because she knew that if she wanted to live peacefully among us, she had to do so silently. None of us wanted to hear her pain, because we couldn't heal it. No one, not even I, really knew the depth of her isolation. For where can emotionally damaged mothers go for solace and protection in this world when they hate their children? Should these women decide to remain childless? Or give their rejected offspring up to others who have hearts open wide enough to love and cherish these children? Or should they desperately struggle alone, like my mother, to parent a child they despise?

Holocausts plant seeds in humans that contain far-reaching destructive powers. We kill, thinking we triumph. Yet our mass murders also destroy us, much the same as nuclear waste decays into half-lives, maintaining the potential to harm for years to come. Our holocausts of Native Americans have led to the human race disconnecting from nature in all continents. Our genocides of the very cultures best equipped to train us in ecological citizenship leave us with no useful memory of how to live on mother earth. Holocausts of the Palestinian, Jewish, African, and Asian people have destroyed rich, useful ethnic legacies. The losses of these voices render terrible effects that will be visited on innumerable future generations of the human race.

I fear we are quickly forgetting what it means to be human. In 2000, the last year of the twentieth century, a six-year-old boy takes a gun from his house and uses it to kill his six-year-old classmate because he's mad at her. After the fact, we learn that this child lived hostage to a terrible world that we—as a society—still neglect to address.

How much does slavery, the holocaust visited on African Americans, have to do with the emotional scars that fester in our collective soul? Its horror has certainly swept through every generation, debilitating some of us, inspiring others of us to overcome, yet fracturing in all of us our ability to love.

Can we ever learn how to break the cycle of pain we inflict on others when we ourselves are often too damaged to transcend our own secret sorrows? No matter how wounded we are, we as a people and a society must right our troubled, entrenched past.

What retribution then is "just" enough? What can our society learn to offer that will heal the lost ones who must learn to mother themselves?

Independence Heights' history revived

Woman's mission to make residents aware of area's past

By ROSANNA RUIZ
Houston Chronicle

Steve Campbell / Chronicle

Monday, Feb. 19, 2001   Houston Chronicle

For the past 15 years, retired schoolteacher Vivian Seals has been on a mission: to let Independence Heights residents know that they are part of a community with a distinct history. Behind her is the oldest house in Independence Heights, built in 1908.

When retired teacher Vivian Seals visited a north Houston school, she was not surprised by what she discovered.

"Not a child knew that they lived in historic Independence Heights," said Seals, 83.

Since 1986, Seals has been on a mission: to let Independence Heights residents know that they are part of a community with a distinct history.

Many are unaware that Independence Heights was more than a neighborhood and can claim rights as Texas' first black city. The town, incorporated in 1915, survived until it was annexed by Houston in 1929.

Seals compiled a scrapbook after years of research so the town would not survive only in the memories of a few original town residents.

"Blacks, and other minorities, need to know that they belong," Seals said, explaining the impetus for her research.

A state historical marker was erected in 1989 at New Hope Missionary Baptist Church on 30th Street to commemorate the once-thriving town.

There are reminders of its early days. Many of the homes and churches still stand today, which helped put the area on the National Register.

"Independence Heights was so little-known. But it's such a great story because it was an enclave and city of its own," said Al Davis, chairman of the Harris County Historical Commission.

There were other neighborhoods that also were once incorporated, Davis said, but none was a predominantly black town.

Independence Heights, more than 300 acres in size, is bounded by 40th Street on the north; 30th Street on the south, now the north Loop 610; Airline on the east; and Yale on the west.

The Wright Land Co. bought the property around 1905 and later sold undeveloped 25-foot lots for $6 down and $6 a month. Seals said the opportunity to design and own their homes attracted middle-class black residents away from the wards.

"You had everything you needed out there. Your own businesses and houses were built by resident carpenters," said Seals, whose father, O.L. Hubbard, served as the town's second mayor. Hubbard was also a teacher at Independence Heights School, now named Burrus Elementary School.

The 1915 election to incorporate passed by a vote of 22-2, according to newspaper accounts. G.O. Burgess, a black attorney, was elected as the town's first mayor. Not long after its incorporation, shops and churches sprang up and the town installed improvements such as shelled streets, electric lights for those with wired homes and a municipal water system.

There are other surviving residents who still live in the neighborhood. Lota Charles, 72, lives on East 33rd, not far from the East 31st home where she was born.

Charles remembers when streets along Independence Heights were unpaved and wooden "plank walks" were a substitute for sidewalks. She and other children would play in the street because hardly anyone there owned cars.

She said she has lived in Independence Heights all these years to be close to family. Her sister lives right across the street and there are other family members in the neighborhood, too.

"I just didn't ever want to leave," Charles said.

Charles' father, Arthur McCullough, served as the town's last mayor. He later helped organize a Baptist church and then founded Salem Missionary Baptist Church, where he was pastor from 1934 until he died in 1974.

The town likely would have gone unnoted if not for Seals' work, which was funded by the Independence Heights Neighborhood Council. Seals often speaks to students and at other events about the town, especially during Black History month. She said she won't stop doing so until her voice or her legs give out.

She knows she has more work to do to teach people about Independence Heights because nothing perturbs her more than some residents' confusion about where they live.

As she thumbs through her thick scrapbook that includes newspaper articles, documents and photos of homes, Seals mentions the names of the families who lived in the homes she photographed to acquire historic designation.

"This was a work of love for me," Seals said. "I did it because I wanted to do it and I knew we needed to be on the books and be a part of history."

MUTATIONS

REM KOOLHAAS
HARVARD PROJECT
ON THE CITY

STEFANO BOERI
MULTIPLICITY

SANFORD KWINTER

NADIA TAZI
HANS ULRICH OBRIST

arc en rêve centre d'architecture

ACTAR

arc en rêve centre d'architecture

Houston ™

Houston

Perhaps no other city in the developed world can claim to be as "wild"—unregulated, unfettered, *neoliberal*—as Houston. American sociologists long ago coined the term "Houstonization" to describe its new organizational effects, particularly as these began propagating to and through other places. The term is a felicitous one because Houston can properly be understood only as a set of protocols and processes. Indeed it is arguably no real city at all but is rather a loose confederation of industrial profit centers that together form an ethereal web of shared infrastructure and economic and statutory partnerships.

Famous for its non-place Aerospace administration and control center (NASA), and for its even larger role as the capital node in a global regime of energy markets, Houston is indeed rooted in nothing more specific or local than the mechanical air-conditioning systems that made it even conceivable as a site of mass inhabitation in the first place. It is now the third largest city in America, yet Houston's entire logic and *raison d'être* is as a profit center, and as such it remains the experimental model for nearly all other developing cities in the world. Houston's famously ruthless "progrowth" policies with zero local and state taxation in exchange for low civic services have resulted in Houston having less per capita parkland and poorer quality water, sewers, streets, and air than any other city in America. Also, though it is more than one-quarter the size of New York City, in 1989 it had only one seventieth the number of public housing units as New York.

More than its lack of taxes, Houston is most famously a city without zoning: indeed it is free of almost any controls on the development and exploitation of its territory for individual and corporate profit. The singular lack of counterforces to balance the free run of market rationality through its ranks has in the past made it one of the "boom-and-bust-iest" cities in the world. Built on an "extraction economy" foundation and riding the extraordinary surges of growth propelled by the combination of extractive booms, a local laissez-faire environment, public subsidies for private expansion, and its significant character as an industrially "specialized" world-market city, Houston's development is uncommonly exposed to economic buffeting and fluctuation at all levels from local and national to global. Today, with an expanded global network (NAFTA) and a diversifying economy (electronics, health care), it has reached a level of greater stability while remaining a true example of laissez-faire frontierism.

Often called the post-industrial city *par excellence* because its economy is highly oriented around the exploitation of advanced technologies—medicine, space exploration, energy—

Houston's urban and economic organization nonetheless remains a strange and precarious-appearing patchwork of still formally distinct micro-ecologies. The Texas Medical Center, a vast, highly concentrated association of healthcare institutions, medical schools, and research facilities, now forms one of the two or three largest complexes of its kind in the world, as well as the largest single employer in Houston. A few miles away, the Houston Galleria, originally a banal real-estate development project, not only integrates a huge upscale shopping mall, several hotels and office towers, pools, an ice rink, heliports, parking facilities, and multiple freeway access in unprecedented density and combination, but anchors a vast set of adjacent suburban business and residential developments that for two decades had helped to bankrupt and displace Houston's languishing "downtown" skyscraper district. The Galleria, too, represents far more than a mere local economic node or phenomenon. Indeed it represents a kind of maquiladora in reverse: its shops, hotels, and spas provide a major monetary anchor for the mobile luxury Latin consumer markets of Mexico and Central and South America. NASA to the south has spawned its own distinct bedroom communities and associated, semi-independent infrastructure and urbanism, just as the West Houston Energy Corridor represents an almost complete linear city-within-a-city itself. The agriculture, livestock, and ranching industries, while not formally based in Houston, nonetheless find in it a venue for their main marketing and promotional enterprise, the twenty-day Houston Rodeo that brings over a billion dollars to the city yearly and buttresses its role as a major linchpin within Texas's vast western and ranch culture. Through a policy of continual rampant annexation and capture of surrounding lands and developments, Houston has been able to extend its territorial growth almost without limit or obstacle, clearing the way for unbridled private development.[1] Entire internal "cities," such as Clearlake, have been owned and developed by single corporations (The Exxon Corp. in the present example).

Despite its parochialism and idiosyncrasies, Houston may well be the "globalized" city *par excellence*: rigorous and pure in its shapelessness, cruel, unforgiving, and utterly delirious in its conviction that cities need be no more than mega-machines for doing "bidness" at ever-expanding scales. It also presents a clear omen and model for all other cities everywhere in the world of what the true destiny and impact of economic globalization could be for human societies.

_1 Even among America's thirty wildly developing "Sunbelt" cities, Houston ranked next to last in per capita expenditure for planning and in number of planners per 100,000 population. Joe R. Feagin, "Are Planners Collective Capitalists?" in *The New Urban Paradigm* (New York: Rowman and Littlefield, 1998).

Houston's "4th Ward" neighborhood began as a "Freedman's Town," a colony of former slaves.
 For decades it was literally camped at the foot of the shiny corporate skyscrapers that house Texas's oil conglomerates. Though this disquieting juxtaposition of First and Third world America was tolerated for decades, in the last 18 months the entire 4th Ward district has disappeared.
The post-NAFTA boom is but the latest regime to frictionlessly reconfigure Houston's profit landscape, replacing a century-old historic district with rows of cardboard executive condominiums in as little as 15 weeks.

Houston's real estate market is perhaps too volatile, too frenetic and too unsentimental to have found time to formally omit old racist clauses from their boilerplate. Rather, rubber stamp disclaimers are perfunctorily impressed onto deeds as testimonials to the cold, swift art of the deal.

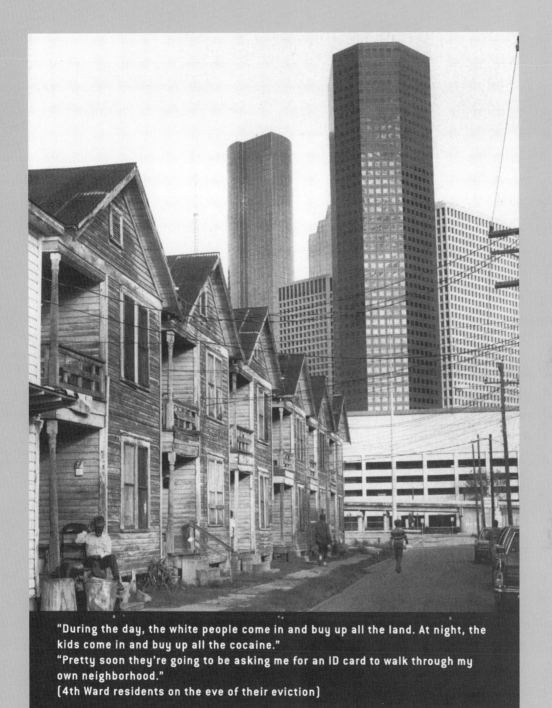

"During the day, the white people come in and buy up all the land. At night, the kids come in and buy up all the cocaine."
"Pretty soon they're going to be asking me for an ID card to walk through my own neighborhood."
(4th Ward residents on the eve of their eviction)

Part IV **Epilogue**

We can love her in the light as well as in the darkness, quiet her frenzy toward perfection and encourage her attentions toward fulfillment. Maybe then we will come to appreciate more how much she has taught us, and how much she is doing to keep this world revolving toward some livable future.

—Audre Lorde,
Eye to Eye: Black Women, Hatred, and Anger

Wed. Oct 15, 1975

Dear Daughter,

It was really good to talk with you, but sorry that you had a cold and that things were not going too well with you.

I wake each morning with you on my mind. I have had two dreams about you. One of which I was forced by some inner power to tell you. I come again to reaffirm the offer of paying your tuition if you care to go back to school to obtain a master in photography. This will enable you to get a teacher's position in some college.

Now, you asked, "how will I get the money?" Carroll Ann, I have always and do now, live by faith. I graduated from high school June 1919. Started to work that same month. Started packing my trunk after my first pay day planning to leave for college in Sept 1919, Sept came and passed but I never lost hope. I knew I would be going I believe the money would be there

Finally Feb 1920 James gave me $50.00. My train fare was more than half of that. When I arrived on Tuskegee Campus I had only a few dollars. Faced with a threat from the dean of women I finally was enrolled in night school. I sight these incidents to show you that human's only interest should be first a _desire_ to do something good and worthwhile, second _believe_ you can do it, third _work_ at it, God takes care of the _how_, the _why_, the _when_, and the _where_. You have the desire, you are working at it, but you must believe

that it will happen. Don't concern yourself about the how, why, when and where that's God's end of the deal. I told you I would pay all tuition, how? I don't know right now but I can and will do it

Love,
Mother

Wed. Oct 15, 1975

Dear Daughter,

It was really good to talk with you, but sorry that you had a cold and that things were not going too well with you.

I wake each morning with you on my mind I have had two dreams about you. One of which I was forced by some inner power to tell you. I come again to reaffirm the offer of paying your tuition if you care to go back to school to obtain a master's in photography. This will enable you to get a teacher's position in some college.

Now, you asked, "How will I get the money?" Carroll Ann, I have always and do now, live by faith. I graduated from high school June 1919. Started to work that same month. Started packing my trunk after my first payday planning to leave for college in Sept 1919. Sept came and passed but I never lost hope. I knew I would be going I believe the money would be there. Finally Feb 1920 James gave me $50.00. My train fare was more than half of that when I arrived on Tuskegee campus I had only a few dollars. Faced with a threat from the dean of women I finally was enrolled in night school. I sight these incidents to show you that human's only interest should be first a <u>desire</u> to do something good and worthwhile, second <u>believe</u> you can do it, third <u>work</u> at it, God takes care of the <u>how,</u> the <u>why,</u> the <u>when,</u> and the <u>where</u>. You have the desire, you are working at it, but you must believe that it will happen. Don't concern yourself about the how, why, when and where that's God's end of the deal. I told you I would pay all tuition, how? I don't know right now but I can and will do it.

Love,
Mother

And I said, not "I forgive you," but "I believe you."
That's what I said. "I believe you."
—Kim Chernin, *The Woman Who Gave Birth to Her Mother*

Dawn

When I was very young, I had a powerful dream that haunts me to this day. It's night in Houston, Texas. A pitch black, dark, quiet night. Everyone is asleep in the house. Safe and snug. The silent air is filled with loosely arranged breathing.

A mass murderer breaks into the house. I am in the back bedroom. I am awakened by the noise of breaking glass, muffled voices filled with terror, then silence. I scramble to hide under the bed.

He is white, slender, and tall, with big feet. Swiftly, he kills everyone but me. After the screams, there is a long and empty silence. Death fills the air. Then he is gone. I crawl out slowly. Scarlet red blood is everywhere. Throats gaping, tight skin split ragged like a full, ripe watermelon dropped by mistake on the ground. My family's eyes are open, dull, with no life within the pupils. I am frozen in fear. And yet, I escape. I run from the house in a cold sweat.

Day is breaking. The morning light is mixed—white pink and platinum blond. I run, fast, hard, so scared. As I run, I feel the dawn at my back.

293

Mollie Carroll Parrott
January 21, 1900 – January 14, 1976

Acknowledgments

Mollie and Fred Parrott's valiant and valuable contribution of their very lives to end hatred and racism and to fill its void with love and justice is my constant beacon. I've had casual discussions on memoir writing with two of my favorite teachers, the late Erik Barnouw and the late Herbert Schiller. Erik Barnouw's *Media Marathon: A Twentieth-Century Memoir* describes the importance of human relationships in shaping lives. Herbert Schiller's *Living in the Number One Country: Reflections from a Critic of American Empire* details the impact of America's global media in shaping individual thought and cultural consciousness. Their wisdom helped shape this book.

Some names in this book have been changed.

My gratitude to: Al Young, Maxine Hong Kingston, Moira Johnston, Fanny Howe (who pointed out the book's title), and the Squaw Valley Community of Writers; Karen Kenyon, Zeinabu Davis, Darlene Clark Hine, Hilary Mac Austin, Howard Zinn, Sidney Baker, Elva Baker, Helen Redman, and Charlotte Houston; Joyce Axelrod, Becca Wilson, Deborah Willis, and Diana Fuller; Adriene Jenik, George Lewis, and Anita Schiller; Jim Burr, José Clemente Orozco, and everyone else at the University of Texas Press; Danah Fayman, Madeline Goldberg, Marsha Kinder, Kathleen MacLeod, and Jimmie and Jeannie Cheatham; Joyce Gattas, Hayes Anderson, Michael Real, Theodore Kornweibel, Bessie Watson, Neil Kendricks, Laurel Scott, Mary Wickline, Catherine Armas Matsumoto, Huimin Ni, Hua Wang; the San Diego State University's School of Communication faculty, and San Diego

State University's Research and Creative Activities Awards; Houston's historians Thelma Scott Bryant, Vivian Hubbard Seals, Sarah Gamble Trotty, Algernita Scott Davis, and Patricia Smith Prather. My gratitude to the Institute of Medical Humanities at the University of Texas Medical Branch at Galveston's and the Harry Ransom Humanities Research Center at the University of Texas at Austin's visiting scholars fellowships program.

A very special thank-you to Vivian Sobchack, who, as a colleague, encouraged me to write according to my vision. As one of the three Constructs Series editors at the University of Texas Press, she helped shape this manuscript with her insightful readings and suggestions. It takes work, time, energy, care, and faith to grow the new. Vivian Sobchack models the best of what is necessary to accomplish the daunting task of birthing the potential of another.

Captions and Credits

Cover: Mandy Richardson quilt. Roni Galgano, photographer; Carroll Parrott Blue, photographer; José Clemente Orozco Farías, designer.

2: Houston Negro Hospital steps. Carroll Parrott Blue.

5: Mollie Carroll Parrott, circa 1919. Carroll Blue Collection.

8/9: Independence Heights, Texas, map, circa 1915. Leona Walls/Vivian Hubbard Seals.

8: *Left,* Carroll family home. Vivian Hubbard Seals. *Right,* Lynching. Center for American History, University of Texas at Austin. CN# 03114, Roy Wilkinson Aldrich Papers, 1858–1955.

9: *Negros Ahorcados.* José Clemente Orozco. Courtesy of Clemente Orozco V. and family.

12: *Left,* Mollie and Carroll Parrott, 1943. Carroll Blue Collection.

12: *Background, Life* magazine cover (8/23/43). TimePix,© 1943 Time Inc. Reprinted by Permission License Usage.

12/13: Lucille Ball, (8/8/43). TimePix/Desilu, too, LLC, © 1943 Time Inc. Reprinted by Permission License Usage. Image of Lucille Ball used with permission of Desilu, too, LLC. All rights reserved.

13: "Negro Division" (8/8/43). TimePix, © 1943 Time Inc. Reprinted by Permission License Usage.

14: Mollie Parrott letter (8/12/43). Carroll Blue Collection.

17: *All,* Mollie Parrott letter (8/12/43). Carroll Blue Collection.

18: *All,* Mollie Parrott letter (8/12/43). Carroll Blue Collection.

22: *Life* magazine cover (8/23/43). TimePix, © 1943 Time Inc. Reprinted by Permission License Usage.

23: "Lindy Hop Dancers" (8/23/43). TimePix, © 1943 Time Inc. Reprinted by Permission License Usage.

24: Lucille Ball (8/8/43). TimePix/Desilu, too, LLC, © 1943 Time Inc. Reprinted by Permission License Usage. Image of Lucille Ball used with permission of Desilu, too, LLC. All rights reserved.

25: "Negro Division" (8/8/43). TimePix, © 1943 Time Inc. Reprinted by Permission License Usage.

28: *Top,* "Storming Fort Wagner: The Massachusetts 54th Infantry Division, circa 1860s." Library of Congress. *Bottom,* Black World War I soldiers. © Emmett J. Scott, 1919/Thelma Scott Bryant.

29: *All,* electronic mail reprinted by permission of Solace Wales. Carroll Blue Collection.

30: *Left,* electronic mail reprinted by permission of Solace Wales. Carroll Blue Collection. *Right, La Nazione.*

31: Carroll Ann Parrott, circa 1946. Lillie Bell Porter Collection.

32: *All about My Mother* production still. Teresa Isasi/Sony Pictures Entertainment, Inc.

34: Mollie and Carroll Parrott, circa 1949. Lillie Bell Porter Collection.

35: New World map. José Clemente Orozco Farías.

39: *Left,* Bilbao, Spain, map. José Clemente Orozco Farías. *Right,* festival postcard. Bilbao International Short Film Festival.

42–48: *Struggles for Representation: African American Documentary Film and Video.* © 1999 Indiana University Press.

49: *All,* Houston, Texas, circa 1900. Houston Metropolitan Research Center/Houston Public Library.

50: *Top,* Houston city police, circa 1915. Houston Metropolitan Research Center/Houston Public Library. *Bottom left and right,* © Houston Chronicle Publishing Co. Reprinted with permission. All Rights Reserved.

54: *All,* Lynching, Before and After. Center for American History, University of Texas at Austin, CN#s 03113 and 03114, Roy Wilkinson Aldrich Papers, 1858–1955.

55: *Top,* James Byrd, Jr. AP/Wide World Photos. *Bottom,* Jasper, Texas, road with circles indicating where James Byrd's body parts were found. Ted Parks, photographer.

56: Main Street, Houston, Texas, circa 1960. Benny A. Joseph and The Texas African American Photography Archive.

57: *Top,* Parrott family home, circa 1949. Carroll Blue Collection. *Bottom,* Parrott family, circa 1950. Carroll Blue Collection/Rev. John A. Moore.

60: Camp Logan postcard, circa 1918. Houston Metropolitan Research Center/Houston Public Library.

61: Camp Logan's "Military Minstrels," circa 1918. Houston Metropolitan Research Center/Houston Public Library.

62–63: The 24th Infantry Division, circa 1916. Jason Holt Collection.

62: *Bottom,* the 24th Infantry Division mutiny route, circa 1917. University of Louisiana Press.

65: Secretary of War Newton Baker's letter to President Woodrow Wilson (8/28/17). Library of Congress.

66: *Top,* the 24th Infantry Division Court Martial, circa 1917. Photographs and Prints Division, Schomburg Center for Research in Black Culture/The New York Public Library. *Bottom,* the 24th Infantry Division under guard, circa 1917. The Fort Sam Houston Museum.

67: *Top,* burial plot map, circa 1917. The Fort Sam Houston Museum. *Bottom,* photo of burial plot, circa 1917. The Fort Sam Houston Museum.

69: *Top,* Black soldier at Camp Logan, circa 1918. Houston Metropolitan Research Center/Houston Public Library. *Bottom,* Houston Riot Investigation Summary (8/25/17). Military Archives Division, National Archives.

70: Soldier T. C. Hawkins. Jason Holt Collection.

71: *All,* T. C. Hawkins's last letter (12/11/17). Jason Holt Collection.

72: *Top left,* Sidney Poitier in *No Way Out* production still, 1949. Courtesy of the Academy of Motion Picture Arts and Sciences. *Right and bottom,* Sidney Poitier 50th Academy Tribute program, 1998. Courtesy of the Academy of Motion Picture Arts and Sciences.

75: Houston Negro Chamber of Commerce, circa 1940s. Houston Metropolitan Research Center/Houston Public Library.

76: Alpha Kappa Alpha Sorority, circa 1940s. Houston Metropolitan Research Center/Houston Public Library.

77: Gulf State Dental Association group photograph (Dr. Fred Parrott, sitting, top right), circa 1949. Johnnye Davis Petersen Collection.

78: *All,* Gulf State Dental Association program, circa 1949. Johnnye Davis Petersen Collection.

79: *Top,* Charles A. George Dental Association's Ladies Auxiliary, circa 1930s. Johnnye Davis Petersen Collection. *Bottom,* Charles A. George Dental Association's Ladies Auxiliary at Parrott home, circa 1940s. Johnnye Davis Petersen Collection.

80: Charles A. George Dental Association's Ladies Auxiliary at Parrott home, circa 1950s. Rev. John D. Moore/Carroll Blue Collection.

82–83: "The Contribution of the Negro Women to American Life and Education," 1954. John Biggers, artist. Courtesy of Blue Triangle Multi-Cultural Association, Inc./Mrs. Hazel Biggers. Earlie Hudnall, Jr., photographer.

86: *Left,* Harriet Tubman, circa 1870s. Library of Congress. *Right,* Henrietta Richardson Parrott, circa 1900s. Carroll Blue Collection.

87: Lena Horne, circa 1940s. Archive Photos.

88: *House Beautiful Magazine.* Reprinted by permission from House Beautiful April, 1998. Hearst Communications, Inc. All Rights Reserved. Vance Muse, writer/ Gerald Moorehead, photographer.

90: Carroll Ann Parrott's sixth birthday party, 8/23/49. Carroll Blue Collection.

92: "A Teacher's Prayer" by Mollie Carroll Parrott. Carroll Blue Collection.

94: *Left,* Mollie Carroll Parrott, circa 1920s. Lillie Bell Porter Collection. *Middle and right,* Houston College for Negroes graduation program, featuring Mollie Carroll Parrott's highest honors designation, (6/9/37). Vivian Hubbard Seals Collection.

95: *Left,* Elementary Grade Card, Carroll Blue Collection. *Right,* Carroll Ann Parrott, circa 1952. Carroll Blue Collection.

96: Blackshear Elementary School faculty, circa 1950s. Carroll Blue Collection.

105: Fred Parrott letter (8/8/51). Carroll Blue Collection.

107: *All,* Fred Parrott letter (8/8/51). Carroll Blue Collection.

108: *All,* Mollie Parrott letter (6/21/53). Carroll Blue Collection.

109: Mollie and Carroll Blue at Niagara Falls, Canada, circa 1954. Carroll Blue Collection.

112–113: *Top,* Niagara Falls, Canada, circa 1900s. Library of Congress.

112: *Bottom, Niagara* movie poster, 1954. Photofest/TM 2002 Marilyn Monroe/CMG Worldwide, Inc., www.cmgworldwide.com.

113: *Bottom,* Niagara Movement Committee, circa 1905. Photographs and Prints Division, Schomburg Center for Research in Black Culture/The New York Public Library.

115: Dorothy Dandridge, circa 1950s. Photofest/Estate of Dorothy Dandridge.

116: Frances Williams, circa 1980s. Carroll Parrott Blue.

118: Rosaura Revueltas, circa 1953. Lia and Paul Jarrico Archives.

122: Pears' Soap Advertisement, 1899. Library of Congress.

123: Pears' Soap Advertisement, 1899. Rare Book, Manuscript, and Special Collections Library, Duke University.

124: *All,* Cream of Wheat advertisements, 1907. Library of Congress.

128: "Self-Portrait" collage, 1971. Carroll Blue Collection.

129: Harry and Julie Belafonte, circa 1957. Archive Photos/Archive Films.

130: Carroll Parrott letter (6/14/57). Carroll Blue Collection.

132: *All,* Carroll Parrott letter (6/14/57). Carroll Blue Collection.

134: Carroll family reunion, circa 1957. Benny A. Joseph/Carroll Blue Collection.

143: Harry Belafonte and Carroll Parrott Blue, 2000. Photograph by Roni Galgano.

146: Susan Kohner, circa 1959. Courtesy of the Academy of Motion Picture Arts and Sciences with the permission of Susan Kohner Weitz.

147: Carroll Ann Parrott, 1960. Carroll Blue Collection.

153–155: "A Hard Lesson From Hollywood's Past," 7/9/00. *Los Angeles Times/*Eric Harrison, writer/Juanito Holandez, photographer.

155: Lana Turner and Juanita Moore in *Imitation of Life* production still, 1957. Photofest.

156–157: Article by Cathy Horyn, Weitz family collection with the permission of Susan Kohner Weitz.

160–161: Fred Parrott letter (9/23/33). Carroll Blue Collection.

162: Lincoln Dental Society, 1944. Carroll Blue Collection.

163: *Top,* Parrott family photograph, circa 1968. Benny A. Joseph/Carroll Blue Collection. *Bottom,* YWCA annual report, 1968. Carroll Blue Collection.

164: Fred Parrott, circa 1973. Carroll Parrott Blue.

170: "A New Song of the South" (11/6/97). Emory Holmes II/*Los Angeles Times.*

175: Fred and Mollie Parrott, circa 1973. Carroll Parrott Blue.

176: *Left,* Mollie Carroll Parrott, 1975. Carroll Parrott Blue.

176–177: "Moroccan Holiday—The French Collection, Part II: #12," © 1997. Reprinted with the permission of Faith Ringgold.

177: *Right,* Carroll Ann Parrott at the International Debutante Ball (9/23/60). Carroll Blue Collection.

178: *Left,* International Debutante Ball letter (8/60). Bethune Council House NHS.

178–179: Carroll Ann Parrott at International Debutante Ball (9/23/60). Carroll Blue Collection.

179: *Right*, Mary McLeod Bethune, circa 1950. Bethune Council House NHS.

180: Carroll Ann Parrott (9/23/60). Carroll Blue Collection.

182–183: International Debutante Ball press release and guest list (9/20/60). Bethune Council House NHS.

184: *Top*, Carroll Ann Parrott (9/23/60). Carroll Blue Collection. *Bottom*, International Debutante Ball invitation (9/60). Bethune Council House NHS.

186: *All*, International Debutante Ball Committee Meeting Notes (8/16/60). Bethune Council House NHS.

190: *Top*, Rodman Rockefeller greets Debutante Ball Queen (9/23/60). AP/Wide World Photos; *bottom*, Photo caption (9/23/60). AP Wide World.

191: "U.S. Art Expert Biddle Expects a Masterpiece" (9/26/60). Joseph X. Dever/ *World-Telegram & Sun*.

194: *Top*, Carroll and Mollie Parrott (12/60). Carroll Blue Collection. *Bottom*, Fred and Carroll Ann Parrott (12/60). Benny A. Joseph and The Texas African American Photography Archive.

197: Carroll Parrott (12/60). Carroll Blue Collection.

198–200: "My Last Will and Testament," Mary McLeod Bethune (8/55). Bethune Council House NHS.

202: *All*, Camp Pendleton landscape and Vietnamese refugees (5/75). Carroll Parrott Blue.

203: Camp Pendleton campgrounds (5/75). Carroll Parrott Blue.

204: *All*, Vietnamese refugee crowd and campgrounds (5/75). Carroll Parrott Blue.

206–207: Mollie Parrott letter (5/28/75). Carroll Blue Collection.

208: Vietnamese refugees (5/75). Carroll Parrott Blue.

209: Vietnamese refugee men (5/75). Carroll Parrott Blue.

210–212: Carroll Blue letter (6/3/75). Carroll Blue Collection.

213: *All*, Vietnamese refugee children (5/75). Carroll Parrott Blue.

214: Two Vietnamese refugee men (5/75). Carroll Parrott Blue.

215: Vietnamese refugee woman (5/75). Carroll Parrott Blue.

216: Vietnamese refugee children (5/75). Carroll Parrott Blue.

217: *All*, Vietnamese refugee woman and camp's bulletin board (5/75). Carroll Parrott Blue.

218–221: Carroll Blue letter (9/30/75). Carroll Blue Collection.

223: Vietnamese refugee woman and child (5/75). Carroll Parrott Blue.

224: *Top*, "Shadow at Funeral" (1/76). Carroll Parrott Blue. *Bottom*, Mandy Richardson quilt. Photograph by Roni Galgano.

228: Yolanda M. López, circa 1975. Carroll Parrott Blue.

229: Yolanda M. López and David Avalos, circa 1975. Carroll Parrott Blue.

233: *Background, Reflections in Black: A History of Black Photographers 1840 to the Present,* © 2000. W. W. Norton & Company/Deborah Willis. *Center,* Jules Lion, photographer/Historic New Orleans Collection.

234: Kathleen Cleaver, Fannie Lou Hamer, and post–shoot out Black Panther headquarters, Los Angeles. Carroll Parrott Blue © 2000, W. W. Norton & Company, 2000.

236: *Top,* People's Temple choir, circa 1975. Carroll Parrott Blue. *Bottom,* Waleed Muhammad at Rally, circa 1975. Carroll Parrott Blue.

237: *Top,* Rev. Jim Jones at rally, circa 1975. Carroll Parrott Blue. *Bottom,* Black Muslim men at rally, circa 1975. Carroll Parrott Blue.

238–239: "Moroccan Holiday—The French Collection, Part II: #12," 1997. Faith Ringgold © 1997.

242–244: "Lights, Camera . . . Affirmative Action." © March 1984, *Independent Magazine*/Renee Tajima-Peña, writer. Photograph, Larry Clark Collection.

245–247: Mollie Parrott letter (4/9/75). Carroll Blue Collection.

248: *Top,* "Shadow at Gravesite" (1/76). Carroll Parrott Blue.

248: *Bottom,* Mrs. Mollie Carroll Parrott's funeral program (1/18/76). Carroll Blue Collection.

252: *All,* Mrs. Mollie Carroll Parrott's funeral program (1/18/76). Carroll Blue Collection.

253: *Top,* YWCA letter (2/6/76). Carroll Blue Collection. *Bottom,* Inga Vickers speech (1/14/76). Carroll Blue Collection.

255: Houston, Texas, Third Ward map. José Clemente Orozco Farías.

256: *Left,* Holman Street tracks, 1975. Carroll Parrott Blue. *Right,* Progressive New Hope Baptist Church, 1975. Carroll Parrott Blue.

257: *Left,* Jack Yates High School, 1975. Carroll Parrott Blue; *Right,* Third Ward children, 1975. Carroll Parrott Blue.

258: *Left,* Parrott home, 1975. Carroll Parrott Blue. *Right,* Mollie Carroll Parrott with family portraits, 1975. Carroll Parrott Blue.

259: Carroll Blue, circa 1972. Dennis Callwood.

260: West Los Angeles city map. José Clemente Orozco Farías.

266: Emory Douglas/The Black Panther Black Community News Service Newspapers.

267: Carroll Parrott Blue/The Black Panther Black Community News Service Newspapers.

268–269: Carroll Parrott Blue/The Black Panther Black Community News Service Newspapers.

272–273: Carroll Parrott Blue, by permission of Rhodessa Jones.

274: Carol Spencer/© 1968–1969 Houston Post Publishing Co. Reprinted with permission. All Rights Reserved.

276: "Crisis in North Ireland—A History of Catholic-Protestant Conflict," January 7, 1976. *The Los Angeles Times.*

277: Mollie Carroll Parrott's notes (1/76). Carroll Blue Collection.

281: "'Independence Heights' History Revived" (2/19/01). Rosanna Ruiz, writer/ Steve Campbell, photographer, © 2001 Houston Chronicle Publishing Co. Reprinted with permission. All Rights Reserved.

282–287: "Houston." *Mutations*/Actar Press: Sanford Kwinter, writer/Paul Hester, photographer/George O. Jackson, photographer/Onezieme Mouton, deed.

288: *Left,* Mollie Carroll Parrott, (10/75). Carroll Parrott Blue.

288–289: *Middle,* Houston Negro Hospital steps, 1975. Carroll Parrott Blue.

289: *Right,* Carroll Parrott Blue. Marc Tule, photographer.

290: Mollie Parrott letter (10/15/75). Carroll Blue Collection.

293: Mollie Carroll Parrott, 1975. Carroll Parrott Blue, photographer.

Quotation Credits.

9: *Bottom,* Abel Meeropol (a.k.a. Lewis Allan), "Strange Fruit."

13: Erik Barnouw, *Media Marathon: A Twentieth-Century Memoir.*

21: *Houston Observer* (10/21/16).

33: *Top,* Paul Hawken/Renee Lertzman, "Down to Business: Paul Hawken on Reshaping the Economy."

33: *Middle, All about My Mother,* Pedro Almodóvar/Sony Pictures Entertainment, Inc.

41: Audre Lorde/The Crossing Press, "Uses of the Erotic: The Erotic as Power." Reprinted with permission from *Sister Outsider,* © 1984 by Audre Lorde. Published by the Crossing Press, Freedom, California.

51: Lucie Eddie Campbell, *In The Upper Room.*

73: Sidney Poitier, *The Measure of a Man: A Spiritual Autobiography.*

99: Jerry Lieber and Mike Stoller, *Hound Dog.*

100: Ferdinand Washington and Don Robey, *Pledging My Love.*

110: Paul Jarrico. "Written By," December/January 1998.

124: *Bottom,* Alphonse Karr, *Les Guêpes.*

125: Sammy Cahn and Gene DePaul, *Teach Me Tonight.*

133: Darlene Clark Hine and Kathleen Thompson, *A Shining Thread of Hope: The History of Black Women in America.*

137, 138, and 140: Billie Holiday, *Fine and Mellow.*

145: Rainer Werner Fassbinder/Thomas Elsaesser, translators, *Six Films by Douglas Sirk.* Reprinted with permission from Thomas Elsaesser and Rainer Werner Fassbinder Foundation.

158: Sidney Poitier, *The Measure of a Man: A Spiritual Autobiography.*

165: André Breton.

169: Barbara Belle, Louis Prima, Anita Leonard, and Stan Rhodes, *A Sunday Kind of Love.*

173: Joe Greene, *Don't Let the Sun Catch You Crying.*

174: Luis Buñuel, "Poetry and Cinema."

177: Heraclitus.

225: Philippians 4:7.

261: Herbert I. Schiller, *Living in the Number One Country: Reflections from a Critic of American Empire.*

275–289: Audre Lorde, "Eye to Eye: Black Women, Hatred, and Anger." Reprinted with permission from *Sister Outsider,* © 1984 by Audre Lorde. Published by the Crossing Press, Freedom, California.

292: Kim Chernin, *The Woman Who Gave Birth to Her Mother.*

This book is set in Bodoni Book,
and is printed on 70lb Fortune Matte paper

Printed and bound by
Thomson-Shore, Inc.

Designed and composed by José Clemente Orozco Farías
on a Power Mac in Pagemaker 6.5 for the
University of Texas Press